ALL THE LOVE

TURNER PUBLISHING COMPANY
Nashville, Tennessee
turnerpublishing.com

ALL THE LOVE

Cover design: Lauren Peters-Collear & Andrea Akers
Book design: Karen Sheets de Gracia

Library of Congress Cataloging-in-Publication Data

Names: Hooper, Kim, author. | Resnick, Meredith, author. | Diep, Huong, author.
Title: All the love : healing your heart and finding meaning after pregnancy loss / Kim Hooper, Meredith Resnick with Huong Diep.
Description: Nashville, Tennessee : Turner Publishing Company, [2021] | Includes bibliographical references and index.
Identifiers: LCCN 2020054607 (print) | LCCN 2020054608 (ebook) | ISBN 9781684425563 (paperback) | ISBN 9781684425587 (epub)
Subjects: LCSH: Miscarriage--Psychological aspects. | Parental grief.
Classification: LCC RG648 .H667 2021 (print) | LCC RG648 (ebook) | DDC 618.3/9--dc23

Printed in the United States of America

20 21 22 23 24   10 9 8 7 6 5 4 3 2 1

ALL THE LOVE

Part memoir — Part therapy session

Healing Your Heart and Finding Meaning after Pregnancy Loss

KIM HOOPER

MEREDITH GORDON RESNICK, LCSW

with DR. HUONG DIEP

TURNER

PUBLISHING COMPANY

"Grief doesn't last forever, but love does."

—Elle Wright

For all those who have lost
and for all the babies who are not with us.

NOTE: For those starting this journey as part of the LGBTQ+ or nonbinary communities, we see you. In this book, the term "woman" or "women" is inclusive of all those who identify as female or were assigned a female gender identity at birth. We standardize the pronouns *she* and *her* for the purposes of simplicity for all readers, but we understand that people of all gender identities and sexual orientations experience this type of loss.

About this book

In 2015, Kim Hooper experienced the first of what would become four pregnancy losses. That ectopic pregnancy was followed by an early miscarriage, the loss of a son in the second trimester, and another ectopic pregnancy. After each loss, two of the friends she turned to were Huong Diep, a board-certified psychologist, and Meredith Resnick, a licensed social worker. She knew they would "get it"—as friends, but also as therapists.

While grieving her losses, Kim was not interested in impersonal self-help books telling her how to feel better. What she wanted was validation for her sometimes ugly, nowhere-near-better feelings. She wanted to hear from other women who had been through similar experiences. She wanted a therapist on her shoulder to help her make sense of the onslaught of emotion every day. In the months following each loss, she felt fragile and unclear of the steps ahead. She knew the experience of her losses would forever change her; what she didn't know is who she would become. As she struggled to come to terms with this, she wanted something she could check in with on a daily basis—not an app or a website, but something tangible, something she could hold, something that could hold her, in a way. When she discovered that no such book existed, the next step became clear: *We need to create one.*

This book is written for you—the person going through this terrible, like-no-other loss. The depth of this loss is a reflection of the love you felt for the baby you will never get to know. We want to focus on that love, the depth of it, what it means for who we become in the wake of profound grief.

It is our hope that reading this book feels like sitting and chatting with someone who has been through a similar experience, while therapist friends listen in to help provide insights and clarity. Even though pregnancy loss is extremely (and unfortunately) common, the grieving process can be lonely. We hope this book is a companion for you during this process, providing you with a haven of validation for the range of emotions that emerge, and offering hope and love even though the future seems—and frankly *is*—uncertain.

There is no right or wrong way to use this book. We have included a detailed Table of Contents so it's easy for you to find entries that resonate with you on a particular day. We hope you find some comfort in these pages. For additional support, we recommend finding a therapist in your area—PsychologyToday.com has a great directory. Also, please consider joining our community of ongoing support at alltheloveafterloss.com, or follow us on Instagram and Twitter @allthelovetalk.

Contents

Kim's story xv
Meredith's story xviii
Huong's story xx

A loss like no other
Why, why, why? 1
It's about the baby—and so much more 3

Different kinds of loss
Chemical pregnancy 10
Ectopic pregnancy 12
Blighted ovum 16
Molar pregnancy 18
First-trimester miscarriage 21
Second-trimester miscarriage 24
Preterm delivery 30
Stillbirth 31

Different circumstances
When the pregnancy wasn't planned 35
When the pregnancy was very much planned 39
When you were pregnant with more than one child 41
When you already have a child (or children) 43
When you've struggled with infertility 48
When you had to make the difficult decision to end a pregnancy 51

The medical part of pregnancy loss

Why didn't anyone tell me about all the blood? **55**

The hormones are real **60**

Dealing with all the doctor's appointments **63**

Looking for answers **66**

When doctors don't say the right things **69**

The care you're probably *not* getting **74**

Shock, guilt, shame, loneliness, anger, despair, anxiety—the gang's all here

Shock and confusion

Is this really happening? **78**

It wasn't supposed to be this way **80**

Guilt and shame

Is this my fault? **83**

I feel like a failure **87**

Loneliness and isolation

If it's so common, why do I feel so alone? **91**

I just want to hide from the world **94**

Anger

My favorite stage of grief **98**

The "It's not fair" tantrum **101**

Betrayal

Feeling betrayed by my body **103**

Feeling betrayed by nature **105**

Feeling betrayed by God **107**

Sadness and despair

Is it normal to be this sad? **110**

Crying all the tears . . . or not **113**

Dealing with depression **116**

Anxiety and posttraumatic stress

    Feeling a loss of control 120

    I'm worried about more bad things happening 122

    Why am I obsessed with death? 127

    Posttraumatic stress: It's a thing 130

Understanding your grief process

What is the "process" anyway? 138

How long is this going to last? 143

Riding the grief rollercoaster 147

Physical signs of grief 152

Grieving in a society that sucks at grief

Feeling pressure to "move on" 156

All the unhelpful things people say 161

When people say nothing at all 171

The Pity Face 174

What I wish people would say 176

Connecting with your baby

Who was my baby? 180

A little ceremony goes a long way 182

Writing to my baby 185

Where is my baby now? 189

Tracking a pregnancy that is no more 191

Connecting with your partner

Grieving differently 194

Understanding your Other Half 202

Can my relationship survive this? 208

Intimacy after a loss 215

When your partner can't give you the support you need 219

When you don't have a partner 221

Thoughts for LGBTQ+ couples 223

Connecting with others

Joining the Pregnancy Loss Club 230

Navigating social media 233

How friendships can change 238

Getting professional help 240

Returning to "normal" life (whatever that means)

Feeling disoriented 246

Triggers at every turn 248

Acting like you're fine (not recommended) 251

Going back to work 253

When grief sneaks up on you 257

Coping with holidays and celebrations 259

Triggering dates 263

Dealing with other people having babies

Why does pregnancy seem to be everywhere? 266

All the triggered feelings—anger, sadness, envy, shame, guilt 270

My kind-of-bitchy open letter to expecting mothers 273

The dreaded baby showers 276

Rediscovering (and loving) who you are

Finding faith 280

Will I ever feel like me again? 284

Self-compassion and self-care 286

Coming back to my body 290

Moments of joy 293

Finding meaning 296

Trying again . . . or not

Should we try again? 301

I want to try again, but I'm terrified 306

When you and your partner aren't on the same page 309

Deciding not to try again 312

Getting pregnant after a loss

When it feels like you're holding your breath for nine months 315

Coping with the anxiety 319

I'm having trouble connecting with my baby 322

To tell people, or not to tell people 326

More unhelpful things people will say 328

Why do I still resent pregnant women? 332

Allowing for hope and gratitude 335

Having a baby after a loss

Giving birth 338

A word about "rainbow babies" 342

I'm still afraid something bad is going to happen 344

Is it normal to *still* be sad? 349

Am I allowed to think the newborn days are hard? 351

What if I forget the baby I lost? 355

How loss taught me about mothering 357

When grief gets (more) complicated

When you have multiple losses 361

When there is no "happy ending" 363

When racial, cultural, and socioeconomic issues come into play 365

When you have a history of loss or trauma 371

When your loss happens at the same time as another loss 373

When your loss feels overshadowed by a major event 375

When your loss causes financial stress **378**

When things get political, religious, or otherwise emotionally charged **381**

Moving forward from here 385

Acknowledgments 386

Bibliography 387

References 389

Appendix

Charities and organizations **403**

Helpful websites **404**

Books about pregnancy loss **404**

Resources for health-care providers **405**

Questionnaires and screeners

Perinatal Grief Scale **407**

Generalized Anxiety Disorder 7-item (GAD-7) Scale **410**

Patient Health Questionnaire-9 (PHQ-9) **411**

PTSD Checklist for *DSM-5* (PCL-5) **412**

Life Events Checklist (LEC) **414**

Patient Stress Questionnaire **416**

Kim's story

I have a confession: For most of my adult life, I proclaimed that I did not want children.

Ironically enough, one of the major things that scared me away from motherhood was the fear of losing a child. Years before I got pregnant, I wrote a letter to my imaginary baby, explaining my apprehensions:

> *The existence of you means that something—the loss of you—could destroy me. Obliterate me. There has never been something in my life with that capacity. I have always prided myself on strength, but you could bring me to my knees. And I'm not sure I'd ever be able to stand up again.*

Everyone told me I would change my mind about having a child, and, begrudgingly, I came to admit they were right. I met my husband (Chris) and sat by his side as both of his parents died when they were in their fifties—his mom had Parkinson's (according to most doctors; there wasn't an accepted consensus), and his dad had a rare genetic type of ALS. Watching their declines awakened something in me: I wanted to live more fully, less fearfully. I wanted a family. In the face of death, I wanted life.

It wouldn't be that simple though. First, I would have to come face-to-face with my greatest fear—loss.

My first pregnancy was ectopic, the embryo stuck in my left fallopian tube. I was rushed into surgery, and when I awoke, I'd lost my baby, my tube, and my faith in a fair world. This first loss was startling, shocking. Suddenly, I felt vulnerable to tragedy in a way I'd never felt before.

With just one fallopian tube remaining, I didn't know if I'd be able to get pregnant again. So, when I did, I proclaimed myself the One-Tube Wonder. Surely, this pregnancy would be successful. But, see, that's not how the world works. There are no "paid dues." There is no fairness. Bad things can happen to any of us.

Early blood testing in my second pregnancy showed the embryo was not viable. I had no signs or symptoms—a "missed miscarriage" it's called (one of many medical terms I've come to know on this long, strange journey). It took weeks before I bled, before I physically parted ways with this life that almost was.

Chris and I went into our third attempt saying, "Third time's a charm" or "Three strikes and we're out." We were trying to be cute, to maintain some sense of humor. Our marriage depended on some levity.

When my third pregnancy went past the first trimester, I thought we were safe. But again, I was fooled. I was left with this startling epiphany that any sense of control I'd had in my life had been an illusion. There is no "safe zone"—in pregnancy or in life. Sometimes, this realization panics me; other times, it makes me feel free.

I carried my son, Miles, for seventeen weeks before his heart stopped. We will never know the medical reason why. When the doctor left the room after telling us that our boy had died, I said to Chris, "This is going to fuck me up. I'm never going to be the same." That was true—it *did* fuck me up. And I am never going to be the same. But I've learned that's not a bad thing, to be changed. Loss is representative of love. Carrying Miles showed me a love I never had before. I can never regret that.

It took me months to decide that I did not agree with "Three strikes and you're out." I wanted to try again. When my fourth pregnancy turned out to be ectopic—again—my doctor shook his head in disbelief. "This is just terrible luck," he said. That was all there was to say.

Chris was ready to give up, throw in the proverbial towel, but I wanted to try one last time. I couldn't help but think of that infamous definition of insanity—doing the same thing over and over again but expecting different results. It didn't make logical sense, given what we'd been through, but there was something bigger than me telling me not to give up.

On October 4, 2017, I gave birth to my daughter. She was born a week before her due date, after a completely normal, complication-free pregnancy. All of the clichés and song lyrics and tired phrases have proven true: She is the light of my life, she is my sunshine, she is the best part of every day.

Even though she is here, my four losses stay with me. Every day I enjoy with my daughter, I am profoundly grateful because, somewhere deep inside, I feel like my time with her might be limited. I document as many moments as I can, motivated by a fear that she will be taken from me. All parents fear losing their child, but for me, the anxiety is heightened.

I think people assume I'm "over" the babies that came before her, but I'm not. I'm still sad about those losses. Watching my daughter grow just makes me more aware of who they could have been—especially Miles, who existed in my head (and heart) as my son.

There are times when Mya whispers to a void of space next to her, as if she has an imaginary friend. I ask her, "Is it Miles?" And she says, "Yes." I have no idea if she even knows what I'm asking, but I like to think she sees him. I like to think that even though she is an only child for all intents and purposes, she has secret siblings by her side.

I saw a psychic once in the midst of our losses, desperate for answers, and she told me, "You have a daughter coming. And the others will be her angels, watching out for her." I don't consider myself a very woo-woo person, but I chose to believe this.

One day, I will tell my daughter about the babies who came before her. One day, she will understand a little more about what her parents were willing to endure for the sometimes-terrifying, heart-exploding pleasure of knowing her.

Meredith's story

If motherhood is a sorority, I am its wayward pledge.

We'd been married almost five years when my husband and I started telling people we were going to adopt an older child. Many squirmed upon hearing the "A" word. Tack on "older child," and the sweating started. Not that they didn't support the "A" word; they did, in theory. They just didn't understand why, in particular, an older child would be a first choice rather than a runner-up.

It seemed to make many moms—grandmothers, new moms, friends' moms, pregnant moms—a bit uneasy. It struck their partners as odd too. They had not adopted or thought about it. They said things like: "Have a baby first, then think about adoption." And: "Why shop secondhand when you can have the original, a little someone who looks just like you?"

Writing that was hard. But that's what people said. To my face! They appeared so grounded in their convictions that I should have a baby. None of their business, you say? Try telling that to the people who believe it is their business. Therapists are not immune to such pressures.

So, we tried. "Trying" is what you say when you're attempting to get pregnant—you don't need to spell it out because people know; they get it (as I'm certain you know). But these others seemed to "understand" motherhood in a way that not only flummoxed but made me question if I was a bit—how shall I put it?—off.

In listening to Kim talk about her pregnancy losses, in sitting beside her as she shared the personal details, and witnessing the pain and suffering she endured, I understood that her feelings of aloneness were universally similar yet singularly different to mine in our parenthood journeys. I never got pregnant, and I adopted two daughters; she endured multiple pregnancy losses and today has a beautiful daughter. And yet it is our emotional experiences that have shared qualities, as they likely do with you.

As a licensed clinical social worker, I've worked with individuals at every stage of the life cycle. Pregnancy or death or illness is not a process you can make neat or tidy, nor is the loss of a child in the womb. But you can give it shape and allow it to be expressed and held. Kim suffered upon losing her babies. She had to come to terms with what was normal and natural for her, which she so openly shares in this book.

Emotions strike each of us differently. This includes grief, which, like any emotion, is dynamic. It wants to be seen and expressed and, in doing so, can bring new perspective and relief. This can be a very solitary process, but in time, we emerge anew.

The verb "adopt" can connote taking on something that doesn't belong in the space where you're trying to put it. It can also mean embracing something new and finding a place where it belongs. Within the pages of this book we've put ourselves, as have you, at the very intersection of grief and love.

Huong's story

I have a confession as well. I am a board-certified psychologist in clinical child and adolescent psychology and have worked with youth for more than twenty years in various capacities as a camp counselor, tutor, nanny, teacher, Peace Corps Volunteer, and now clinical psychologist. But, here I am in my forties, and I will most likely not have biological children. I love kids and appreciate their innocence. I even love teenagers, which is my area of expertise. I love the way their brains are slowly melding together as they begin to question, "Do I want to continue to believe the same thing my caregivers have, consciously or subconsciously, passed to me?" all while dealing with raging hormones and emotions. Children make me laugh at their frankness and honesty, but they also frighten me with their needs, incessant demands, and fragility.

I am experiencing what you, dear reader, will come to read more about as "ambiguous loss" for a child or children that I don't have. I have never carried a child (to my knowledge), and I have no idea if I am capable. Am I part of the club of women with no children by choice, or did life circumstances make a choice for me? I want to be honest with readers that I have not personally experienced a miscarriage, but in some basic ways, a miscarriage is a plan or idea that did not materialize. I can relate to that.

In my clinical work, I am privileged to be witness to my clients' traumas that they so willingly share on my couch. They share with me their pain and worries, stories that they do not share with others for fear of judgment or pity, or because they cannot bear to have someone in their everyday lives to remind them with that "look." My office is a safe space where, for forty-five minutes, they can put down their backpack of pain and unzip it, and we can examine together. I encourage them to leave a few things in the office if they can, and I remind them that they can always pick it back up at a later time. Some leave a little. Some leave a lot. But it is a place where their pain is seen, validated, nurtured, and ultimately transformed.

In my personal life, I am privileged to have female-identified friends, some whom I have known since my teenage-braces days. These women have struggled (often silently) with infertility, miscarriages, IVF "miracle" babies, and the resignation but quiet acceptance that life does not always proceed on a straight and narrow path and that the journey to becoming a "mother" is filled with joy and misery. I applaud my friends for having the courage to "decide to have your heart go walking outside of your body," as Elizabeth Stone puts it.

One of my goals here is to highlight and serve as a voice and ally to several underserved and under-represented groups at the miscarriage conversation table—the BIPOC and LGBTQ+ communities. I identify as a Vietnamese-American, heterosexual and cisgender female, meaning that my current gender identity matches my assigned sex at birth. I am privileged in my ability to navigate this world as an able-bodied, overeducated individual. When Kim and I discussed this labor of love (pun intended), I immediately knew I wanted to discuss the invisible experiences of the BIPOC and LGBTQ+ communities and to talk about the impact of being a minority within a minority. I am thankful for this opportunity.

A loss like no other

Why, why, why?

It just doesn't make sense.

I am a storyteller at heart. I've been writing books since I was a kid. I like beginnings, middles, and ends. I like stories to have an arc. I like characters to develop. I like plots to "make sense." So, when my pregnancies ended, I couldn't help but wonder what this meant for "my story." Why did these things happen to me? What did they mean?

Confession: Before my losses, whenever I heard of someone having a miscarriage, I wondered if it was something she did (or didn't do). Maybe she didn't eat the right things or take the right vitamins. Maybe she let stress get the best of her. Maybe her marriage was unhealthy, and her body "knew" she shouldn't have a baby. Because I've thought these things before, I know other women think them. And it's not because we're cruel. It's because we don't want to think something bad can happen *without* a reason. It's much easier to have a reason than to consider that sometimes pregnancies just end, randomly and unpredictably.

"I am done trying to reason with it. For now, at least. There is no reason. There is nothing to understand. There is no could-have or should-have because there is only what is."

—Nora McInerney, *It's Okay to Laugh (Crying Is Cool Too)*

My losses were so distressing because they made me painfully aware of the randomness of things, of how little control I have (See "Feeling a loss of control"). I did everything "right," and I still had these things happen to me.

I did everything "right," and I still came up on the wrong side of the statistics—not one, but *two*, ectopic pregnancies, a loss in the second trimester when 99 percent of babies at that stage make it full-term. I was especially unnerved when I saw others who did things "wrong" and had easy pregnancies and healthy babies.

Did all of this mean something? Was I not cut out to be a mother? Did I not deserve a baby? Was my marriage not strong enough? Maybe my losses happened because I'd had too many successes and needed a fair dose of failure. Maybe they happened because I didn't treat my body well in my twenties. Maybe they were a much-needed, harsh lesson in losing control.

"We are a meaning-seeking species . . . We are also a storytelling species. The brain's language centers have a natural proclivity for coherent stories—grand narratives with an overarching point and a satisfying end. Things must happen for specific reasons; they must have a point. The brain is not satisfied with pointless randomness." —Ralph Lewis, MD, *Psychology Today*

What I've come to understand is that my losses didn't really *mean* anything, not in and of themselves. They didn't happen for any particular reason. They just *happened*. People tried to assure me that "everything happens for a reason." They tried to force meanings on me. When I was in the thick of my grieving, I wasn't ready for that.

In my own space, on my own time, I did find meanings, or I created them. That's what we do as humans—we make meanings. Meaning is the lemonade of life's lemons. From my losses, I've gained confidence in my own resilience. I've realized the fragility of life, which has motivated me to live more fully, less fearfully. I've traded my illusions of control for more perspective and compassion for others. So, yes, I've found meaning in my losses (See "Finding meaning"). But any positives I've managed to extract from the rubble of my grief don't make up for the heartache. It doesn't work like that. Put simply: There is no answer to the question of "why" that makes the grief any less painful.

It's about the baby—
and so much more

There are layers to this type of loss.

You know what they say—a woman becomes a mother the moment she sees a positive pregnancy test. This was true for me. There was instant attachment. I began to develop a strong, like no-other bond with my baby-to-be once I saw the two pink lines.

I see the agony of my losses as a reflection of the emotional investment I'd made. Each loss was the loss of a dream. My babies represented a future. I had fantasized about what life would be like with them. I had seen them in my mind, begun thinking of names. The profound sorrow I felt was in response to the loss of those fantasies. I'd never get to know those individual beings. With each loss, I had to grieve a relationship that ended before it really began.

I also felt a huge loss of innocence and faith. I was forced to realize that bad things can happen even when we do all the right things. Any control I'd felt before was an illusion. This was deeply unsettling to the very foundation of who I was. In a way, losing a baby was losing myself. It was losing the way I'd always seen the world.

In the midst of all this loss, I felt very alone. I knew, logically, that pregnancy loss was common, but it was such a lonely experience for me. There were two reasons for the loneliness: one, I was shy about discussing my losses because I felt like they were indicative of some way I'd failed; two, I felt like people didn't really "get it." I felt a lot of pressure to "move on," the implication being that my losses weren't that significant. Even my husband seemed dismissive of the depth of my pain—"I know it sucks, babe, but you have to start moving forward."

I knew other women had experienced losses like mine, but when I looked around, I didn't see anyone else hurting. My assumption was that I wasn't handling it well, that there was something wrong with me. I started to become depressed about the fact that I was depressed. Like I said, there are layers to this thing.

It took me a long time to realize that there *are* other women hurting; they are just hiding, feeling just as isolated as me.

"Pregnancy ending in a death just leaves you broken. The puzzle you're left with is how to assimilate this turn of events: the death of someone who never lived but who was all in your imagination; who was real, and who opened up an enormous space inside you, but will never fill it. The world you discover in the aftermath of miscarriage seems so impossibly empty."

—Miranda Field, "My Others," featured in *About What Was Lost: 20 Writers on Miscarriage, Healing, and Hope* (Jessica Berger Gross, editor)

Meredith

The immediate loss of the pregnancy—your baby—is the easiest to identify and apply frameworks for grief, healing, and resiliency to. This is because it is a tangible loss. The loss of innocence is more nuanced and painful, transcending different levels of the self, way back to childhood. This is more evident as the freshness of the wound lessens. But you must feel the pain in all its rawness to receive a deeper understanding of what it will eventually mean for you and you alone.

As Kim says, many women may begin to feel an intensely deep connection to their baby when they find out they are pregnant. This connection is based on biological forces kicking in, but it is also based on the fantasies the woman begins to have—the planning, imagining, wondering, daydreaming.

What Kim describes here is the loss of the fantasy of parenthood. Folded into that is the excruciating longing to know your child, *this* child. That existed before, and it continues. But now, where does this love go?

"It's a primal loss." —Traysi Handel, LCSW, USC School of Social Work

When the baby was conceived, took root, and began to grow, something inside you began to shift—very deeply. Like tectonic plates deep in the earth. Now, with the loss, those plates have abruptly assumed a new position. Something foundational inside you has broken apart. Pieces that once fit smoothly now have jagged edges—emotionally, physically, spiritually.

These otherwise "steady" plates—your worldview, your spirituality, your religion, maybe even your partner—have provided structure and focus that may have worked, and worked well, in your life. Those things have been good to you, but alone they may not explain a loss like this.

"There is no recovery from the loss of life's possibilities."
—Shannon Gibney and Kao Kalia Yang, "Reclaiming Life," in *What God Is Honored Here? Writings on Miscarriage and Infant Loss by and for Native Women and Women of Color*

Sometimes, a loss like this can shatter something that may well have needed to be broken or, at the very least, examined more closely. To grow in new ways. To make something strong—you—even stronger.

Unfortunately, we don't get to choose when these existential events happen or what triggers them. Pregnancy loss is one such trauma.

One moment you are embracing that tiny fertilized egg deep inside, reading up on its development week by week, finding a way to acquaint to this tiny human—as I've heard Kim refer to the embryo, then baby—inside whose cells are growing, multiplying, and dividing, week after week after week.

"I experienced these losses as an assault on my sense of self."
—Linda Layne, *Motherhood Lost*

And then it just ends. So many levels of promise are upended. That is why it hurts so much.

Of course, some women may *not* feel an instant connection to their baby. Some may have complicated feelings about being a parent. Some pregnancies may have been unplanned or even unwanted. That does not mean that the loss of the pregnancy is without distress. These women may feel great distress over, say, the lack of control they have over their bodies. If you did not feel an instant connection to your baby, for whatever reason, you may feel guilty about your loss. You may feel unentitled to your sadness. You may feel angry. These are all valid.

Huong

Another thing that makes this loss particularly hard is the ambiguity of it. Some questions my clients ask themselves are: *What went wrong? Why does it hurt so much to lose someone I never knew?* In the psychology world, we often classify pregnancy loss as an ambiguous loss, "inherently characterized by a lack of closure or clear understanding."

Psychologist Pauline Boss, PhD (1999), coined the term "ambiguous loss" and described two types of ambiguous loss. The first is when a person is physically present but psychologically absent (for example, as in those individuals with dementia). The second type is when there is a physical absence but a psychological and emotional presence. According to Boss, "I intention-

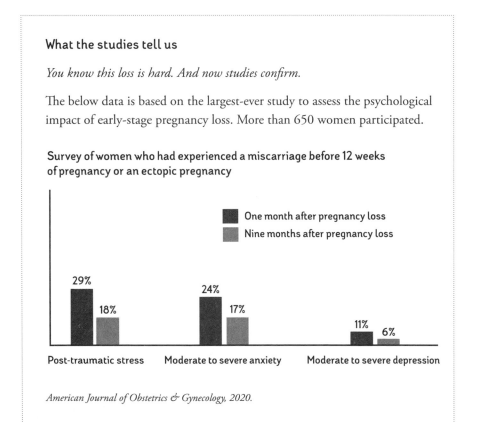

What the studies tell us

You know this loss is hard. And now studies confirm.

The below data is based on the largest-ever study to assess the psychological impact of early-stage pregnancy loss. More than 650 women participated.

Survey of women who had experienced a miscarriage before 12 weeks of pregnancy or an ectopic pregnancy

■ One month after pregnancy loss
■ Nine months after pregnancy loss

	Post-traumatic stress	Moderate to severe anxiety	Moderate to severe depression
One month after pregnancy loss	29%	24%	11%
Nine months after pregnancy loss	18%	17%	6%

American Journal of Obstetrics & Gynecology, 2020.

ally hold the opposing ideas of absence and presence because I have learned that most relationships are indeed both." This sentiment is consistent with stories from parents who have experienced pregnancy loss(es). They describe the feeling of the presence of a child they have never physically met but who will always be a part of their hearts and psyche. However, the same parents also experience the absence (both physical and emotional) of a child they will not be able to see grow up.

What we know from research and clinical work is that ambiguous loss is related to a *lack of facts* surrounding the loss of a loved one. Therefore, in the case of a pregnancy loss, the lack of facts can be related to "Did I do something to cause this?" or "Was there something more I could have done?" or "If I would have taken this vitamin or exercised more (or less) or done [fill in the blank], would I have had a successful pregnancy?"

I remind my grieving clients that those questions are related to our natural desire for a sense of control. Although it is painful to inflict self-blame for a pregnancy loss, for some it is easier to self-flagellate (which perpetuates the myth that we have control over all of our life outcomes) than to accept the randomness of life and the lack of answers.

Another component of ambiguous loss may be a lack of support from others, who also may lack a clear understanding of the loss and what it meant to you. Maybe people didn't know you were pregnant. Maybe they did know but can't understand why you are so grief-stricken. Many people find it hard to intuitively understand how the grief for a child who did not live outside the womb (or died shortly after birth) could be so prolonged or intense. The ambiguous loss and subsequent pain are often exacerbated and worsened by the way others dismiss the loss or judge the griever.

In this way, there are two traumas—the trauma of the pregnancy loss and the trauma of others' reactions to that loss. The invalidation of others can leave some women second-guessing their feelings. Or, even if a woman is secure in how she feels, she may second-guess the relationships she has with people who do not take her sadness seriously. The end result: loneliness.

I remind my clients that trauma *is* trauma and that they are experiencing a *very* normal reaction to an abnormal event. I also remind my clients that if someone does not react in the way you need, it is best to establish boundaries and to perhaps distance yourself for some time.

As both a card-carrying member of the human race and a psychologist, let me say that personally, it has been difficult to sit with the pain of some of my best friends and loved ones as they share with me their pregnancy losses. Our natural inclinations are to soothe the pain, either through words or actions. However, I remind myself and my clients that there are no words that can take away pain. Pain is an emotion that needs to be felt thoroughly. It needs to have motion. To be examined. To be respected. It is a part of the human experience. And in trying to alleviate someone's pain, you may be unconsciously asking them to expedite their grieving and healing.

Imagine your cocoon
I sometimes walk my clients through an exercise where I have them imagine themselves cocooning and being wrapped with love and protection. Who would they want in that inner sanctum? What do they need to hear, feel, touch, smell, and see during that time? I then encourage them to honor their innermost needs without questioning themselves or allowing others to judge them.

Different kinds
of loss

Chemical pregnancy

A loss is a loss is a loss.

With my fourth pregnancy, I started spotting a few days after seeing those two pink lines on the test. I called my doctor, concerned because the last time this had happened, my pregnancy turned out to be ectopic. He said, "Well, it might be just a chemical pregnancy."

Just a chemical pregnancy.

I still bristle at the "just." I also bristle at the term "chemical pregnancy"— as if it was a science experiment gone wrong.

Meredith: Sometimes doctors, even ones we truly like, live deeply in the world of data and do not pay enough attention to their patients' emotions. This leaves many women feeling dismissed, overlooked. As far as I'm concerned, "just" should apply to things like "just a cup of sugar" or "just a minute." Not "just a chemical pregnancy." (See "When doctors don't say the right things").

I googled "chemical pregnancy" and learned that it's an early pregnancy loss that occurs shortly after implantation. Chemical pregnancies account for the vast majority of miscarriages (50 percent to 75 percent).

My suspected chemical pregnancy turned out to be another ectopic pregnancy, which received more attention from my doctor because it was, you know, *life-threatening*. Had it been "just a chemical pregnancy," he likely would have had nothing more to say to me.

People assume that chemical pregnancies aren't a big deal because the woman wasn't pregnant for long and didn't experience pregnancy symptoms like morning sickness. But, in my mind, all pregnancies are a big deal. They represent a spark of life, however brief. And for me, each spark was attached to so many hopes and dreams and plans. I was pregnant, and then I wasn't. The emotional whiplash of that left me reeling.

Meredith: From soaring exhilaration to crushing disappointment—that's what being forced into grief feels like. Just as the love begins, you are forced to let it go.

Ectopic pregnancy

Been there, done that. Twice.

My husband, Chris, and I made the decision to start a family in early 2015. After a couple months off the pill, I peed on a stick and, three minutes later, felt a jolt of excitement throughout my body.

That excitement turned to unease when I began spotting a few days after the positive test. I called my doctor. They weren't concerned, said, "It's probably just implantation bleeding" (this led to lots of googling on this subject). Blood draws over the course of two weeks showed the embryo was growing . . . until, suddenly, the growth slowed. "We need to do an ultrasound," they said.

It goes without saying that my first ultrasound was nothing like what I pictured it to be. There was no magic wand passed over my belly, no tiny bean of a human on the screen. Instead, the doctor inserted something inside me as if she was doing a pap smear (which felt invasive; I worried she was harming my already endangered baby). The doctor sighed upon seeing the blip of my baby on the screen: "It's ectopic."

Ectopic is Greek for "out of place," which felt accurate in so many ways. These types of pregnancies are relatively rare—about 2 percent of pregnancies. In my case, the embryo had taken up residence in my left fallopian tube—a terrible oops of nature.

My doctor recommended emergency surgery because of the size of the embryo (just a sweet pea, but too big for a fallopian tube). There was risk of my tube rupturing, which can be a life-threatening situation. Ectopic pregnancies are the leading cause of first-trimester maternal death.

"I found it very hurtful when people would dismiss what had happened. Most people didn't even understand what an ectopic pregnancy was. They would just say, 'You had a miscarriage, don't worry . . . You'll get pregnant again.' People didn't understand how traumatic that was to me . . . Having surgery due to the blood loss made me feel that I was so close to death. Also, it meant the possibility of not being able to get pregnant again, the fear of having another ectopic pregnancy."—Deysi De La Cruz, on her ectopic pregnancy

This surgery ordeal was terrifying for me. I'd only been under anesthesia once before, as a teenager, when I had my wisdom teeth removed. The whole process was awful—getting vials and vials of blood drawn, having an IV inserted through my hand, answering questions about my advance directive. And then the electricity went out at the hospital, and I had to wait in a hallway, lying there on the gurney, for two hours before they could operate.

When I woke up, the doctor said I had already started bleeding internally, meaning the tube would have ruptured "at any minute" if they hadn't operated. In hindsight, I was having shoulder pain, which can be indicative of internal bleeding (apparently when blood in the abdomen irritates the diaphragm, pain may be felt primarily in the shoulder).

Physically, I could barely move for a few days. With laparoscopic surgery, they pump you full of air so they can see and maneuver around. I was so bloated and uncomfortable. In a bit of cruel irony, I looked about five months pregnant for several days. It hurt to sit up. I fainted during my first attempt at walking (my husband splashed water all over my face, something that seems laughably dramatic now). The only thing that felt OK was lying flat, staring at the ceiling.

After this traumatic, "out of place" experience, I was terrified to try again. When I expressed my anxieties to a good friend who is a doctor, she said, "It won't happen again. I've only seen that, like, twice in my career."

Famous last words.

I had a *second* ectopic pregnancy a little more than a year after the first (there were two other losses in between). As Elizabeth McCracken says in her memoir, *An Exact Replica of a Figment of My Imagination*, "Once you've been on the losing side of great odds, you never find statistics comforting again."

With my second ectopic pregnancy, the embryo was so small that my OB-GYN couldn't see on ultrasound where it had implanted. He assumed it was in my one good tube, the right tube, but he didn't know for sure. Some ectopic pregnancies occur on the ovary or the cervix, or even in the abdominal cavity. Any surgery would be exploratory, so they gave me a shot of methotrexate, a drug that's normally used to treat cancer. It works by stopping cells—cancer cells, embryonic cells—from dividing and growing.

Meredith: So much related to health care goes unexplained to patients. A routine test doesn't make it less of a test, or less of an anxiety-producing test. When you are in the midst of a pregnancy loss, you already feel like so much is out of your control; it is your right to ask for explanations of procedures so you feel more agency in the situation.

See "The medical part of pregnancy loss" for more information about how to navigate doctor's appointments and feel more empowered as you go through what is very much a medical event.

I had to get blood drawn every couple of days to ensure my pregnancy hormone levels were dropping. At one point, they increased, which scared me. Finally, they started to drop. It was painfully slow. It took *two months* for me to officially become unpregnant. In those two months, I still had to go to work and social activities. I had to celebrate my damn birthday with a party that my husband had planned before this mess began. I had to act like everything was fine, though I knew my embryo was slowly dying.

To this day, I consider this one of the most excruciating experiences of my life.

Huong

Another way to frame Kim's (and, perhaps, your) experience and the pain (physical and emotional) of an ectopic pregnancy or pregnancy loss is through an intersectional lens.

The concept of intersectionality was first coined by Kimberlé Crenshaw in 1989 to describe how race, class, gender, and other individual characteristics "intersect" with one another or overlap. Intersectionality is also used in critical theories to describe how oppressive institutions (racism, sexism, homophobia, transphobia, ableism, xenophobia, classism, and others) are interconnected and cannot be examined separately from one another.

In my clinical practice, I use the theory of intersectionality as a framework to understand the multiple layers that one has to navigate, or the multiple balls that one must juggle, due to the unique intersection of their challenges and the larger societal context.

For some ectopic pregnancy losses, there is the intersection of the loss of the child, the potential physical danger to the mother, the numerous medical appointments, the lack of trauma-informed care by the medical providers, and the obvious and subtle differences in power dynamics between a medical provider and patient, among other factors, including race, class/socioeconomic status, sexual orientation, and gender identity.

Meredith: Just like a routine test doesn't make it less of a test, that an event is "rare" is no consolation when it happens to you. After reading Huong's explanation of the concept of intersectionality, take a moment and think about your personal intersections and how they made your pregnancy loss more difficult to navigate.

Blighted ovum

Yes, it "counts." Of course it does.

A friend of mine had a blighted ovum, and I had no idea what that was. When she explained it to me, my first thought was, "Why call it a 'blighted ovum'?" What a terrible name for a loss.

A blighted ovum happens when a fertilized egg attaches itself to the uterine wall but the embryo does not develop. You still get a positive pregnancy test, and you assume things are going as they should. A diagnosis usually isn't made until an ultrasound shows either an empty womb or an empty gestational sac. What an awful moment—sitting at your first ultrasound, hopeful and eager, only to hear and see that there is no baby.

"Some people might say that a blighted ovum is not a 'real' pregnancy, so it's not a 'real' miscarriage. That there was never a fetus so it doesn't count. I tell you that's a crock of shit. Loss is loss."

—Olivia Lasting, This West Coast Mommy blog

What's so cruel about anembryonic pregnancies (I prefer this term to "blighted ovum") is that the body recognizes that the pregnancy cannot continue (usually due to chromosomal issues), but the message is delayed in getting to the brain. You have no reason to think anything is wrong . . . until that ultrasound.

My friend said she felt silly grieving a "non-baby pregnancy." But I called bullshit on that. She was clearly distraught. She had been envisioning a life with a baby, and now she was left to grieve that dreamed-of future. I could feel her grief like a brick in my own stomach; it was familiarly heavy. I knew what she was going through was profound and life-changing.

"For ten weeks, my slightly bulging belly gave me the impression that I was pregnant, when in fact, I was simply carrying an empty home."
—Elsa Valmidiano, "Blighted," featured in *What God Is Honored Here? Writings on Miscarriage and Infant Loss by and for Native Women and Women of Color* (Shannon Gibney and Kao Kalia Yang, editors)

Molar pregnancy

I'll say it again—it counts.
Of course it does.

Molar pregnancies are rare (one in one thousand pregnancies), so if you have one, it can feel especially lonely. These types of pregnancies, like ectopic pregnancies, also carry medical risk for the woman, which makes them even more distressing.

If you've had a molar pregnancy, you probably don't need me to explain it, but I'll offer a short explanation for those who want it or don't know what it is. A molar pregnancy is where an abnormal fertilized egg implants in the uterus. The cells (called trophoblasts) that should become the placenta grow far too quickly and take over the space where the embryo would normally develop.

There are two kinds of molar pregnancy—partial and complete. With a partial molar pregnancy, two sperm fertilize the egg instead of one. There is too much genetic material for the baby to develop. With a complete molar pregnancy, one sperm (or even two) fertilizes an egg that has no genetic material inside. There are not enough of the right chromosomes for the baby to develop.

In a very small number of cases, molar cells burrow deeply into the uterus or spread to other parts of the body. This can develop into a rare type of cancer. WTF, right? Fortunately, the cancer has a cure rate of almost 100 percent . . . but still.

A molar pregnancy must be deeply unsettling. My ectopic pregnancies were medically scary, in addition to being emotionally fraught, and I imagine molar pregnancies are similar. Having your innocence taken away by experiencing something like this sucks. Then you have to deal with nobody really understanding what you're going through, because very few people know what a molar pregnancy is. Or if they do know what it is, they might dismiss it as "not a real pregnancy." For me, each pregnancy was very "real."

Meredith

When the "statistically rare" anomaly is yours, life takes on a surreal quality. You are in another category, shuttled down another hall, isolated in a room where you are about to learn an entirely new vocabulary—and experience an altered reality. It's not what you or any woman expects or wants. On top of everything, it can feel very lonely, particularly when you're first presented with the specifics.

Emotions cannot be assigned to one loss and not another. They do not work that way. How come it is OK for a woman who is trying to get pregnant to weep when her period comes, while a woman who sees a positive pregnancy test but has a blighted ovum or molar pregnancy feels silly? Both are valid experiences. Both matter. Both count.

Grief is not an overreaction. That is the truth, whether others "get it" or not. Who is the Judge over what a "real" pregnancy is? Who can know, but you, of the unseen attachment you felt, the preparations you made? You. And you are enough.

Huong

F.O.D. First. Only. Different.

In her memoir, *Year of Yes*, Shonda Rhimes talks about being an F.O.D.—first, only, different—as both a source of privilege and also a burden. I often use this concept in working with my clients, especially those with unique experiences that place them in the F.O.D. pregnancy loss club.

You may be the *first* patient of a particular medical provider to experience a molar pregnancy. You may be the *only* person in your pregnancy loss support group to have a blighted ovum. And you may feel *different*—very different—as if you are in a different club, a club where you are both the president and sole member.

In January 2008, I provided my first therapeutic session as a therapist-in-training. It has been more than a decade of hearing hundreds and hundreds of stories of pain and sorrow. I have come to realize that our pain is ours and ours alone. Due to our unique genetic makeup, upbringing, personality, and life choices, no one will experience our pain in the way we do.

So while it can be lonely to not have another human being to reflect our pain to us and say "me too," I encourage you to stand in front of the mirror and look at who is staring back at you. That person deserves all the compassion you can muster.

"… the fact that it was a molar pregnancy has been hard to deal with as all I can think is how can I feel this way, love something that wasn't really there? But on the other hand I think there was a baby there …" —Shared by Jade on MiscarriageAssociation.org.uk

First-trimester miscarriage

When things seem to be going fine . . . until they don't.

After my ectopic pregnancy, my doctor said, "You should try again. But, just know that miscarriage is very common." She retired shortly after that appointment, so I never got to ask her if she's psychic.

With my second pregnancy, there were no worrisome symptoms, but early blood testing (done as a precaution because I'd had an ectopic pregnancy and was therefore "high risk") revealed the embryo was not growing fast enough. An ultrasound confirmed the embryo was in the uterus—a good thing—but a miscarriage was "imminent." The doctor said I could have a D&C (dilation and curettage, a procedure to remove tissue from the uterus) or I could pass the baby naturally. I liked that word—*naturally*. I asked how long that would take, thinking it would be a few hours or days. He said it could be up to *a month*.

"At ten weeks, it's hard not to already have so many hopes and dreams for your future child, and when that book gets shut quickly, emotionally that can be very hard." —Michaela, on her first-trimester miscarriage

Before this, my limited understanding was that miscarriage involved sitting on the toilet, expelling some blood, and feeling sad for a while. I thought it was this nice, tidy experience. I was so naïve. I had no idea there could be this scenario of knowing a baby is dead and waiting for my body to realize this fate—a "missed miscarriage" or "missed abortion," they call it. As if you made an appointment to terminate the pregnancy and didn't show up.

Meredith: I don't think we realize how painful the suffering is for someone who has lost a pregnancy, nor do we realize the myriad ways it can occur. We, as a society, seem to have this naïve and somewhat lacking understanding of miscarriage, including the physical and emotional toll it takes.

The doctor said he could give me something to "expel the embryo" (I don't know why they continue to use such terrible language in these situations). That medication, Cytotec (generic name misoprostol, used off-label for incomplete first trimester miscarriages) works for 80 percent of women, but I found myself on the wrong side of the statistics (again). When the pills didn't work, I waited and waited and waited. It was weeks later when I finally passed the embryonic sac. It was obvious when it happened—I saw the blob, like a small red egg yolk, on the toilet paper. I took a picture of it, desperate to commemorate this failed life. Then I flushed it down the toilet—because I was shocked, because I didn't know what else to do. Nobody had prepared me for this.

Meredith: Programs like hospice and palliative care help prepare for death. They might present rituals that help mark the ending of life but also provide a bridge to get us thinking about consciousness and the soul as the person is dying.

Pregnancy loss needs more of this. But because it can occur so suddenly, there is less time to prepare. It is more akin to having a loved one die unexpectedly, a very traumatic event. Even so, we have rituals in place for deaths, even sudden ones. Pregnancy loss remains a very undeveloped area of grief, mourning, and transition. Women may feel confused about the steps they are supposed to take, including the very basic step of what to do if they lose the embryo at home. Sadly, many women are left having to decide for themselves.

It seems like first-trimester miscarriages are easily dismissed, waved off as being "so common." I think people don't understand the magnitude of the pain if they haven't gone through it themselves. For me, when I saw the positive pregnancy test, I was on my way to motherhood. The fantasy had begun. The loss, even at "just" six weeks, was crushing. It didn't help to hear statistics about chromosomal abnormalities. It didn't help when people said,

"At least it was early." I don't care how early the loss is—there is no "just." There is no "at least."

"According to science, it was an unviable fetus; according to my heart, it was my baby." —Soniah Kamal, "The Face of Miscarriage," featured in *What God Is Honored Here? Writings on Miscarriage and Infant Loss by and for Native Women and Women of Color* (Shannon Gibney and Kao Kalia Yang, editors)

Second-trimester miscarriage

A loss that makes you realize there is no "safe zone."

My third pregnancy was different from my first two. I took pregnancy tests every day for the first couple weeks, analyzing the test strips to see the line getting darker. I was constantly feeling myself up, confirming my breasts were still tender. Most days, I had morning sickness, which was really an all-day queasiness that made me feel like I was on a boat in rough waters. On the days I wasn't as queasy, I was convinced the baby was dead. Every trip to the bathroom raised my blood pressure. I closed my eyes when I pulled down my underwear, then opened them, preparing to see red. When the doctor called with my first blood test results, I felt dizzy, like I was going to pass out. My hCG levels were good, though.

At eight weeks, I saw my very first heartbeat on ultrasound. Up until that point, ultrasounds had given me nothing but grief. I started crying tears of relief. I'd done enough googling to know that hearing a heartbeat is a big deal—only 1.6 percent of pregnancies end after a heartbeat is confirmed. This time, I thought, I would be on the right side of the statistics. I had to be. When we crossed into the second trimester, "the safe zone," I let myself breathe a sigh of relief.

I had every test done to ensure the baby was healthy. He was—and, yes, the baby was a boy. We named him Miles. Over the course of a few ultrasound appointments, we saw him grow limbs; we watched those limbs flail about on the screen.

And, then, at the four-month mark, something was wrong.

On ultrasound, the black sea of amniotic fluid was mostly gone. There was nothing for the baby to float around in, like you see babies doing in all the ultrasound photos people post on Facebook. He was squished between small pockets of black. He was tucked in on himself and so contorted that it was difficult to know what we were looking at. His heart rate was fine, but he was measuring a couple weeks behind—without the space provided by the fluid, he couldn't stretch and grow.

The doctor explained that there could be a deformity with the baby's kidneys or urinary tract, meaning he was swallowing the amniotic fluid but not processing and excreting it properly. That's what amniotic fluid is, basically—fetal urine. He said it could also be a problem with the placenta, or a tear in the membrane, leading to leakage. When I asked him what would happen if the fluid levels didn't improve, he said the baby would likely press against the umbilical cord, reducing the blood flow and causing death. He said even if that didn't happen, there was a risk of birth defects from vital organs (heart, kidneys, and liver) getting compressed.

There was nothing to do but wait and see. I don't think people realize how much "wait and see" there is with later losses. The in-limbo phase is agonizing.

The doctor sent me home with an ultrasound photo, as if this were any other prenatal appointment. In it, Miles was staring out at us, his eyes big black holes. He looked alien and terrified, as if pleading with us to save him. For months, this photo gave me nightmares.

At home, I commenced staying off my feet and drinking a gallon of water a day (which is what some women on message boards recommended for low amniotic fluid). I bought a fetal doppler online so I could check Miles's heartbeat. When it arrived, I lay in bed, squeezed gel on my belly, and moved the wand around. There it was—a strong heart rate of 159. It sounded like a muffled recording of a horse galloping.

The next day, I tried for hours to get a reading and I couldn't. I didn't want to call my doctor, because I thought he would chastise me for buying the monitor (I envisioned him saying, "Leave the monitoring to me"). I tried not to worry because so many women on the "pregnant-and-worried" message boards said they had trouble finding the heartbeat. "The baby moves around a lot," they said. "You're probably not doing it right," they said. Still, the day after that, I wrote in my journal, "I woke up this morning not feeling pregnant. I think the baby has passed."

A woman's intuition is a powerful thing.

Still, during the two weeks of bed rest, I overrode my intuition and convinced myself that the baby would be fine. I didn't have any symptoms that he *wasn't* fine. No bleeding, no cramping. It would just be so bizarre if he died. I kept asking myself that jinx of a question: *What are the chances?*

Meredith: We think of pregnancy as being natural and therefore not fragile. However, here we are awakening to the reality of the unthinkable—the fragile state of pregnancy, even a pregnancy that passes the first-trimester mark. Loss in the second trimester is not common, but it is more common than we like to think. Out of one hundred pregnant women, between one and five of them will lose a baby in the second trimester.

The doctor asked me the usual questions about how I was feeling, then started the ultrasound. A few seconds in, he sighed and said, "I'm not seeing a heartbeat." I was shocked. It was April Fools' Day. For a brief second, I thought he was playing a sick joke on me.

All I said, and it came out as a shriek, was, "What?"

He interpreted this as an actual question and went on to explain:

"The way the baby is measuring tells me he died shortly after the last appointment," he said. "Do you see how blood is no longer going to the baby?"

He continued moving the transducer around my belly, investigating. The medical interest on his face disgusted me.

"Can you stop?" I screamed.

Months later, when I was finally ready to get my medical records, I'd see that he wrote, "The ultrasound procedure was terminated due to patient request after finding out about the absence of the fetal heart rate." I read this as disappointment on his part, like he would have continued examining my dead baby for hours if I'd let him.

Meredith: We are all human—even health-care providers. But lack of acknowledgment and the disregard of pain and suffering is not what medicine is about. When a physician takes an extra five minutes to sit with you, answer your questions, and listen to your concerns, you might still be angry, but it would be directed at the appropriate target—the loss—and not at how you were treated which, in turn, becomes an unnecessary distraction.

He handed me a box of Kleenex. My husband was clutching my ankle. I was still lying on the examination table.

"I'm so sorry, Kimberly," the doctor said.

Nobody calls me Kimberly except for my grandma. This man did not know me at all. It took everything in me not to say, "My name is Kim, you asshole."

The pregnancy was too far along for a D&C, so there were two options: A D&E (dilation and evacuation), which involves dilating the cervix with medications and/or instruments then taking apart the fetus and removing it through the dilated cervix; or labor induction. I couldn't imagine giving birth to Miles. I wanted to see him in my mind as a healthy baby, not a lifeless, gray, very miniature human. I opted for the surgery. I still wonder if that was the right choice.

My doctor said he didn't perform D&Es, which made me painfully aware of how uncommon my predicament was. I had to see another doctor at another hospital for the surgery. The surgery involved some preparation—I had to have small rod-like devices placed inside the cervix so it would be dilated enough for them to remove the baby. This was as excruciating as it sounds. In addition, I had to take prostaglandin medications to further soften and thin the cervix.

On the day of the surgery, two words were written in black marker on the packet they gave me: FETAL DEMISE. I can't imagine a more depressing pair of words. I was put under anesthesia, something that was no longer unfamiliar to me. When I woke up, I was crying—bawling. Was I crying because of pain, or because I knew, even in my unconscious state, that they were taking my baby?

I asked the nurse to make sure they tested the fetus for any infections or genetic problems. We'd already discussed this with the doctors and they assured us they'd "get to the bottom of it." I was desperate for answers. The nurse nodded distractedly, handed me a cup of ice chips, helped me into a wheelchair, and pushed me through the halls to the parking garage, where my husband's car was waiting.

In the days that followed, my breasts were engorged and sore because my body thought I'd given birth and needed to feed the baby. I didn't leak milk, thankfully. Some women do. My belly was a pooch of failure, its protrusion reminding me every second of what I'd lost. I couldn't sleep, even with the sleeping pills prescribed to me. It was like I was wired to listen for a crying baby who wasn't there.

We never found out why Miles died. The lab apparently "lost" him. I was so infuriated that I threatened to sue the doctor; I even went to the local courthouse to file paperwork. In the end, I didn't. In the end, I didn't have the energy.

I no longer obsess over why Miles died. I've found peace with not knowing. I do think of him often. He remains in my heart as the son I never got to hold.

_____

"At fifteen weeks along, I found out the fetal heartbeat was slowing down (below 70) to a point which indicated the baby would likely not survive . . . The most difficult part of losing this baby was probably the two-week stretch where the heart rate was 'too slow to probably make it' but 'not yet stopped' . . . I had to slowly wait for the life inside of me to die."

—Jessica, on her second-trimester loss

Meredith

What Kim describes is a stunning example of how the stages of grief sneak in when you don't realize it, at a time when you might not have thought you would need to be grieving at all. One day, a powerful heartbeat; the next, no reading at all. *Am I holding the monitor correctly? Maybe the baby turned on his side? Is this me worrying too much?* While the intuition directs us very specifically, it can be so difficult to follow it. Plus, disparities in clinical symptoms that can occur simultaneously add a level of confusion. Amniotic fluid is gone yet the heartbeat is strong. How to make sense of something like this? Fear is so natural.

In this case, I do not see the denial of intuition as black or white. It is not as simple as, "You did not trust your intuition, and that is bad." Sometimes, distrusting one's intuition is part of a delicate dance of self-protection.

Denying that you were experiencing a monumental loss of life, a life growing inside of you, protected you just enough, at a time when you needed protection. It provided a tiny window of energy to drive yourself to the doctor, press the elevator button, sign in at the front desk. These are steps that are familiar, doable. *I am going to find out if anything is wrong.* That is how denial is supposed to work, as a kind of protective shock absorber in the shortest of terms.

When intuition slices through that denial, it can be frightening and alarming. *Trust myself? What if I'm wrong? Or what if I'm right?*

Julie Russell is a registered nurse and Reiki Master who has done more than eight thousand Reiki sessions, including sessions for women going through pregnancy, infertility, and loss. She says, from an energy perspective, it is very difficult for human beings to see past the loss in the moment it is occurring. They fixate on a decision that wasn't made, a step that wasn't taken, or, as we can see, an intuition not followed. Try to set that aside, or at least find more ways to view what you did or didn't do. "There is no good or bad. Rather, this is a way for the soul to learn and grow. The soul does not live by duality, by good or bad." In fact, a deeper connection and trust of your intuition *might* be one of the more profound and bittersweet lessons of pregnancy loss.

"I fought tooth and nail to be a mother ... I suffered several miscarriages including two at five months. That's when you have the clothes already picked out, the nursery is already painted. They ask you do you want a funeral or do you want the cremation."—Wendy Williams, television host

Preterm delivery

When your baby arrives much too soon.

I've talked to a few women who have been through the torturous experience of preterm delivery, and their stories bring me to instant tears. I can only imagine how terrifying it must be to feel contractions or have your water break *months* early. There is this helplessness—oftentimes, there's nothing the doctors can do. The goal is to keep the baby inside as long as possible for the greatest chance of survival. But, sometimes, there is no choice in the matter; the baby is coming.

Extremely premature babies (born at or before twenty-five weeks) have to fight for their lives from the moment they emerge into the world. Watching this fight must be excruciating. Suddenly, you're not just recovering from the trauma of an early delivery, but coming face-to-face with the trauma of watching your tiny baby struggle to survive.

With this type of loss, you did get to meet your baby. You got to see him or her, hold him or her. You got to say hello and then had to say goodbye. This can feel like a blessing and curse; you are given the briefest of introductions to your child, then promptly denied more. You are left with all that comes with a death—paperwork, planning a service (if you choose), telling people what happened (all the pressure to explain). You are burdened with worry for any future pregnancy—how will you do anything but hold your breath for those nine months? Doctors may throw around obnoxious terms like "cervical incompetence," leaving you angry with your doctors or your body or God or all of the above. You may have symptoms of posttraumatic stress (See "Posttraumatic stress: It's a thing"). There is no way around it—you will be completely heartbroken.

Stillbirth

The briefest hello; the most terrible goodbye.

My therapist said to me once, "Kim, tragedies can't be ranked." Loss is loss is loss. But, I don't know. To me stillbirth seems like one of the worst losses that can happen to someone. There are all those months of pregnancy, of hope. There is labor and delivery. Then silence. Then tears.

I have an acquaintance-friend whose son was born still at thirty-six weeks. I reached out via Facebook, feeling like a moron because I was at a loss for what to say (and I'm supposed to know about this stuff). I cried about his son for days. I confess to still stalking his social media accounts (and his wife's) to check in on how they are doing. I just can't imagine their pain. My heart breaks for them.

"My perspective on life instantly changed after the loss of Ella. I realized I wasn't immune to life's negatives and that loss, death, and grieving were as true to me as life, hope, and joy."
—Georgie, who had a stillborn daughter (Ella) and two first-trimester miscarriages

I always assumed stillbirths were exceedingly rare. But in doing research for this book, I learned that about one in 160 pregnancies end in stillbirth. That's far more than I thought. This kind of loss is particularly brutal because it often involves the physical and emotional toll of labor and delivery (vaginally or via C-section). It involves a death certificate and funeral planning (if you choose). There are often so many medical questions—how did this happen? How do we make sure it doesn't happen again? In many cases, there is no absolute conclusion to be drawn, or parents are given a less-than-satisfying explanation (such as, "there was an issue with the umbilical cord" or "there was a problem with the placenta"). Not that any explanation could be satisfying.

With a stillbirth, you see and hold your baby. You are given a brief time to bond before saying goodbye. I cannot imagine this moment, the giving over, the letting go. I have to assume the real giving over and letting go takes a lifetime.

Meredith

Conception, pregnancy, and childbirth are the ultimate creative acts. An egg and sperm join; zygote becomes embryo becomes baby. We don't just hope, we expect that we will meet and love and cherish this most extraordinary baby.

Loss of a baby who arrived too soon or was born still defies all that we expect of this creative process. Everything is turned not only upside down but inside out. For example, the skin-to-skin contact immediately after birth we think of as primarily beneficial for the baby's attachment to mom becomes the first step in a fraught and difficult goodbye. When you leave the hospital, your arms and heart will search for things to do—again, where does all that love go?

Increasingly, hospitals are recognizing the need to honor the life of the baby who died, and also the experience of the mother who carried and lost that baby.

Traysi Handel, LCSW, USC School of Social Work, explains that when hospitals incorporate rituals to also honor the loss and trauma experienced by the parents, it helps support the grief process at the earliest stages. Some hospitals, for example, provide memory boxes for parents who have lost a child born prematurely, who have given birth to a stillborn baby, and who have miscarried in the hospital.

At some hospitals, these memory boxes include, when appropriate, photographs, an artistic rendering of the baby's brief stay on earth, in the arms of the parents or in their hospital bassinet. The box also contains the infant's hospital wristband, newborn hat, and delivery blanket. Parents are allowed to pick up their baby's box only after one year has passed, when their grief is less fresh, and time has provided some room for recovery.

When you lose a baby born prematurely, or you give birth to a baby born still, you are left with difficult decisions to make, many of them logistical. Before twenty weeks' gestation, the loss of a pregnancy is considered a miscarriage. After twenty weeks, it is considered fetal demise or fetal death.

There will be specific reporting requirements based on the laws in your state.

It's likely you will wrestle (or have wrestled) with questions like: Should you view the baby's body or not? Is it wrong not to want to? Are you expected to know? Will you hold the baby? How will you say goodbye? Will spending time with the baby make the final farewell easier or harder? How will you find the courage to walk out the door without your baby in your arms?

How far along you were with your pregnancy might influence your answers to these questions. But your desire to view, touch, and hold the baby will be completely personal to you. Some hospitals offer Cuddle Cots, which are cooling devices that preserve the body of a baby who has died in a bassinet or crib so that he or she can remain up to five days in a hospital room with the parents as they navigate decisions and as the mother receives the aftercare she needs.

"... the death of a baby to stillbirth is the ultimate paradox for providers and patients—the convergence of life and death."
—Joanne Cacciatore, *Seminars in Fetal & Neonatal Medicine*

There are no rules, of course, except what feels right for you in that moment. Trust that whatever decision you made was the right one in that moment. Throughout this process, trust that you will do the best for yourself that you can. In the weeks to months following the loss, you will discover new ways to connect with your child that could include but are not limited to: talking to your baby, writing notes and love letters to them, and/or creating a time capsule of trinkets and goodbye notes from you, family, and friends.

Huong

There is one more thing I wanted to touch on. Some of my clients have told me it was scary for them to see their stillborn or deceased baby. Perhaps there was a deformity. Perhaps the baby was purple and blue. Some parents then felt guilty that they had such "disgusting" and "inappropriate" thoughts about their child. I remind clients that our minds are constantly creating stories and chatter (also known as the monkey mind), and so if you find yourself bombarded with thoughts, please know that is a natural part of your survival brain. There is no need to feel guilty or doubt the love you have for your baby.

Different circumstances

When the pregnancy
wasn't planned

Wanting, not wanting, and something in between.

Though it may seem counterintuitive, feelings of ambivalence can surface during the grieving process. It can be confusing.

I see ambivalence in grief as somewhat of a second cousin to the "bargaining stage" in Kübler-Ross's model (See "Understanding your grief process" for an overview of this model). You might be familiar with bargaining, like "If I had only . . . " and "What if I hadn't . . . ?"

Ambivalence, or the state of mixed feelings or contradictory ideas about something, is interwoven in daily life even without loss. And it's hard to articulate. Ambivalent feelings that surfaced during your pregnancy may have surfaced even if the pregnancy wasn't lost. The nature of your ambivalence might have been different (but maybe not); your loss brought everything to the surface. As you grieve, you're bound to encounter a range of feelings, not only about your loss but about how you view yourself and your life.

Emotions are not linear. Ambivalence can make you feel a little fragmented. How, after a tremendous loss, could you feel relief as well as sadness? How can you be happy for your friend who is pregnant with twins but also privately wish she'd struggle in her pregnancy too? You might understand all this on an intellectual level, but reconciling (and actually living with) these feelings can be more than a little uncomfortable and . . . make you feel incredibly stuck.

Processing difficult feelings is far from being stuck. Turning over thoughts and reflecting shows movement; movement means life, change, and ultimately renewal.

Researchers found something interesting about ambivalence—examining it can help people recover after a major loss. This means that by looking at the many feelings you have—some that are opposite and contradictory—you may grow stronger and become even more resilient. A very good thing.

Here are some scenarios that encompass ambivalence from the start. But keep in mind that though the details of your pregnancy and loss might differ, ambivalence, as we've established, is still universal.

Kim: With each of these scenarios, there is also the difficulty of others' reactions, like, "I didn't think you guys even wanted a baby." There is this implication that it shouldn't be a big deal because you weren't pining for a child. Society has little tolerance for ambivalence. We like things to be black and white; the gray area of this type of loss is confusing (for the griever and the people around them). They may feel "unallowed" to be sad. They may try to tamp down grief, which we all know doesn't really work. I wish people were better at acknowledging the gray area. I wish they would just say, "I'm so sorry you're going through this."

Unplanned but wanted

Perhaps you were going to wait. But this surprise, albeit early, was a welcome one. Getting pregnant was easier that you thought it would be. The emotion and joy surrounding preparation—so much to do and so little time—was by turns exhilarating and awe-inducing. Your life was about to grow in ways you were excited to explore. And then everything changed. In an instant your joy was replaced with anguish. Or confusion. A feeling of being lost. Wait. What just happened? And why?

Passive acceptance

Your period was late, the pregnancy test was positive, and you (somewhat passively) decided to keep the baby, a choice made almost out of convenience. Admitting that, even to yourself, was difficult. But despite not having a maybe-someday plan to have a baby, something started to change for you. You were starting to become "OK" with this pregnancy. Maybe not 100 percent but, you told yourself, who in this circumstance is? For you, the loss of this pregnancy has been steeped in guilt. Did you not want the baby enough?

Unplanned and unwanted

Perhaps you didn't want to be pregnant. At all. Maybe your pregnancy was the result of a sexual assault. Maybe the sex was consensual, but you regret it. Maybe the sex was with a loving partner, but your birth control failed. For you it wasn't about ever being ready; you didn't want a baby. You were not conflicted about that. So why is the loss of the pregnancy so damn hard? You might feel an element of relief coupled with a flare of shame and, with that, guilt. You might cycle through those emotions in a matter of minutes. Holding that tension while coping with the effects on your body is difficult and exhausting.

All these circumstances have one thing in common: the whiplash effect of something unexpected seeming like a guarantee, and then that surprise being violently taken away. You are left coping with the nature of the pregnancy and the equal shock of losing what you hadn't planned for. Both events are destabilizing to the core.

Kim: This whiplash effect is what's so painful and disorienting—you're pregnant, you're starting to envision your life going down a certain path, you're planning, you're preparing. Then, you're not. It takes awhile for the brain (and heart) to catch up to reality; it takes even longer for acceptance.

This much we know:

- Losing this baby hurt in ways that you never imagined it would.
- The guilt of not having wanted it now might haunt you. This is human, so try to be kind to yourself.
- A part of you might worry you brought on the loss with your thoughts. But that kind of thinking tells me that a person is trying to not fully acknowledge how they really feel, whether that be powerless, helpless, impotent, lost, scared, guilty, or something else. Thoughts alone did not end your pregnancy. The temptation to believe that they did may be a way of trying to package an explanation for something that cannot be explained.

Kim: In her memoir, *Poor Your Soul*, Mira Ptacin talks about exactly this. She writes:

"Are you sure this isn't your fault? You weren't really that happy about the pregnancy in the first place. What if you willed this to happen? What if you did this with your mind? I can just see it: *Pregnant woman eliminates unborn child by telekinesis*. A baby killer."

With my own losses, I preferred to think I was somehow at fault. In a way, that was easier than the truth—which is that these things just happen. There was nothing I could have done differently that would have changed the outcome. I think we're wired, as humans, to believe in our own power, our sense of control. Realizing that we do not have as much power and control as we thought is so unsettling.

When the pregnancy was very much planned

You wanted this baby so much.

You planned. That's what responsible adults do, especially when it comes to having a baby.

You counted days. Looked at long-term and short-term goals. Prepared your body. You saved. Created room in your nest. All you needed, wanted, was that precious little someone to fill the space you'd tended.

Kim: This—the planning, the taking of the right steps—made my losses so hard to understand and accept. I had spent years thinking that if I did X, Y would happen. I'd always been a smart, capable person, a high-achiever who rarely encountered difficulties when I put my mind to something. I did not understand how I could fail so miserably when I had done everything "right." My losses forced me to come to terms with a disturbing truth—it doesn't always matter if I do everything right; some things are completely out of my control.

You must trust that your desire and attention to this process still has value. The attention you've paid has opened a space inside you. Perhaps you'll try again. Perhaps not. But the care you took to provide for this baby, this pregnancy, is still meaningful in and of itself. Hopefully, the excitement you once felt will hold a special place, alongside the new emotions you are exploring and honoring. Through the sadness you are deepening. Your willingness to receive this grief, to pay it the attention it deserves, will open you in new ways.

For now, spend time with your sadness. Don't fear it. You will intuitively know when the time is right to try again, if that is what you want.

Kim: Yes, this is so true. The steps I took to prepare for a baby—stopping certain medications, taking vitamins, adjusting my lifestyle, preparing financially—changed me. I began thinking beyond myself to this future child. Just that shift in mentality made me a more selfless, loving, compassionate person.

"You never know why these things happen … All you know is that it brings you closer together, it breaks you open, it opens up your heart, it deepens your appreciation. It makes you more human."

—James Van Der Beek, after he and his wife lost a son in the second trimester

When you were pregnant with more than one child

One (or more) makes it; one (or more) does not.

You are pregnant with twins or multiples, and one (or more) has died. In addition to the grief of the loss, you may be experiencing the natural fear of getting attached to the other(s) who remain. What if you lose them too? You're scared, concerned, fretful. The fears give your mind something to clamp onto at a time when you're desperate to clamp onto something.

If you have older living children, you may find yourself worrying about them too. According to a review of several studies, "Many parents reported feeling emotionally guarded about their living children for fear of losing them and going through repeated grief. The long-term impact on siblings, surviving twins, and subsequent children also included survivor guilt as they felt that they had to live their life for two people."

Your fears, and the pressures a child may feel to fill the empty space in your life as a result of your miscarriage, are real. However, awareness of their potential is all that's required to begin to address them and get the help you may need to make the process a bit easier.

When your womb is left empty

Losing a baby by itself is destabilizing. Losing multiple babies, as can happen naturally or with fertility treatments, further complicates grief.

You might find yourself wondering, "Why couldn't just one of them make it?" You might find yourself feeling especially cheated. You may cycle between hopefulness and helplessness, wishing your emotions would land in the former and stay there. But they haven't, not yet. Trust that, within the turmoil of your grief, the parts of you that are the strongest, the parts of you that understand that you will get through this are very much with you, perhaps more than you think. Likely, you intuitively know that surrendering your timetable for grief is one of the most self-loving moves you've got. As you shed tears or bite back angry words or stumble through the confusion that is so natural with loss, be kind to yourself and let yourself know how proud you are of yourself and of your fortitude, your grace, and your willingness to confront this pain.

Kim

Yes, gypped, cheated, angry. There were two (or more); then there were none. It just doesn't seem fair (See "The 'It's not fair' tantrum"). I imagine when you find out you are pregnant with twins (or triplets or more), you go into preparation mode—figuring out finances, space planning (maybe even buying a larger home), purchasing two or three of all the usual supplies. Being pregnant with multiples takes planning to another level. After expending all that time, energy, and effort, losing the pregnancies must be absolutely devastating. Rage-inducing. It doesn't seem fair because it isn't. It absolutely isn't.

And, I would guess, you might not feel like people "get it." If you have a surviving baby, others are likely to dismiss the loss: "At least you have the one!" This probably leads to ambivalence, maybe even guilt. Yes, you have "the one." You feel pressure to feel nothing but immense gratitude. But the other (or others) mattered too. You grieve for them, for who they could have been. You vacillate between this grief and the gratitude, which must be confusing and heartbreaking.

I have a friend who was pregnant with twins, then found out one had died. On ultrasounds throughout her pregnancy, she had to see the dying twin gradually fade. It sounded awful. She said it caused her immense grief, but she didn't really talk about it. She didn't think people would understand, because she was still obviously pregnant (she went on to deliver a healthy baby). When she did confide in select friends and family, they encouraged her to "focus on the positive." Really, though, she wanted to focus on the baby she had lost.

When you already have a child (or children)

You have so many feelings to consider—yours and theirs.

That is what's hard—balancing your needs with theirs, separating your sadness from theirs. According to one study of the psychosocial impact of stillbirth published in the journal *BMC Pregnancy & Childbirth*, "Some parents reported feeling torn between managing their own grief and parenting siblings, whilst others found comfort at the time of grief from existing siblings."

Let's consider the two parts separately—your feelings and theirs.

Part 1: Your feelings

Know this: You don't have to cure grief with gratitude.

You think: *I should be thankful I already have a child.*

Then you realize: *I already am thankful.*

Then you wonder: *Should I be more thankful?*

You even make a list of all the things you're thankful for.

Except the pain isn't getting erased.

So, what's going on?

You are merging two ideas into one, that's what.

Though many women will find solace after a loss if they already have a child, that child does not replace the baby or babies you lost. One does not cancel out the reality of the other. If someone were to tell you to "feel better" about losing a baby because you already have children, it would feel insensitive. There is still a loss, and that loss is important to grieve.

Gratitude in and of itself is wonderful! But using it with the belief that if you're grateful for one thing your grief due to another will dissipate might actually prolong your suffering.

Connecting with grief is the only way to process it. The more you try to apply the solution of gratitude for the child you have, the more you miss the opportunity to connect with the grief you feel over the child you lost.

Your child is their own person. I know you KNOW this, but reminding yourself helps articulate that your sadness over losing the baby is its own process. Practice gratitude for your ability to see each child and the loss of the baby that was growing inside as separate and in need of different kinds of attention. Both live in your heart, but the one who is living and breathing and growing needs you to see them for all their individuality. This may deepen your grief at times, but that is because you will be consciously tending to it.

That is something to be grateful for.

Part 2: Their feelings

Painful, difficult, complicated. How and when to talk to children after a pregnancy loss is all those and more. The discussion, if done, may serve as a foundation to how a child processes and internalizes grief in their life. Carl Jung believed that nothing infuses children more than the silent facts in the background of the home.

This is your child's loss, too. If they knew about the baby, you will need to talk to them. If they did not know, they may pick up on your emotion, and you will need to help mediate that for them. This may even come up with children who are born later too.

Studies that have looked at stillbirth tell us that experiencing the birth of a stillborn child can create anxiety over one's other children and subsequent pregnancies. It is reasonable to think that even a miscarriage, ectopic pregnancy that was ended, or other loss in the womb could have similar effects. Still, parents can (and do) develop resilience around such loss. And so can their children. In fact, children can have incredible insights about loss and sadness. Invite them to share; let them guide you as well.

Kim: Resilience, yes. It's deeply upsetting for adults to experience a pregnancy loss because of all that it brings up in us around mortality and loss of control. It must be even more unsettling for children to try to understand this. However, there is the lesson of resilience, of gaining confidence in one's ability to withstand the bad things in life that happen without rhyme or reason.

Here are some things you may want to keep in mind:

1. Let the child's needs guide you. If your child was aware of the pregnancy and identifying as the older sibling, find simple, uncomplicated ways to talk to them about what happened. Listen to their concerns.
2. The goal here is to be child-centered, picking up on cues and addressing them—hours to days, to weeks to months to years later, gauging their capacity to understand.
3. Help them separate who they are from the baby you lost. Likewise, help them separate you from the baby. Children and even adolescents are still trying to figure out who they are apart from their parents. This developmental process is ongoing. At times of trauma, a child might become fearful they, too, will die like the baby did. A book that may help children with their fear is *The Invisible String* by Patrice Karst (author) and Joanne Lew-Vriethoff (illustrator). If you notice that their fear lingers, seek professional guidance.
4. Do not confuse your needs with theirs. As parents—as humans—we risk this happening whenever we are not attuned to our own needs. It's our own shakiness that makes us want to control and direct. So be aware of what you truly need as you move through the mourning process—to have private space to cry, to question the unfairness, to feel your anger. This will help reduce risk of inadvertently confusing your grief with your child's.
5. If the child did not want a sibling, they might experience a kind of guilt that the baby died. Reassure them it was not their fault. Talk to them about how they feel, also assuring them that no one takes their place.
6. If the child was too young to understand you were pregnant, be mindful of your feelings and give yourself space to grieve. Perhaps a friend or relative could watch your little one to give you time and the opportunity to experience the intensity of your loss out of the child's presence.

"I can remember setting my daughters up in front of *Blue's Clues* and other cartoons for hours. I was depressed, and I was afraid I wouldn't be able to function as a healthy mother anymore. I cried a lot and walked out of the room so the kids wouldn't see me. I felt numb mostly. Scared that the beauty of life had been stripped away for good."—Wendy, on tending to her daughters after her two first-trimester miscarriages

7. You may tell your child that "God must have needed another angel" to explain the loss or death. For some children, the idea of presenting this as *the* reason could evoke more confusion. Even if the beliefs in the home center around this, when it is used to explain a real death, especially of another child or sibling, it might evoke a different kind of guilt: *Why did God not want me? I don't want to leave my mom and dad anyway, so is there something wrong with me? Does that make me a bad kid?* Speak to your child in ways she can understand, and tell her that together, you will get through this. Children are resilient, and the more you invite their conversation, the more they will understand it's OK for them to take time to figure out what the loss means to them too.

Explaining the loss to your child is a process that might resurface for months to come; it's not a one-and-done—nor need it be.

Kim: Grieving for adults is a process that can resurface for months (or years) to come, so it makes sense that a child would wrestle with it over time too.

Huong

First and foremost, you need to take care of yourself. As they say, parents need to put on their oxygen mask first before they can tend to their children. Children will pick up on the mood and tension in the home. They are less likely to listen to what you say than they are to act the way you do.

Remember, be kind to yourself. Allow for the range of feelings (See "Riding the grief rollercoaster"). You can be both grateful for the children you have AND also grieving the baby you lost. You can be annoyed with your living child AND also want another child.

When talking to children about loss, my advice is always to follow the child's lead. If they ask questions, then try to answer in the most age-appropriate way possible and remind them that the loss is NOT their fault. Some books I recommend to help children understand and process grief: *Something Happened* by Cathy Blanford, *Molly's Rosebush* by Janice Cohn, and *We Were Gonna Have a Baby, But We Had an Angel Instead* by Pat Schwiebert.

Kim

I'm a big fan of gratitude—being mindful of all that is good in my life. But nothing irked me more during my losses than people encouraging me to "count my blessings." It felt so dismissive. Why couldn't I be grateful for all those blessings and *still* be sad and angry about what I'd lost? There has to be space for both. It doesn't help when people say things like, "At least you have [your child's name]." That's like saying to someone who loses their house in a tornado, "At least you have your car!" Like, duh. That doesn't mean the loss of the house isn't devastating.

A friend of mine who has a toddler and lost a pregnancy said she felt like the implication was that she was "greedy" for wanting another child. She started to feel guilty for her grief, thinking that maybe she shouldn't feel so sad because, like they said, she had her daughter. Then she felt guilty because she had a hard time being "on" around her daughter because she was sad. So much guilt. Her grief was valid. She's allowed to want another child. She's allowed to be sad. She has a vision for the family she wants—a certain number of children, a certain amount of time apart in age. She's allowed that vision. She's allowed to grieve that vision.

"My kids knew something was wrong. Each time I saw them, my eyes would well up. Each time I saw them I thought: If I can't keep a baby safe inside of me, how am I going to protect these two who are out and about in the world?"
—Soniah Kamal, "The Face of Miscarriage," featured in *What God Is Honored Here? Writings on Miscarriage and Infant Loss by and for Native Women and Women of Color* (Shannon Gibney and Kao Kalia Yang, editors)

When you've struggled
with infertility

*You've gone to so many lengths
to conceive, and now this.*

Grief can be multiplied exponentially when infertility has been a factor.

Efforts spent trying to conceive often begin with hope and excitement but can become draining emotionally, physically, and financially. You may have visited numerous practitioners—alternative, mainstream, healing, intuitive—each with their own timetables and protocols and constraints. You may have undergone extensive testing and tracking. You may have spent a significant amount of money on specialized diagnostics and procedures. Or, you may not have been able to afford treatments you wanted to try. No matter what, you likely endured so much waiting and longing.

And then you got pregnant. You believed the hard part was behind you. And then you lost the baby.

Before you were pregnant, there was the hope you'd become pregnant. Now you are no longer pregnant. The hope has been dashed, possibly not for the first time.

The loss of this baby echoes the loss of the missed conceptions that occurred month over month, year over year. So you are not only grieving this baby, but those other months, possibly years, of loss too.

Research has told us that conception, pregnancy, and childbirth are critical transitions for women. Infertility and perinatal loss, referred to together as reproductive trauma, can change a woman's perception of herself and be a major source of stress that often has psychological consequences. There is a cumulative effect of the stress.

Infertility is a unique area of loss. Honor that, and you.

There is a cumulative effect of the stress. I can vouch for that. After my third loss, I began undergoing extensive testing to try to determine if there was something besides "bad luck" to explain my losses. Opening the door to infertility specialists was overwhelming. This was a whole new world—with high financial cost, complicated medication regimens, and demoralizing statistics. My husband and I quickly realized that entering this world would require a significant investment from us emotionally, physically, and financially. I worried our marriage wouldn't survive it.

Testing showed that my egg quality and quantity was extremely poor. I was given this information via email at the end of a Friday, right when the doctor's office was closing. I sent a scathing reply along the lines of, "Thank you for giving me this distressing news at a time when I cannot get ahold of you. I appreciate your consideration of my feelings!" That doctor called me over the weekend (I must have really made her feel bad) and agreed to see me the next week. She said, verbatim, "It appears that your embryos are destined to die."

I consulted with other doctors. One said we would never conceive naturally and that IVF had less than a 5 percent chance of success. Another said, "Well, you keep getting pregnant, so I have hope. You're like someone with a terrible résumé who keeps getting the job."

At one point, we considered a donor egg, meaning another woman's egg would be joined with my husband's sperm and the baby would grow in my uterus. I explored databases of women selling their eggs and could not get comfortable with the idea. So many of them had patchy educational backgrounds . . . or cringe-worthy tattoos.

"You become used to living in a constant state of fluctuating despair and hope. And this doesn't turn off when and if you get pregnant. It doesn't turn off when you hear or see the heartbeat. My son is 3. I'm still trying to turn it off."
— Regina Townsend, "The Lasting Trauma of Infertility," the *New York Times*

I decided to focus on improving my eggs with the hopes of doing IVF. I wouldn't even be eligible to do a cycle if I didn't have enough follicles to start with (follicles basically house immature eggs and can be stimulated to produce mature eggs). So, I took all kinds of weird supplements. I gagged on shots of wheatgrass every day. I did acupuncture every week for months. Despite all this, my follicle count was never good enough to do IVF. We were left with no option but to keep trying on our own.

And then we had our daughter.

Strangely enough, she was conceived during the same cycle when they said my eggs weren't good enough for IVF. Moral of the story: Who the hell knows how this conception stuff works?

I know my story is nothing compared to what others go through. I have friends who have used Clomid and gotten shots in the ass for months to try to conceive. Some tried intrauterine insemination (IUI) or IVF. Some were successful, and others are still waiting. That's the thing—there is so much waiting (and waiting and waiting). When you finally do conceive, you must feel as if you've won the Super Bowl. You must feel as if the hard part is over. Losing the pregnancy after all that time and effort must be soul-crushing.

Couples who embark on infertility treatments are motivated by hope. I used to tell people, "I'm a closet optimist." On the surface, I was cynical and sarcastic, saying things like, "We'll probably just keep losing babies. I appear to be good at it." But, deep down, I kept going because of hope. So much hope. That's what's invested more than money or time—hope. A loss can put a wrinkle in that hope, and I imagine it takes awhile to iron that out and decide what's next.

" ... Our life was less and less like the lives of our married friends, who had entered a new and somewhat exclusive world of playdates and birthday parties and bedtimes. But our life did not resemble our single or childless friends' lives either. We lived in a constant state of waiting." —Belle Boggs, *The Art of Waiting: On Fertility, Medicine, and Motherhood*

When you had to make the difficult decision to end a pregnancy

You might question if you did the right thing. Or you might know you did but still be overcome with grief.

The baby was not developing. There was a significant chromosomal, musculoskeletal, or organ deficit that would have made it impossible for them to live outside the womb or subjected them to a life of ongoing pain. Even with the best medical technology in the world, there was nothing to be done.

Maybe your health was in danger. Maybe you did all the correct things, but you became sick. Or maybe, like Kim, your pregnancy was ectopic, which brought with it a series of serious complications that had to be addressed within hours. Maybe your own life was at stake.

What if you were raped or a victim of incest and became pregnant as a result? What if your religious community, who is against termination, ostracized you for getting pregnant despite your victimization and then condemned you for considering terminating the pregnancy?

What if you are pro-life and feel extremely conflicted about the choice you had to make? What if you are pro-choice and still feel extremely conflicted?

Coming to a decision and then leaning into the decision to garner the strength needed to proceed in situations like this is so difficult. You bounce between rumination and fear. You bombard yourself with questions: Are you doing the right thing? Do you have a choice? How will you know? What if you made the wrong choice? And on top of everything, what if you have to deal with others' judgment (See "When things get political, religious, or otherwise emotionally charged")?

If you have felt this way, know that the pain of rumination is natural and normal and may be helpful to your growth. In fact, according to a 2020 study in the *Journal of Psychological Trauma*, rumination is important in adjusting to traumatic events, namely the end of pregnancy: "Evidence suggests that deliberate rumination predicts posttraumatic growth." This means that techniques like reflective thinking, reviewing the narrative of what happened during your loss, and discussing fear openly truly helps women heal and grow.

This idea of growth is further supported by research published in 2017. That research assessed anxiety and posttraumatic stress related to ending a pregnancy due to the health of the fetus and found that "following traumatic events individuals may experience growth." They found that "positive reframing" was a significant predictor of posttraumatic growth and suggested that Cognitive Behavioral Therapy (CBT) may be beneficial in helping women with this positive reframing. (See "Getting professional help" for more information on CBT and other therapies).

Remember this: You were given less-than-ideal circumstances at best, terrible circumstances at worst. The difficult choice you made was to terminate the pregnancy. You took on an unimaginable pain to prevent future pain for you and/or your child. You were "given a choice" but not between two things you wanted to choose between.

And you made the best choice you could.

"I hear only one single, solitary truth about this warped, colossal calamity: that this baby just ain't going to be. That this sweet and scary, gigantic and tiny new kind of love growing inside me won't be developing much more. That the end of the road is right up ahead of us, or so it seems."

—Mira Ptacin, *Poor Your Soul*

Kim

In *Poor Your Soul*, Mira Ptacin writes about how she learned of her daughter's severe defects around halfway through her pregnancy: "Their facts were incessant. Words I couldn't pronounce. *Holoprosencephaly*. Images I cannot forget. *Clubbed feet. Deformed spine. Collapsed skull. Broken heart*."

What the studies tell us

According to a study of parental coping four months after terminating a pregnancy due to fetal anomaly:

- Women and men showed high levels of posttraumatic stress symptoms (44 percent and 22 percent, respectively) (See "Posttraumatic stress: It's a thing").
- Women and men showed high levels of depression (28 percent and 16 percent, respectively) (See "Dealing with depression").

(Prenatal Diagnosis, 2007)

"Risk of complicated grief was found to be especially high after termination of a pregnancy due to fetal abnormality." *(Dialogues in Clinical Neuroscience, 2012)*

Note: Complicated grief is defined as severe, prolonged (> 12 months) grieving. *(American Journal of Hospice & Palliative Medicine, 2020)*

She is left with a decision—give birth to this child who has no chance of survival, or undergo a D&E (dilation and evacuation). She wrestles with the decision, feeling uncomfortable with the "violence" of the procedure but equally uncomfortable giving birth to her daughter. She mentions the complicated feelings she has about the D&E, a procedure usually associated with late-term abortions.

I had similar complicated feelings with the loss of my son. His heart had already stopped, but I still wrestled with whether to have the D&E or give birth to him. It upset me that my hospital (with a strong religious affiliation) did not perform D&E procedures. If I wanted that (and eventually I did), I had to go to a medical center I'd never been to before. It left me feeling like I'd somehow done something wrong. The whole thing felt strangely clandestine.

Like I said, my son's heart had stopped. I did not need to have conversations that involved weighing his chances of survival. I can only imagine the heartache of that—the guilt, the questioning, the uncertainty. Anguish—that's the word that comes to me. Anguish.

The medical part
of pregnancy loss

Why didn't anyone tell me about all the blood?

So. Much. Blood.

After my first ectopic pregnancy, I thought I wouldn't have heavy bleeding because I'd had surgery to remove the embryo (and my fallopian tube). I called my doctor in a panic when I soaked a pad after just a couple hours. She assured me it was normal, that it was the uterus shedding all the lining that had built up to house the baby. Lining? This was news to me.

Even with this experience, I was still a little shocked at the amount of bleeding with each of my losses. I bled for weeks, walking around with thick pads between my legs, feeling like an invalid wearing a diaper. I distinctly remember celebrating my birthday (or trying to) while bleeding profusely. I kept thinking, "If these people at my party only knew . . . "

I cannot figure out why doctors tell women that a miscarriage is "like a bad period." They should elaborate. They should say, "You might bleed for weeks. Or a few months." They should say, "You will pass clots and tissue." I suppose they don't want to scare you, but that's silly. You're going to be scared anyway. The emotional pain of a loss is hard enough. It's made harder by the physical discomfort, which nobody really prepares you for.

A friend of mine was going through a miscarriage at the same time I was going through my second loss, and we texted back and forth to exchange information. We asked questions like, "How do you know when you've passed the sac? What does it look like?" It felt like we were trading underground information. This exchange made me feel less alone, less bewildered.

"So let's get it out in the open. To start, what does a miscarriage really feel like? Despite how they're portrayed in movies, miscarriages can involve a lot more than a rivulet of blood. There are clots, sometimes the size of golf balls. There are cramps that feel more like labor contractions—an upsetting reminder, perhaps, of the birth one will not have. The process can go on for weeks, even months, leaving women in a strange purgatory between pregnant and not." —Lauren Kelley and Alexandra March in their *New York Times* Opinion piece, "You Know Someone Who's Had a Miscarriage"

I also found comfort on message boards. I didn't seek them out initially, but when I googled things like "bleeding after miscarriage," I was presented with links that connected me to threads of discussions between women who seemed to "get it." I felt a huge amount of intimacy in these forums, even though I didn't know many of the women's full names or what they looked like. In "real life," women came out of the woodwork and confessed their own miscarriages once I mentioned mine. It was like I found myself in this community I'd never known existed (See "Joining the Pregnancy Loss Club"). To this day, I'm grateful for this community. Until the medical community can get on board to provide more guidance and support to women in the midst of the physical process of pregnancy loss, women have to band together to guide and support each other.

Meredith

A while back, I read an article in the *New York Times*, "Facing End-of-Life Talks, Doctors Choose to Wait." The research suggested that "many doctors, especially older ones and specialists, say they would postpone those conversations" (meaning end-of-life conversations). Saying doctors "choose to wait" or "postpone" the discussion makes it sound like their action is always altogether rational, planned, and born out of ethics. But if you read between the lines, I think you'll see the truth is out—doctors are human like the rest of us, and like the rest of us, timid, ill-equipped, and perhaps even scared to talk about death in a personal way with patients.

The same goes for pregnancy loss. That is not to say all specialists behave in such a manner, but having worked in hospitals and in-home health, with children and adults, I can say I've seen this across the board.

"I wish I had known how massively traumatic it could be. I was essentially in labor for 12 hours . . . I think there should be miscarriage midwives." —Jenna P., featured in the *New York Times* Opinion piece, "You Know Someone Who's Had a Miscarriage" (Lauren Kelley and Alexandra March)

My experience working with dying patients, visiting hundreds of people diagnosed by their physicians with end-stage diseases who had months or weeks to live, taught me that even—or especially—the most brilliant (and often the nicest) doctors are more frightened of discussing death than their patients are. I know, a bold statement to make. But as a clinician, there was nothing more painful for me than being dispatched to a patient's home or hospital room only to have the patient's family—or the patient—tell me in tears that they *can't get the doctor to tell them anything*. Meanwhile, the doctor's office had ordered home health and wanted the social worker (me) to explain what hospice is. The scared and now more confused patient wants to know why the social worker is talking about hospice, about *death*. "My doctor told me we were going to wait and see how the chemo/radiation/surgery worked," he says.

Based on my years working with doctors and interviewing professionals, I can say with certainty that doctors struggle with loss, with death, with breaking difficult news to their patients. Seeing the pain in a patient's eyes and feeling helpless against it is a real issue for physicians. Countertransference—when a therapist projects his or her feelings unconsciously onto the client—appears to occur between doctors and patients as well. It can center around the physician's ability to heal or not heal the patient, and the doctor's guilt or sadness when healing does not occur. I believe it can cause doctors to become curt, cold, and unreachable—three things patients often complain about. Doctors may also avoid the subject or provide only fragments of information so as not to "worry" patients. But a patient will often sense the gap, and this creates more anxiety.

When I was new to the field, more seasoned social workers and nurses told me that doctors only like to focus on solutions—that if the doctor couldn't find a solution, it was a sign of failure—and that this explained why many shied away from discussing "what if" with their elderly patients, even the seriously ill. *What if*, as in, *What if the treatment doesn't work?* "That's your job," my colleagues told me, almost as if they were relieved someone new was coming in to relieve them of broaching the subject with a patient when a physician hadn't.

This is to tell you that if you are not getting the answers you need from the doctor, you may well need to ask again and again. You may need to ask to speak to a nurse or the practice manager. In the hospital, a social worker can help, as can shift nurses, and, if necessary, the ombudsman.

"It seemed like the bleeding would never end. All of that pain and discomfort only to return home to emptiness. All for nothing."

—Jessica, on her second-trimester loss

In the hospital and in-home health, it is a social worker's job to help the patient process end-of-life issues, to help the parents prepare for the death of a child, and to help the mother who has a miscarriage. But how many OB-GYNs have a social worker in the office?

It is completely understandable if you have felt that the information you've been provided has fallen short. This, I think, is one of the harder things to grapple with as a patient. It compounds the grief you're already feeling. You will need to untangle that disappointment from your loss. Express your disappointment directly, share the hopes you had, and avoid blame unless the doctor is at fault for more than being an insensitive jerk. You do this not to let them off the hook right now, but to disengage yourself from that stream of energy. Later, once you've tended to your immediate needs, you can address these issues with your doctors, if it still matters to you and if it feels right.

Huong

This is part of a much larger problem with the medical system and the medical training system, which is a self-selecting journey in terms of the rigor of the training and the personality types that it attracts.

Medical schools and training programs are trying to model compassion and trauma-informed care. However, at the end of the day, medicine is also a business, and the bread and butter entails keeping a patient alive.

If you have watched any episodes of shows like *Grey's Anatomy* or *ER*, you've seen that medical doctors are humans too—humans with their own drama, pain, and confusion. It's possible the doctor sitting across from you may have just experienced her own pregnancy loss and cannot bring herself to discuss yours. It's possible your doctor is afraid that if they show too much compassion, they will break down and cry in the office and be deemed unprofessional. Or maybe their heart wants to sit down, grab a box of Kleenex, and talk to you, but they are also aware they have been running an hour behind all day and they will not meet their productivity or billing requirements if they sit down.

"It is often difficult for women to process this trauma because they receive strong messages from society that these details are too disgusting to talk about and should be silenced. This can make many women feel a sense of shame around their bodies and their experience." —Rayna Markin, psychologist and associate professor at Villanova University, to Huffington Post

In my opinion, this conversation needs to go higher. To the administrators. To the CEOs of large hospitals. To the government. There needs to be space and time for women to have their medical and emotional needs met.

The hormones are real

But they are separate from grief.

In the wake of my first loss, my husband latched onto "hormone fluctu-ations" as the reason for my emotionality. I understand why. It was easier to blame a biological, physical process than to consider that my loss—our loss—had had a profound, possibly permanent, effect on me. It comforted him to think of these "hormone fluctuations" as temporary, something that would pass. It comforted me, too, at first. I mean, my sadness was excruci-ating. I liked the idea of it being something I could explain away, something that wouldn't last long. But when I didn't "get a grip" after time had passed, when my hormones had conceivably "leveled out," I realized that it was naïve to chalk up my mood swings and tears to hormones alone. I was deep in grief. That's what it was.

This is not to say that hormones don't play a part. They do. When I lost my pregnancies, my body went through huge changes. To put it simply, my body (and hormones) were preparing for one thing, and then this other terrible thing happened. Like, *whoops, just kidding, U-turn.* My body had been infused with hCG, the major pregnancy hormone, and then that hormone became unnecessary and plummeted, along with levels of estrogen and progesterone. The change was abrupt, and the chemical shift in my brain triggered feelings of sadness and anxiety. It took weeks for my body to adjust.

With each of my losses, my period returned after about six to eight weeks, which is when I assumed things were "normal-ish" again, at least hormonally. I know some women may have wonky cycles (or no cycle) for a while—ask your doctor about this if you're in this boat.

When my regular cycle returned, it was unsettling for me to realize that I was still so sad and anxiety-ridden. At that point, I could no longer blame my hormones. I had to face my grief head-on. So, yes, the hormonal changes are real, but, for me, the shifts in my mood were about much more than hormones.

Meredith

After you lose a pregnancy, your body's hormones plummet in the same way as if you'd given birth. This biological cascade can trigger an emotional flood that overwhelms the system—sadness, anxiety, anger, and despair. The tears seem never-ending, fed by a well that refills instantly and without warning. It can be disconcerting, confusing, and at times frightening. *Is this really me?* Yet, as hormone levels regulate, moods eventually will, too.

Here's the catch: emotions that are triggered by hormones can look the same as those triggered by grief. These two sets each have their own paths, and they run on parallel and overlapping tracks inside you after you lose a pregnancy. This means you are traveling both at the same time. Imagine walking with one foot on each as they intersect, widen, and double up. Each set needs its own care and attention, which is difficult on every level!

Or, think of it this way: you've got two identical sets of sadness, anxiety, anger, and despair, each of which would be overwhelming enough on its own. One belongs to your hormonal fluctuations; the other belongs to your grief. As hormones stabilize, the emotional ebb and flow from the hormone set begins to neutralize. You may notice this as feeling a bit more centered and connected to your body again.

Except if you're grieving.

Your grief has its own timetable separate from the timetable on which your hormones regulate. The sadness, anger, anxiety, and despair you feel related to your loss are still there. "Ah-ha," you say. That feels about right.

Understanding the difference between the causes of these identical emotions can help you learn to identify what's causing your feelings—and trust that you know *you* better than anyone.

It can also help you know if you need help, and the type of help to seek.

"Prior to the menstruation post-miscarriage, there is a physical component to the sadness where it almost feels like the sadness owns you. After the hormones get resettled, there is a shift and it will start to feel like you own the sadness." —Kristen M. Swanson, RN, PhD, dean of the College of Nursing at Seattle University, apa.org

When life takes a turn no one expected, human beings crave order and seek measurable results. Hormones can be quantified. You take a blood test and find out if you've got the right or "normal" amounts. If they fall "within normal limits," they can be monitored and tracked to make sure they stay that way. If they're not, doctors will keep an eye on you. Medicine is good for that.

Unfortunately, grief doesn't work that way. Grief cannot be measured or quantified, and "normal" varies from person to person (See "Understanding your grief process").

Dealing with all the
doctor's appointments

I had no idea so much was involved.

Of course I'd heard of miscarriage before I had one of my own. But my understanding of all that it involved was very limited. To put it simply, I was naïve, blissfully ignorant. I really did think that a miscarriage involved a woman bleeding while on the toilet and that was that. Just typing that makes me want to add the wide-eyed embarrassed emoji.

I've had a range of pregnancy losses—ectopic pregnancies, first-trimester miscarriage, second-trimester miscarriage. Each came with its own special surprise procedure or medication or complication. Each one involved a number of doctor's appointments that put me in the same waiting room as women who were healthfully pregnant. Can't they have separate rooms for those of us who have just experienced loss, or are still in the process of losing?

Nobody talks about all the appointments, how the medical part of loss can go on for weeks, months. I know for some it's not this way, but none of my losses were neat and tidy. Here are just some of the appointments that added to my stress:

- Blood draws to monitor hCG levels. I must have had at least fifty over the course of my pregnancies.
- Lots of ultrasounds—transvaginal, transabdominal, 2D, 3D, basically any ultrasound known to man
- Two hysterosalpingography (HSG) procedures to assess my fallopian tubes and uterus

- Salpingectomy (surgery to remove my fallopian tube)
  - Follow-up to get stitches out
- D&E (dilation and evacuation surgery with general anesthesia)
  - Appointment before to dilate my cervix
  - Follow-up appointment to check on uterus
- Methotrexate injection
  - Follow-up appointment

I had to schedule these appointments around my work schedule, often sacrificing lunch breaks or waking up early to be the first one in the door at the lab or clinic. To add insult to injury, the appointments came with bills that kept arriving for months, reminding me over and over again of the nightmare I was living (See "When your loss causes financial stress").

"And now, in the waiting room of an OB/GYN office for a postmiscarriage checkup, I feel like a soldier in a field of visual landmines. Nowhere is safe to look. Not the black-and-white photos of cherubic babies on every single wall, or the rounded bellies protruding from proud mothers-to-be, all glowing and puffed up with their success of carrying a baby nearly to term..." —Colleen Oakley, *You Were There Too* (in this novel, the main character, Mia, endures multiple miscarriages)

All of this, cumulatively, resulted in so much stress for me—on top of the stress of grieving. At the time, I was going through motions, doing what my doctors told me to do. Maybe that "doing-ness" was good for me in a way, but I do remember that I was exhausted. Every day with a scheduled appointment felt like a marathon.

Meredith

Doctor appointments can be a double-edged sword. With the loss of a pregnancy, as with illness, when you need care, you hope you can get it and that it's the right care—for you.

Even if the care is good, stress about visiting the doctor can start when you pick up the phone to make an appointment. If you're already feeling worried or vulnerable, relaying the details to the person on the other end—

and hearing yourself speak them aloud—can exacerbate those feelings. If you are fortunate to get the doctor on the phone, you might feel a flash of ambivalence—*I'm glad she called, but wait; maybe something is really, really wrong?* Merely seeing your doctor's name on the office door and pregnant women in the waiting room can once again drive home the reality that you're dealing with something worrisome, causing you to feel (naturally) overwhelmed in new ways and anxious about what the doctor will do, find, and say. As if that weren't enough, this taps into underlying insecurities about losing control.

"What folks on the outside don't often understand about pregnancy loss is that beyond the emotional pain, women are often undergoing physical procedures to remove the excess tissue from the pregnancy, and these medical interventions can and often do compound the trauma." —Haley Neidich, a licensed psychotherapist specializing in perinatal mood and anxiety disorders, to Scary Mommy

In an ideal world...
Practices would offer childcare. This would not have to be all day or even every day, but on certain days during specific hours. This would make it simpler for women to attend appointments and get the care they need if they cannot afford a sitter or do not have a nanny or daycare center. Too often, women are unable to tend to their own medical needs due to childcare issues. This offering would make appointments a little less stressful for women dealing with pregnancy loss while also taking care of a child or children.

Looking for answers

And hoping they make the pain more bearable.

I spent so much time, energy, money, and effort in search of answers. *Why did this happen? Why does this keep happening?* I talked to a dozen different doctors—OB-GYNs, fertility specialists—and consulted with holistic medicine practitioners, acupuncturists, psychics (yes, psychics), you name it. I was desperate.

My first ectopic pregnancy was explained to me as "a fluke." They didn't see any obvious anatomical issues when they looked around during my salpingectomy (surgery to remove my fallopian tube). When we decided to try again, I had a hysterosalpingography (HSG) done to make sure there were no blockages in my remaining tube and no visible issues with my uterus. This is supposed to be a relatively painless procedure, but it was excruciating for me. They placed a thin tube inside my cervix, then injected contrast dye through the catheter so that it flowed into my uterus and fallopian tubes. On X-ray, the contrast dye highlighted the shape, size, and function of my tubes and uterus.

This procedure revealed no issues with my remaining tube or uterus, so we tried again. When I was told the embryo wasn't viable with my second pregnancy, this was again explained as "a fluke," likely a chromosomal abnormality (though no testing was done). I accepted this as fact and went into our third attempt thinking there couldn't possibly be something else that would go wrong.

Except it did. Losing Miles was the most heartrending of all because it was such a mystery. Everything had been going fine, then my amniotic fluid was low, then he died. They were supposed to save his remains after my D&E, but that didn't happen. Someone made a mistake. I was told the lab "lost" (read: discarded) him.

It's likely we never would have known what happened even if they had run the tests. Because of my previous two losses, I'd had all the blood testing possible done as a precaution, and Miles appeared to have no chromosomal defects. Whatever happened was probably related to an issue with my placenta or an anatomical irregularity with Miles. But we'll never know, and that took me a long time to accept.

My fourth loss was also a mystery. They could tell by my hCG (pregnancy hormone) levels that the pregnancy was ectopic (not in the uterus where it was supposed to be), but they couldn't find the embryo on ultrasound. I still don't know what happened. If the embryo hadn't implanted in my tube, where was it? When my doctor mentioned it could be "anywhere, really, maybe your abdominal cavity," my eyes bugged out. I had never heard of this. He didn't want to do surgery because it would have been exploratory, in search of the embryo. So I got a shot of methotrexate to slowly kill the embryo. It still baffles me that I had two ectopic pregnancies. I can make no sense of this.

"Our human nature is wanting to know why."
—Dr. Christine C. Greves, OB-GYN at Orlando Health Winnie Palmer Hospital

I had another HSG done to double-check there was no blockage in my one tube. They said it was fine. Then I got pregnant again and had a totally normal pregnancy. Go figure.

That's all I can say—go figure.

I know why I was so desperate for answers. Answers would have given me some kind of control, or at least a *feeling* of control. I wanted to be able to say, "Oh, that's what happened. That makes sense." But I was never able to say that.

Some women do get clear answers—testing reveals a specific genetic defect, for example. I assume getting this type of answer helps reduce some of the self-blame. But I doubt it takes away the pain and sorrow, which is what I was hoping it would do for me.

Meredith

One of the keys to healing—processing and integrating the experience so you are no longer constantly at the mercy of it—is knowing that your path is going to be different than someone else's even though you share the same reason for being on that path in the first place.

One woman may not need or want an explanation of why the pregnancy ended, while another will. In this way you share a collective experience but you are also very much your own person, an individual. Navigating that tension and weaving the personal within the collective together to better understand and honor your experience—and you—is what your journey needs to be about.

What the studies tell us

According to a national survey, 78 percent of people reported wanting to know the cause of their miscarriage, even if no intervention could have prevented it from occurring. *(Obstetrics & Gynecology, 2015)*

Miscarriage may be considered common, but that doesn't make the loss less painful or perplexing. Studies show that many parents feel tremendous guilt when a miscarriage happens. Tests that examine DNA sequencing of fetal tissue may be able to answer some of the questions of "why" a miscarriage happens. Of course, as Kim has shared, tests can't answer everything.

Trust that you will know when you've found sufficient explanation for your loss—for you. You may reach a point where you no longer need to dig for answers or "ask better questions." Science may deliver an explanation, and your psyche may deliver its own. You may rely on religion—or find that the answers don't sufficiently address the depth of your suffering. The point is this: trust your ability to discern when the reasons matter, when you need a different way to frame and understand why, and when letting go of needing to know matters.

You can always change your mind.

When doctors don't say
the right things

*You would think that given how common
these losses are, doctors could do better.*

After my first ectopic pregnancy, when I saw the doctor to have my stitches removed, she was weirdly excited to show me pictures from my surgery. "That's the ectopic, right there," she said, pointing at this bulge in my fallopian tube, like a mouse traveling through a snake.

"You mean my baby?" I said to her.

She nodded, uncomfortably.

"It was a body, though no one ever said that word, only 'matter' and 'tissue,' rendered shapeless, ungraspable." —Miranda Field, "My Others," featured in *About What Was Lost: 20 Writers on Miscarriage, Healing, and Hope* (Jessica Berger Gross, editor)

After we lost Miles, the doctor assured us they would do extensive testing to determine why he died. Some weeks later, when I hadn't heard anything, I called the office and was told by a nurse that the "products of conception" had been lost at the lab. Products of conception—like something sold alongside the condoms in a brightly lit aisle of Walgreens.

I asked the question I'd asked my first doctor: "You mean my baby?"

I may have yelled these words. The nurse stumbled over what to say before promising the doctor would call me. When the doctor called, he said, "I'm sorry. These things happen." That kind of phrase should really only be used when someone steps in a puddle on a rainy day or spills coffee on their shirt before a big meeting.

After losing Miles, I started seeing fertility doctors to investigate why I couldn't seem to sustain a pregnancy. I was told that the quality and quantity of my eggs was horrible. One doctor told me my embryos were "destined to die." Seriously. I still wonder if I should write her a letter, telling her how hurtful her words were. I'd also like to tell her that she was very wrong. I had a daughter.

I know doctors see pregnancy losses all the time, so these losses have very little effect on them, but I wish they would consider the emotional impact for the patient. I also wish they would stop using such dismissive clinical words and phrases. I don't even like the term "miscarriage." It seems to blame the mother for failing to carry the baby. Nobody failed! It just happened.

Here are a few other terms that irk me:

- **Cervical insufficiency/incompetence.** Any woman going through a loss does not need to hear about how any part of her is incompetent or insufficient.
- **Irritable uterus.** What does this even mean? No woman wants the word "irritable" attached to any part of her.
- **Early pregnancy failure.** Can we just say "loss"? Nobody failed.
- **Terminated.** I think this term is insensitive even when we're talking about job loss. When we're talking about pregnancy loss, it's just unacceptable.
- **Not viable.** It just sounds so cold and businesslike. It's a word I hear in work meetings—"that's not really a viable option."
- **Expel the embryo.** I heard these words while the doctor was explaining options to deal with my missed miscarriage. "Expel" is such a violent word. Why not just say, "Help your body let go of the baby"?
- **Fetal demise.** These words were the diagnosis on my surgery packet before my D&E (dilation and evacuation) after Miles died. The reality for me was that my baby's heart had stopped beating. The clinical term just made it seem like a standard medical event.
- **Advanced maternal age** (sometimes called a "geriatric pregnancy." Seriously). If you're over thirty-five, you get to hear this term a lot. It felt like a preemptive explanation, like if something went wrong, my age was the reason, like maybe I was stupid to consider having a child after thirty-five.

- **High risk / low risk.** Being classified as "high risk" (due to age or another reason) can make the pregnancy fraught from the beginning. On the other hand, being labeled "low risk" and then experiencing a complication can be blindsiding. Can we just accept that pregnancy always carries some risk and get rid of these labels?

"During my first miscarriage, the ER doctor rattled off statistics at me as though trying to communicate this happens all the time. Then he insensitively went on with the whole 'it happens for a reason' spiel, hinting that there was something likely wrong with the fetus. His finger was inserted in my vagina at the time. No. Just no."
—Wendy, who experienced two first-trimester miscarriages

"The doctors and specialists stopped sounding as if they were talking about a baby, but rather about something made out of metal." —Mira Ptacin, *Poor Your Soul*

Maybe doctors use these weird clinical terms because they think it's helpful? Do they think we will forget we are losing babies if they just refer to the babies as embryos and fetuses? I never thought of my pregnancies as embryos and fetuses—I thought of them as babies, for better or worse. I wish my doctors had acknowledged the attachment I felt. I wish they understood that I didn't just lose an embryo or a fetus; I lost a dream.

Meredith

It's fair to view the Hippocratic oath as encompassing the emotional needs of patients—and many doctors do. But when they don't, and it happens to you, particularly during a sensitive and fraught medical time, it hurts. How could it not?

Inherent in our collective culture is the belief that doctors are experts. That may be true when it comes to medicine, but doctors are human.

When a pregnancy is lost or a baby is stillborn, it is also a loss for them. Even doctors who encounter loss daily might be afraid of death on an emotional level. That is not an excuse for being insensitive, but it sheds some light on how a person can behave curtly or clinically. They cut off—from themselves and you. This can even trickle down to the staff, who may adopt the physician's attitude, though some physicians may have patient, compassionate front desk employees who compensate for the doctor's cold demeanor. It can happen both ways.

We hold physicians in high esteem and give them our trust precisely because they are experts in their field. You're already in a vulnerable state when you wind up at the doctor's office; there is already a kind of power differential in play—professional to personal, intellectual to emotional. For a physician and her staff to effectively meet a patient's emotional needs during such a time, that physician needs to have a general understanding of her own needs, as well as her patients'. Some do far better than others.

"An OB-GYN compared me to a dog and how they often have multiple puppies and lose one or two along the way." —Sarah Crawford, featured in the *New York Times* Opinion piece, "You Know Someone Who's Had a Miscarriage" (Lauren Kelley and Alexandra March)

Doctors are people. And like all of us, they will not always say the right thing. But if we can find physicians who value the relationship with their patients and who view the doctor-patient relationship as a partnership, then if that doctor says something that hurts, you'll be able to talk about it with them and let it go.

Tip: When interviewing doctors, ask how they view the doctor-patient relationship. See what they say and how you feel about it. There is no place for ego in medicine.

Huong

Language is so powerful. In my clinical practice, some of my clients speak English as a second language, which further compounds the pain and potentially adds confusion to the experience of being informed of a loss. Some hospitals and clinics have medical interpreters, but they may not be specifically trained in delivering painful news in a culturally informed and trauma-informed manner.

Trauma-informed care is currently a buzzword in the medical and mental health world. It is defined as practices that promote a culture of safety, empowerment, and healing and take into account an individual's personal history of trauma. For example, a medical office or hospital can be a terrifying experience for someone who has experienced previous trauma, which may include previous pregnancy losses and/or negative experiences with medical providers.

As a fellow health-care professional, I have interacted with numerous medical providers who run the gamut of bedside manner. Some never received any sensitivity training; others have personality traits that do not lend themselves well to empathy. In my role as an educator, I oftentimes remind medical providers that while this may be their hundredth or thousandth time informing a patient of a pregnancy loss, they are handing their patients a brand-new reality.

"Medical people are trained to think things through medically and often have the emotions of a ruler. They may offer words of condolence, but more often than not, they're looking at you like a textbook, not an emotional being. Or at least that was my experience 90 percent of the time." —Georgie, who had a stillborn daughter (Ella) and two first-trimester miscarriages

---

It's important for health-care professionals to find a balance between medical jargon and human emotion. I encourage physicians to pay attention to the patient's language and mirror that back to them: If they say baby, I say baby. If they say fetus, I say fetus. If they say loss, I say loss.

The care you're probably *not* getting

And the care you just might need.

It's strange—pregnancy loss is so common but there's a lack of structured support for people going through it. Technically, my OB-GYN was there for my pregnancy; when my pregnancy ended, was he still my doctor? It wasn't clear. When I called with questions in the wakes of my losses, I felt like I was a bother. But I didn't know who else to call.

Even when I was medically "dealt with," there was still the issue of my mental health. Nobody seemed to think that needed attention. Nobody suggested I speak to a therapist. Nobody gave me a list with phone numbers or websites or other helpful resources. There were the requisite follow-up appointments to assess any physical issues, and when those were over, that was it. I felt like I was a box on a to-do list, checked off and forgotten.

My experience seems to be common. In an article in the *Washington Post*, Johnna Nynas, an OB-GYN whose work and research focuses on pregnancy loss, said, "As long as there are no complications . . . from a medical standpoint, there is generally no need to do any specific follow-up as long as women get their periods back. But, what we are not addressing . . . is that women are grieving, and that women have a lot of fears and frustrations, and are dealing with a lot of emotions often times after these losses and we are not following up on that."

Nope, you are not following up on that.

I sought out therapy on my own. I'd been in therapy before, so it wasn't hard for me to reach out for this type of help. But I assume it's hard for some. I assume some could use the encouragement and support of their doctors (and insurance companies) to get the help they probably need. I wish there had been more structured support available for me.

With this book, I'm hoping to raise awareness so it can be available for others. For more, see "Getting professional help."

Meredith

"Talk to your doctor." That's what drug ads for depression symptoms and public service announcements for mental health awareness say to do. So, how do you bring it up? When you're sitting in a paper gown awaiting test results that will determine the course of your pregnancy? What if your doctor says (kindly or curtly) that it sounds like you need to talk to someone and leaves it at that? You're not likely to want to broach the subject again in that office.

The psychological impact of miscarriage is sometimes overlooked because miscarriage is so common. Caring for the needs of women who miscarry is considered medically straightforward (by physicians, anyway). If your OB-GYN asked about your stress level and mood and even inquired about how your partner was doing, this is wonderful. If she didn't, you're not alone. Despite evidence of the substantial emotional stress women go through with early pregnancy loss, doctors don't routinely provide—or even mention—follow-up care.

There are different explanations why. Primary care providers, family physicians, obstetricians, and other doctors may be uncomfortable discussing stress, and they may lack the training required to assess risk for mental health problems following miscarriage. Studies that separately explored the ability to recognize mental health issues and acknowledge them to the patient—two entirely different things—suggest that even though some physicians *are* able to assess their patients' moods (and with relative accuracy), they subsequently fail to raise these concerns with those patients. Denial, a general discomfort with emotions, and the perception of sadness or anxiety that arise during a medical issue as transitory and temporary are some reasons this can happen. Women are the ones responsible for seeking medical attention following miscarriage. This explains why so many find the approach to mental health in the aftermath of loss to be inadequate.

So, in order to take good care of yourself now *and* going forward:

- **Expect** that medical issues will, in varying degrees, affect your emotions and your ability to manage them. See this as natural.
- **Be aware** that, given the research cited here, your doctor might not address your mental or emotional health after a loss.
- **Remember** that, no matter how your physician behaves, your mind, body, and spirit are intricately interwoven.
- **Create** a self-care plan that is holistic in nature that you refer to in concert with your medical care plan.
- **Proactively research** licensed therapists in your area who specialize in pregnancy loss, high-risk pregnancy, fertility, and loss. Do this before you need one, knowing you may not need to call. Check out their websites and call for information. Ask close friends or people you trust for referrals to their therapist.
- **Ask your OB-GYN** to share resources related to pregnancy loss, support groups, and educational information. Check your local hospital for community education and lectures, as this is a good way to connect to others who know what you're going through.

Huong

There is still so much shame and stigma around mental health. Physicians may fear asking questions. They may think that if they ask a patient if they are going to hurt themselves or if they have thoughts of ending their life that it will cause the patient to contemplate self-harm and suicide. They think that exploring mental health with a patient is like opening Pandora's Box.

Conversely, patients think that if they talk about pregnancy loss and their grief for their baby they will never get over it. People fear their own unknown feelings. It is a natural reaction to want to protect ourselves, but we may be doing ourselves a disservice by not seeking help to peer into our inner unknown.

Shock, guilt,
shame, loneliness,
anger, despair,
anxiety—
the gang's all here

Shock and confusion

Is this really happening?

It can't be.

I have to admit, when I first learned about the stages of grief, I didn't really understand denial. I thought, "People actually believe something *didn't* happen? I don't get it." Now I get it.

When the doctor told my husband and I that our son had no heartbeat, I remember thinking, "No, he's joking. It's April Fool's Day. Ha ha." Even when the doctor stared at me with seriousness all over his face, I clung to this (dis)belief. A couple days later, during the torturous waiting period before my D&E (dilation and evacuation), when I was just walking around with my dead baby inside of me, Chris and I went to a pub in an attempt to get our minds off things. I couldn't bring myself to order a beer. "What if he's still alive?" I said. Logically, I knew he wasn't. But on another level, I didn't know. Or I didn't want to know.

With each of my losses, I woke up the day after finding out the terrible fate thinking, "It was just a nightmare. Everything is fine." I would have to ask Chris to confirm that this was not the case. I just could not believe it.

For days, I walked around in this haze of disbelief, waiting to wake up from a bad dream, waiting for something to be undone, for someone to tap me on the shoulder and say, "Gotcha!" It took several days before I said to myself, "This is actually happening."

In a way, I felt like my body was in denial too. With my miscarriages, I had no symptoms, no signs of anything being amiss. My baby had died, and my body refused to accept this fact. It took weeks and weeks for my body to let go, to acknowledge the death.

For me, the intensity of the denial reflects the level of attachment that existed. In a way, denial is a sign of love. When you love something so much, of course you don't want to believe when it's gone.

Denial serves a purpose for us. It is a shock absorber. It is a form of self-protection when we cannot face our reality. Coming out of denial can be like emerging into broad daylight after days underground. You instinctively cover your eyes or turn away because the brightness hurts.

As denial about the loss begins to fade, something else can emerge: anxiety. *How can I organize all this inside me?* Turning inward also brings a constant reminder of who is no longer there, the love that you lost. How will you live with this new reality? These are the types of questions that come next on your journey.

The shock and denial that I see in many of my clients after a pregnancy loss is also very much linked to culture. We're getting there with talking about pregnancy loss more openly, but we still have a ways to go. This means that women are often not prepared for the reality of a loss (hence, the denial).

Results from a study comparing responses of women in Qatar versus women in the United Kingdom highlight some of the cultural differences that can impact a woman's response to pregnancy loss.

In Qatari culture, reproduction is a central part of a woman's role. The women are expected to have large families, and therefore, they tend to experience multiple pregnancies and, subsequently, increased exposure to pregnancy loss. Miscarriage is not perceived as a shocking event; it is considered a normal and common event in a woman's life. According to the research, the women were sad following the pregnancy loss but tended to not dwell on the loss: "Although birth control is available, women saw pregnancy as the expected outcome of sex with their husbands, and miscarriage as part of the normal experience of a woman's reproductive journey."

"Denial helps us to pace our feelings of grief. There is a grace in denial. It is nature's way of letting in only as much as we can handle." —Elisabeth Kübler-Ross and David Kessler, *On Grief and Grieving*

On the next page, we'll talk more about how our culture has left many women reeling after a pregnancy loss.

Shock and confusion

It wasn't supposed to be this way

I feel blindsided.

In retrospect, I feel a little silly for how utterly shocked I was with my first pregnancy loss. Of course I knew people lost pregnancies, but I really didn't think of it as something that would happen to *me*.

When I think about why this is, several factors come to mind. One, I think we all have a bit of a sense that we're immune from certain tragedies (or we like to think we are). I had been privileged to go through life without any major events to disrupt this belief. I still had some of that invincibility that comes with youth.

Two, I wasn't hearing anyone *I knew* talk about pregnancy loss, so it *seemed* like a rare thing. Now I know that many women in my life had lost pregnancies, but they did not talk about them because nobody else did. Shame breeds silence breeds shame breeds silence, and on and on.

Three, everything I was seeing and hearing was telling me that loss wasn't common, that motherhood was right around the corner. There were baby bumps all over Facebook, emails from companies trying to sell me things the moment I'd created a profile on a pregnancy site, apps encouraging me to bond with my baby when he/she was just the size of a poppy seed. All of this reinforced so much early attachment, which is both good and bad—good if your pregnancy leads to a healthy baby, but painful if your pregnancy ends.

Sometimes I think about women in the olden days who may not have known for weeks if they were pregnant. Maybe they didn't notice a missed period, for example. Maybe they only became aware of their impending motherhood when a bump began to grow. If a woman miscarried early, she probably didn't even know what had happened—just chalked it up to a period. When my grandmother was pregnant in the 1950s, she didn't know she was having twins until two babies magically arrived. Doesn't that seem absurd?

We have so much technology these days. We can pee on sticks before our missed periods and be aware of our pregnancy so early. Sophisticated ultrasounds allow us to see the poppy seed before a heart has even started beating. That heart can be heard as early as six weeks. I don't think any of this technology is *bad*; after all, at least two of my losses would have led to my death without medical technology. But some of the advances may have given me a false sense of security. When I saw the poppy seed on-screen, I thought I was on a sure path to motherhood, and that just wasn't the case.

"When you find out you're pregnant, you immediately think of yourself as on a very well-established narrative track. When you go through pregnancy loss . . . it's a sudden, abrupt deviation from the standard narrative. That can be completely disorienting." —Dr. Rebecca Kukla, Professor of Philosophy, Georgetown University, "Don't Talk About the Baby"

All this goes to say that I'm not surprised I felt blindsided; I'm not surprised that most women feel blindsided, even though the statistics are out there, even though we hear about pregnancy loss more. There is more talk of it these days, which is good, but I'm guessing more women feel like me—silly for their shock, like *I should have known this could happen*. What I've decided is that I did know it could happen. I stored this knowledge so far back in my head because I didn't want to consider it. I wanted to live in hope. I wanted to believe all the subject lines in those company emails: *You're going to be a mama soon!*

Meredith

In her book *The Myth of the Perfect Pregnancy*, Lara Freidenfelds makes clear that the majority of miscarriages are caused by chromosomal abnormalities that render the embryo incompatible with life. They are largely random and unpredictable. "All in all," Freidenfelds writes, "early pregnancy losses are part and parcel of childbearing. However we think about pregnancy, we need to take miscarriage into account."

But, so often, we do not take miscarriage into account. The perception we seem to hold both societally and individually is that miscarriage is a rare freak occurrence. *Obstetrics & Gynecology* (2015) reported that survey respondents "erroneously believed that miscarriage is a rare complication of pregnancy, with the majority believing that it occurred in 5 percent or less of all pregnancies."

This disconnect between truth and reality can exacerbate shock and confusion when a pregnancy is lost.

"In a society that has so many advances at our fingertips to enable women to become pregnant, we need to pay more attention to the emotional toll when these advances ultimately fail us." —Lara Freidenfelds, *The Myth of the Perfect Pregnancy*

Huong

I often use the concept of demoralization with my clients as a way to frame pregnancy loss. Demoralization, as described by the psychiatrist Jerome Frank, is experienced as an inability to cope, together with the associated feelings of helplessness, hopelessness, meaninglessness, subjective incompetence, and diminished self-esteem. It is often used to describe pregnancy loss.

In Michelle Obama's memoir, *Becoming*, she describes her emotional distress after a miscarriage, an experience she described as "lonely, painful and demoralizing almost on a cellular level." A twenty-five-year-old pop singer, Halsey, has also described her miscarriage as demoralizing. Meghan McCain wrote an opinion piece in the *New York Times* where she described herself as "demoralized" following a pregnancy loss.

Demoralization is associated with the breakdown of how a person views and understands the world. Some individuals feel generally disoriented (Which direction is up, and which direction is down?) and unable to locate meaning, purpose, or sources of need fulfillment (Why even bother? Everything is futile). One may begin to question their former beliefs, and previous convictions dissolve into doubt, uncertainty, and loss of direction.

One way I describe demoralization is what happens to us when the supposed "rules of the game of life" change on us, often without any warning. For some of us familiar with the board game The Game of Life, there are certain "rules" to follow such as buying life insurance and going to school to make a bigger paycheck. We all believe that we understand the formula for happiness and success.

Pregnancy losses disrupt all the rules we have internalized and come to believe are true. It can be life-altering.

Guilt and shame

Is this my fault?

*I was stuck on this particular
question for a long time.*

A tiny part of me still wonders what I did wrong. I'm a thin person (my hips have never, and probably will never, be described as "childbearing"); was I not strong enough to sustain a pregnancy? Were my losses some kind of karma, payback for not treating my body well enough in my twenties? Did I wait too long to start a family? Apparently, thirty-five is "advanced maternal age" (I guess that's a slight improvement on the old term—"geriatric pregnancy"— but both terms seem to carry with them accusation, blame).

In addition to tormenting myself with those questions, I latched on to certain other things to blame, certain things to make it my fault. On the next page is just a short list of things I still obsess about.

"Mis-carry: The word itself creeps with guilty error, as if you've carelessly dropped something you were meant to hold. Pregnancy comes with a list of dos and don'ts, and doctors and the women's health movement like to emphasize the responsibility we have for our bodies. So, when you miscarry, it's hard not to feel like you did something wrong." —Emily Bazelon, "I Went Out Full," featured in *About What Was Lost: 20 Writers on Miscarriage, Healing, and Hope* (Jessica Berger Gross, editor)

"I was convinced it was my fault . . . that perhaps I had mistreated my body too much in my past and that it was paying me back by making my body uninhabitable to the baby." —Jessica, on her second-trimester loss

First pregnancy:

- I had a cold and took over-the-counter medication in those two weeks between ovulation and a positive pregnancy test.
- I had a few beers during that two-week wait.
- I went in a jacuzzi for twenty minutes before I knew I was pregnant.

Second pregnancy:

- I had pizza with goat cheese topping—was the goat cheese safe? It was cooked, but maybe not enough?

Third pregnancy:

- I felt a weird pull in my stomach when I was swimming at the gym— did I tear a membrane?
- I exercised too much.
- I exercised too little.
- I let work stress me out too much.
- I slept on my stomach too often.

Fourth pregnancy:

- I didn't put my legs up after having sex so the egg got stuck somewhere.

It was easier to blame myself than to confront the more terrifying reality— my losses just happened, for no reason. They were beyond my control. My first OB-GYN shrugged off my ectopic pregnancy as a "fluke."

"Guilt is a mixture of anxiety, sadness, and anger: anxiety that you failed, sadness that you didn't measure up, and anger at your own self. Guilt arises from your belief that you should be able to protect your children."
—Deborah L. Davis, *Empty Cradle, Broken Heart: Surviving the Death of Your Baby*

Even now, this is still hard for me to accept. Even now, when I openly share my losses, I still wonder if people judge me, if they assume I did something wrong to cause my losses. I know if they do assume that, they are struggling to accept the same thing I am—the loss of control we all want to believe that we have (See "Feeling a loss of control"). As another doctor said to me, "It's just one of those things." Being human means living through so many of "those things."

"I did go back and think, did I do anything that might have prompted it? Is it because I am a lighter weight? Should I have stopped having caffeine? Is it because I run? It's very easy to go down a rabbit hole of what ifs when you want answers to something that 'just happens.'"

—Michaela, on her first-trimester loss

"I remembered the things I'd done wrong:
I hadn't been off the pill for long before I got pregnant (two weeks).
I had a couple of drinks (five weeks).
I had to stop to breathe during a tough bike ride (ten weeks).
I lost control of a fight with Karim (fifteen weeks).
I went to a concert in a smoky bar (seventeen weeks).
I was bad about prenatal vitamins (most weeks)."

—Seema Reza, "Pity," featured in *What God Is Honored Here? Writings on Miscarriage and Infant Loss by and for Native Women and Women of Color* (Shannon Gibney and Kao Kalia Yang, editors)

Meredith

When terrible things happen, we naturally try to find ways to organize, to put order to that which does not play by the rules of linear cause and effect.

The pain of your loss defies depths inside yourself that you've experienced before. And why wouldn't it? You've lost a child, a child who was—is—real. You are forever connected. The depth of your sorrow may leave you feeling desperate to find reasons for your loss.

Sometimes self-blame is a place we go when no other explanations work; sometimes we blame others. But in your heart, deep down, I think you know that blame (of yourself or others) does not alleviate the pain.

Your grief is, in a way, an extension of life in that you are alive and present to feel this pain. Throw out the expectations that this should be a "gift." That is a cliché you needn't bother thinking about. You will be the one to determine when—and if—you ever think of it that way.

It may make you feel vulnerable and uncomfortable, but when you find yourself looking for the reasons—obsessing over them—turn instead to the natural state of your grief. Connect to your baby and allow yourself to experience the longing. If you don't overthink your grieving process, your thoughts and actions will guide you to what will help soothe your pain. You will know when something doesn't help and gravitate toward what does. Perhaps that is a morning reflection, a letter to the baby you lost, or planting a garden in their memory and honor. The pain is healed by creating a metaphoric "space" inside you and tending to that space over time. It has infinite room for spirit—both yours and your baby's.

What the studies tell us

According to a national survey:

- 47 percent of people who'd had a miscarriage felt guilty.
- 41 percent of people felt they had done something to cause the loss.
- 28 percent of people felt ashamed.

Many people believe that pregnancy loss is caused by specific things:

- 76 percent believe it's caused by a stressful event.
- 64 percent believe it's caused by the pregnant person lifting a heavy object.
- 28 percent believe it's caused by previous use of an intrauterine device.
- 22 percent believe it's caused by oral contraceptives.

(Obstetrics & Gynecology, 2015)

Guilt and shame

I feel like a failure

I mean, wasn't my body "made for this"?

Because I've always been a high-achiever—the typical Type A who got straight A's—I was used to efforts translating to rewards. This is one of many reasons my losses knocked the breath out of me.

Each of my losses felt like a personal failure, like my body screwed up doing the very thing it was supposedly designed to do—create and carry a child. Nobody said to my face, "It must be something you did," but I felt like that was the undercurrent of platitudes like "Everything happens for a reason."

"I couldn't help thinking I had let everyone down; they were expecting the happiest news and I had given them this."
—Elle Wright, *Ask Me His Name: Learning to Live and Laugh Again After the Loss of My Baby*

I felt an immense amount of shame about my losses, especially when one loss turned into two, then three, then four. I *had* to be doing something wrong. I was convinced everyone felt that way, that they pitied me and thought I was pursuing a foolish dream. I felt angry at them (and the judgments I imagined them having). I felt angry at my body. I felt sad for my babies, for letting them down, for being incapable of carrying them to term.

Meredith

Believing that your body "screwed up" is a way of assuming personal responsibility for your loss. It is also a way of contributing to the narrative that miscarriage is rare and within a person's control. In this way, you've internalized an expectation that society places on you—an expectation to become a mother. And by blaming your body, you say to society, "I failed. I didn't do what I was supposed to do." These thoughts have a way of merging with the natural feelings and emotions that arise with grief.

"For years after (and even today to some extent), I felt like a complete failure. I couldn't even protect my unborn baby. I wasn't able to do what millions of women are able to do." —Tracy P., featured in the *New York Times* Opinion piece, "You Know Someone Who's Had a Miscarriage" (Lauren Kelley and Alexandra March)

It *almost* seems like a natural response of self-protection. You isolate yourself as "the deficient one" so that the rest of us do not have to consider the randomness of pregnancy loss, that it could happen to anyone. It's a harsh way to punish yourself for something that is not your fault.

The shame Kim describes makes me think of the collective burden she and so many women carry upon experiencing miscarriage. Shame is a painful feeling of humiliation or distress caused by the consciousness of wrong or foolish behavior. But nothing here, in the loss of a child, points to anything remotely shameful.

"The earliest and most undeniable proof of our finiteness and mortality is the perception of the body. The body prevents any attempt to transgress its limits, constantly crushing any illusions we might have of omnipotence." —Aldo Carotenuto, *To Love, To Betray*

When the body falters, we try to find meaning. At the same time, we are afraid of what we might discover—that we have so little control over so many things. We may fear this lack of control is due to some kind of deficiency within us. And that can lead to shame. It's a chain reaction built on a falsehood.

It doesn't work, and it isn't true. So unsubscribe from that burden. No one has control over this type of pregnancy loss. Note what thoughts come to mind, what feelings surface, and explore those instead. This will take you deeper, and depth is where the healing occurs.

It is important to understand the difference between guilt and shame. Guilt is "I did something wrong"; shame is "I am bad." In the case of pregnancy loss, neither is true.

If you find yourself stuck in thoughts of guilt and/or shame, Cognitive Behavioral Therapy (CBT) can be very helpful. This type of therapy is based on the idea that the way an individual perceives a situation is more closely related to their reaction than to the actual situation itself. It is like the Anaïs Nin quote: "We don't see things as they are, we seem them as we are."

Consider this triangle:

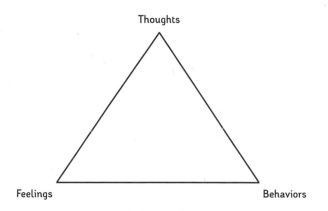

Thoughts

Feelings   Behaviors

Our thoughts are basically what we think about an event/situation, and they can affect how we feel and act. In the case of a pregnancy loss, if your thought is "I am worthless" or "This is my fault," this can lead to the feelings of sadness, guilt, despair, hopelessness, and also the behaviors of self-isolation, self-criticism, overeating/undereating, and more.

Our behaviors or actions also affect how we think and feel. For example, if you are lying in bed and crying following a pregnancy loss, you may start to think, "I am so weak, I can't even get out of bed to go to work," which could cause you to feel sadness or anxiety.

Lastly, our feelings and emotions can also affect what we think and how we behave. Some may engage in a pattern called emotional reasoning, where we believe our emotional reaction is true, regardless of evidence to the contrary. For example, "I feel overwhelmed and hopeless, therefore my problems must be impossible to solve," or "I feel inadequate after this pregnancy loss. I am a worthless person if I can't be a mother."

With my clients, I ask them to keep a log of their daily thoughts (it is incredible how many negative thoughts we have) and to start to challenge them by asking questions such as:

1. Is this thought true?
2. Does having this thought serve me?
3. Is there another explanation or way of looking at things?
4. What advice would I give to a friend that has this thought?

"How much we know ourselves is extremely important but how we treat ourselves is the most important." —Brené Brown

Loneliness and isolation

If it's so common, why do I feel so alone?

Because many of us are suffering in silence.

It's commonly reported that nearly one in four pregnancies end in loss. About one in 160 pregnancies end in stillbirth. If that's not startling enough, some believe rates of pregnancy loss are even higher, as women may miscarry before they realize they are pregnant, or they miscarry at home and do not report it. In 2018, evolutionary geneticist William Richard Rice of the University of California, Santa Barbara, reported that *most* human pregnancies end in miscarriage. As one of my obstetricians said, in an attempt at consolation: "Ask ten women if they've miscarried. Nine will say yes, and the tenth is lying."

"Miscarriage might just be the loneliest experience that millions of women have faced." —Lauren Kelley and Alexandra March in their *New York Times* Opinion piece, "You Know Someone Who's Had a Miscarriage"

And yet, despite *knowing* this information, my losses *felt* like a personal affront. That's the thing—knowledge and emotion are two very different things.

In recent years, there has been more in the news about miscarriage, emphasizing how common it is. The message is, "You are not alone." And, yes, it is nice to know that other women also go through this. But, I still feel like we are all going through it privately. We are all in our own personal hells, concealing from the world the truths of the physical and emotional pain we are enduring.

I think some of the silence around miscarriage starts with the silence around pregnancy in general (at least pregnancy in the first trimester). There is an unofficial "rule" that women should not announce their pregnancy until it's past the precarious first-trimester mark. I abided by this rule without considering why. Now when I consider why, I'm left to conclude that women associate embarrassment, shame, and guilt with losing a pregnancy, so we think it's best to remain tight-lipped. The problem, of course, is that when I did suffer a loss, I felt alone because nobody had even known I was pregnant. It all seemed like too much to explain. And, yes, there was the embarrassment/shame/guilt factor. Talking about my losses felt like shouting from the rooftop, "Hey, I totally failed to do this thing that my body was supposedly made to do!" (See "I feel like a failure").

Meredith: In some cultures, superstition dictates that the news not be shared, that showers not be thrown, that baby furniture not be purchased. These beliefs, held over generations, may not necessarily have anything to do with shame but with fear of loss. In addition to these feelings, the fear of profound sadness should a pregnancy be lost or a miscarriage occur may keep women from sharing. We might call this a protective measure—she's not ready for questions because she is only just trying to sort through the answers herself. Another reason is that different women will experience the loss with varying degrees of intensity. Others may simply be more comfortable being private; for them privacy does not indicate isolation or shame.

When I started sharing my losses with other women, the vast majority of them said something like, "Oh, yeah, I had a miscarriage when . . . " Even my mom confessed that she'd had a miscarriage. To this day, every time someone tells me of their own loss, my reaction is one of shock. How did they go through this, and I had no idea? Why are we all hiding?

I don't want to hide anymore. I don't want to just say, "I lost four babies." I want to talk about the nitty-gritty details of those losses. I want other women to feel free and empowered to do the same.

Meredith: It is wonderful that we have come to a place where more and more women are advocating for openness, sharing their rage at being silenced, and talking about their losses. Some who had losses years ago may be finding there is finally room for their voices to be heard and valued.

"I felt lost and alone, and I felt like I failed. Because I didn't know how common miscarriages are. Because we don't talk about it. We sit in our own pain, thinking that somehow we're broken."
—Michelle Obama

"Shouldn't we be talking openly about this much more often, so that we're better prepared for the grief when it hits us?"
—Emily Bazelon, "I Went Out Full," featured in *About What Was Lost: 20 Writers on Miscarriage, Healing, and Hope* (Jessica Berger Gross, editor)

"The silence makes us feel as if there is something fundamentally wrong with wanting and needing to remember our children, no matter how short their lives may have been . . ."
—Shannon Gibney and Kao Kalia Yang, "Reclaiming Life," in *What God Is Honored Here? Writings on Miscarriage and Infant Loss by and for Native Women and Women of Color*

Loneliness and isolation

I just want to hide from the world

You have my permission.

After each of my losses, I hibernated. I've always been a bit of a homebody. I'm a classic introvert—energized by alone time, drained by too much social interaction. My introversion was exacerbated by my losses. I needed time and space to work through my grief. Grieving is such a personal, solitary endeavor. Yes, sharing can help, but I needed to be alone.

Part of the reason I wanted to hibernate is that I felt so misunderstood. People were bombarding me with all these cliché phrases, force-feeding me positivity: "It'll happen when the time is right!" and "Don't give up!" and "You just need to keep trying!" (See "All the unhelpful things people say"). I could not handle this assault of optimism. I just wanted a minute (or a billion minutes) to be sad.

"For the friends that I told, I made it crystal clear that I needed to be left alone. I didn't want to see anyone, I couldn't face it."
—Elle Wright, *Ask Me His Name: Learning to Live and Laugh Again After the Loss of My Baby*

The loss of a pregnancy, more than other types of loss, seems to bring out the positivity in others. It's very confusing for the griever. The implication seems to be that you can just move on from this type of loss. So, when I felt devastated, I started to wonder if something was wrong with me, if I was "overreacting." When I realized I couldn't move on like everyone kept implying I should, I felt like a failure (again), on top of being really freaking sad. So, I isolated. *Peace out, world, you're too much for me right now.*

I know all the experts will probably say that isolating isn't good, but it was downright necessary for me. I didn't want to deal with people saying the wrong things—and I knew they would. I didn't want to be expected to socialize in any "normal" way when all I could think about was my sadness. I felt mentally safer in my own semi-predictable bubble. I was (understandably) depressed and, as the medication commercials say, uninterested in the things (and people) that used to give me pleasure.

I had to indulge my desire to isolate, at least for a while. I had to remove all external factors and find some stability within the safe boundaries of my own home before I was ready to venture out. And when I did venture out, I started with dog walks and errands. My advice: Go easy on yourself. The world will be there when you're ready.

"Parties and gatherings have become impossible for me to endure. I stay home as much as I can. I'm glad when the weather dips below zero and automatically cancels all my social obligations."
—Miranda Field, "My Others," featured in *About What Was Lost: 20 Writers on Miscarriage, Healing, and Hope* (Jessica Berger Gross, editor)

Meredith

Grief can be exacerbated by silence. Sharing feelings is painful, but allowing them to build up is draining in the long run.

If you absolutely do not want to see people *yet*, do something to get the emotion out. You can do this in different ways for each level of your being—body, mind, and spirit. Here are a few ideas:

Body

Move your body so the sadness, worry, anger, and angst can't settle in one spot too long. You don't want it to get theoretically (or literally) lodged in place (as in backache, headache) if there is a chance to avoid that. Sometimes there is.

- Take easy walks, or do some slow, gentle stretches.
- Take a restorative yoga class (there is typically not much conversation in these types of classes, and people tend to slip out after class without

talking in an effort to prolong that quiet space within).

- Or, check out what classes are available online through YouTube, a streaming service, or a studio. There are thousands of videos that feature gentle, restorative postures that allow you to slowly deepen into postures while lying on your back or while seated.

■ Try child's pose. This sweet, nurturing posture can be extremely soothing. Slip that into your daily routine every couple of hours, and notice the relaxing benefits.

Whatever movement you do, notice the sensations in your body as the muscles open and blood and breath flow through your limbs, carrying life force. Movements like these open the space inside you to hold new experiences apart from, and side by side with, the grief. By moving your body, you help create that space.

Mind

Give your mind something different to focus on while letting it know you take its concerns seriously.

■ Draw, paint, scribble, write, collage, and give your feelings a voice.
- Play music if you want, but choose something of the easier-listening variety or without words. Songs that have a gentle melody are good for this. (Try to avoid music with prominent beats, language, voice, dissonant chords, including certain classical music, rap, and hip-hop.)

■ Return to your renderings throughout the day, and look at them anew.
■ Turn them upside down: what do you see, feel, and experience when you examine your creations? These creations carry your voice from deep within.

Appreciate the innate voice your grief has. Trust that the pain you're in will get better and that one day—perhaps not that far from now—you'll have perspective that might seem difficult to fathom right now. Trust; it will come in its time.

Spirit

Here are two distinct ways to commune with your inner sense:

Inner sense and focus
1. Find some time in a quiet spot at home or outside (or in your car) and, well, just sit there.
2. Sit with the intention of doing nothing except to notice whatever you see. It might be a bird or a flower.
3. Now, notice what bubbles up from inside. Listen to those sensations, impulses, associations, and longings—they are expressions of you.
4. Think of these messages as though they were a song.
5. Don't try to direct, change, or stop them.
6. Just notice and honor them.

Inner sense and refocus
1. Find a space that is quiet and secluded.
2. Sit with the intention of doing nothing except finding one object to look at. Or you can concentrate on your own breathing or a particular prayer or meditation that you may repeat over and over.
3. If your mind drifts to what is bubbling up from inside, gently refocus on your object, your breath, or your prayer.
4. Here the point is to practice in small increments how to gently but actively cultivate peace within yourself.

All these will help you connect more fully to yourself and help you join these different levels within.

Huong

As a matter of fact, not all the experts would say to socially connect.

We are all wired differently, and we all react in different ways to coping with trauma and loss. Honor your body and your needs. Only you know what you truly need.

However, if you start hearing your brain saying things like, "You are alone, no one else understands you, just stay home alone," then that is the time to think about reaching out. There is a big difference between self-preservation mode (which is about honoring your unique needs) and self-isolation mode (which could ultimately get in the way of meeting your needs).

Anger

My favorite stage of grief

Oh, yes, anger.

I wasn't just angry after each of my losses, I was full of vicious rage. It was ugly and startling and, in retrospect, completely understandable. Here are just a few sources of my anger:

- My body—Why the hell couldn't it do this thing it was supposedly made to do?
- Pregnant women—Why did they all seem so chipper and blasé?
- Mothers—Did they even realize how lucky they were?
- My job—How was I expected to show up and give a shit about work with all I was going through?
- My husband—Should I even stay married to someone who clearly does not understand me at all?
- Doctors—Could they be any more insensitive and unhelpful?

While I was grieving, I became that person giving the finger to people on the freeway and whispering curses under my breath in long grocery store lines. I overreacted any time something didn't go as planned. When a pipe broke in our house, I ranted and raved while my husband looked on with concern, likely wanting to say "calm down" but knowing that things did not go so well the last time he'd said that. Once, in response to one of my verbal lashings at the world, he said, "It must be hard being you," and I could feel the fire coming out of my eyes as I looked at him and said, "It's about to be real hard to be you." I almost hit him.

If sadness was this heavy weight pressing on my chest that made me want to stay in bed all day, anger was the jolt I needed to keep moving. Anger is the Red Bull of grief, the energy-giver. Anger made me feel invigorated and alive at a time when part of me wanted to die. So it was necessary. It still is, sometimes.

"Anger is like fire—it rages and burns and needs to be released, and when it does, it's like the gates of hell have been flung open. My rage burned, it bled through my veins and hurt like hell, but it made me feel ten feet tall and bulletproof."

—Georgie, who had a stillborn daughter (Ella) and two first-trimester miscarriages

---

This is not to say it's good to be angry long-term. Much of the reason I sought therapy was to deal with my anger. I spent the majority of most sessions talking about how unfair everything was and discussing my hatred of baby showers. It helped. I needed to vent. I had to get through the layers of anger to uncover the despair that was hiding. That's the thing—there's always something beneath the anger. It's usually the stuff that hurts the most.

Meredith

Anger has life force inside it. The mere flash of anger reverberates through the body, buzzing, thrumming, echoing. That is life.

But many of us are conditioned not to express anger. We are taught to disown it (and call it ugly). We do not understand the purpose of anger. By extension, we don't understand how to express it or, in some cases, let it go.

Part of this stems from family patterns and caretakers (parents) who had difficulty expressing, holding, and working with their own anger. Sound familiar? If anger was used in your family to inflict pain, intimidate, and control, then you might develop an aversion to it, in others and in yourself. The opposite can happen too: anger, say, cloaked in sarcasm or cynicism, for example, might become a tool to bully or domineer.

Missing from all this is the understanding that anger is a natural emotion. It's a normal emotion that requires processing. But many of us reach an impasse—within ourselves—about how to do that. Yet it is still there inside, waiting for its due attention from us.

When I've worked with clients and when I've worked at processing my own anger, it has often taken repeated attempts to drill down to the core of the emotion. Where did it come from? Is it an echo from the past as well as of the current loss?

The point of expressing anger is not only to get it out. It is to get it out so it can be examined, reflected upon, and understood. It can teach us valuable lessons about what we can or want to tolerate. Anger that shows up solely in the expression phase does not accomplish this. Take anger very seriously. If you don't, you can get stuck in it. When we get stuck in it, we risk losing perspective on it. We risk lashing out and sliding into resentment.

Out of anger can come transformation, but only if we tend to our anger. Pay attention to these feelings that might at times make you want to rise up and destroy whatever is the trigger. Often the reason one is angry is beneath the obvious. Ask yourself: What is beneath the obvious? What wants your attention?

"Anger is strength and it can be an anchor, giving temporary structure to the nothingness of loss. At first grief feels like being lost at sea: no connection to anything. Then you get angry at someone. Suddenly you have a structure— your anger toward them."

—Elisabeth Kübler-Ross and David Kessler, *On Grief and Grieving*

Anger

The "It's not fair" tantrum

*Maybe if I stomp my feet hard
enough, I'll feel better?*

I feel like we all *know* life isn't fair, but I don't think we *believe* it. I think, in our hearts, we think (or want to think) that bad things won't happen to us if we are good people.

I talked to my therapist extensively about my obsession with fairness. I just could not wrap my head around how this could happen to me when I'd done everything "right." She told me about the Just World Hypothesis. According to the wise internet, this hypothesis is the assumption that "a person's actions are inherently inclined to bring morally fair and fitting consequences to that person, to the end of all noble actions being eventually rewarded and all evil actions eventually punished."

"When a loss hits us, we have not only the particular loss to mourn but also the shattered beliefs and assumptions of what life should be."
—Elisabeth Kübler-Ross and David Kessler, *On Grief and Grieving*

I clung to this principle because I really wanted to believe there was a formula to life: If you do X, you get Y. A formula like that is comforting in its simplicity. My pregnancy losses showed me that life doesn't work like that. Life doesn't always make logical sense. Here I was, someone who had taken all the correct steps to get pregnant, and I was suffering while there were drug addicts having perfectly healthy babies (I had to stop watching the TV show *Intervention* because it infuriated me).

The truth is, sometimes bad things happen when you do everything right, and good things happen when you do everything wrong. This realization rocked my world. It was like in addition to grieving my babies, I had to grieve my belief in a fair world.

"Ours is a generation of women who are uniquely captive to the illusion of control: If you study for the test, you'll do well. If you take the Kaplan class, you'll get into good schools. If you drink your V-8, the baby will be fine. That's how we run our whole lives. But pregnancy doesn't work that way. It just doesn't." —Dahlia Lithwick, "I Went Out Full," featured in *About What Was Lost: 20 Writers on Miscarriage, Healing, and Hope* (Jessica Berger Gross, editor)

Meredith

We live in a results-driven, do-er society. We can attribute part of our conception of fair/not fair to that. We are bombarded with information about planning a pregnancy and having a healthy baby. We are inundated with tips and recommendations of everything one is supposed to do to get the "right" results. These authoritarian voices masked in self-help preach to parents-to-be that being vigilant, or avoiding this food, or doing that treatment, or [fill in the blank] is *the* key to a healthy pregnancy. We have placed value on the visible goal being achieved and have paid far less attention to the emotional cost of that. If you are more inclined to logical thinking, it can be especially upsetting when your outcome does not align with your plan; essentially, your belief system has failed you. If you are more of an intuitive thinker, you might want to believe that if you had approached the pregnancy with more of a plan, things would have been different.

Now, hold all that off to the side as you explore the unique circumstance of your own suffering. If you are a logical, step-by-step thinker, how can you invite your more intuitive, less goal-oriented side to flourish? How can you use grief as a catalyst to expand your belief systems? If you are more intuitive, how can you channel your experience into something useful that might help others cope with the loss you're enduring and, in the process, give voice to your experience? These tiny adjustments utilize the agency you do have and open up choices to pursue to help you heal.

Betrayal

Feeling betrayed by my body

Why can't it just do what it's supposed to do?

In my quest to blame something for my losses, my body was as good a target as any. After all, I'd come to believe women were "made" for pregnancy. Our bodies were designed to house babies, to be safe havens for growing humans. With each loss, I couldn't help but think that I'd gotten a lemon in the body department.

After my first ectopic pregnancy: *Stupid fallopian tube, trapping my would-be baby. You fucking idiot.*

After my missed miscarriage: *Body, did you not get the memo? The embryo died. LET IT GO.*

After my second-trimester loss: *Is my womb just inhospitable? Did my placenta fail? What the hell?* With that loss, I distinctly remember grabbing the small pouch of my left-behind belly and cursing at it.

After my second ectopic pregnancy: *Are my eggs blind? Why can't they find my uterus? Millions of eggs have found their way to millions of uteruses (uteri?) since the beginning of time. Why can't my body get this right?*

Blaming my body was easy. My body was a convenient recipient for my rage when it was too hard for me to accept that these things just happened, that there was nothing to blame.

I wish I hadn't been so mean. After all, my body went through the losses with me. It wanted to grow a healthy baby so badly. It produced all the hormones. It made sure my breasts were prepared to nurse. It grew a placenta. It lined my uterus to nourish the embryo. It tried so hard. Even now, I get emotional thinking about what we went through, my body and me, together. I'm happy to say that, eventually, we made peace (See "Coming back to my body").

Your body has held a promise for you—for months, years, or decades—as it does in different ways for everyone. You made a promise to treat your body well, and you kept that promise. You took vitamins and ate healthy foods, went to the doctor, watched your health. You trusted your body. You had faith in it.

Your body is both the betrayer and the betrayed. And you can't even take a break from it to decide whether or not you can trust it again because, well, in simplest terms, you're in this together.

Your body is a living, breathing, amazing organism. It, too, grieves the loss of this pregnancy, this baby. It doesn't want to disappoint you, and a part of you, deep down, knows this. Like Kim, you will eventually understand the heroics of your body and the champion it truly is. You are in this together.

"I felt angry at my body and ashamed of my brokenness."

—Jessica, on her second-trimester loss

Betrayal

Feeling betrayed by Nature

I thought Nature was supposed to be kind and good.

After my first miscarriage, the doctor told me what most doctors tell women who experience miscarriages: "There was probably a chromosomal abnormality. This is just nature's way of dealing with things." I guess this "nature's way" spiel was supposed to be some comfort, but it just left me feeling vulnerable to nature's dark side. To put it simply, I came to think of Mother Nature as a total bitch. She made everyone think she was warm and nurturing when the truth was she's ruthless and cruel.

In December 2016, bitter and sad after my first two losses, I came across an article in the *New Yorker* ("Rewriting the Code of Life" by Michael Specter). The article is about Kevin Esvelt, a biologist and assistant professor at M.I.T Media Lab who is dedicated to exploring how we can rewrite DNA to make mice (and eventually humans) immune to the bacteria that cause Lyme and other tick-borne diseases. Specter writes: "Part of his job, as he sees it, is to challenge what he describes as 'the ridiculous notion that natural and good are the same thing.'" Another Esvelt quote that stood out to me: "The idea that nature is the essence of goodness . . . is so foreign to my perception of the world that I can't even conceive of how people can think that way. There is a such a fantastic degree of suffering out there."

Yes, a fantastic degree of suffering.

Losing a baby has complex layers of mourning; mourning the idea of nature as "good," mourning one's sense of safety and protection, is just one of those layers. I don't hate nature. I fear it a little. I respect it. But I'll never see it as inherently good again.

What is natural is sometimes beautiful, but not this. Not a miscarriage. Nature, like the Universe, holds all things, and some of those things can be violent and devastating.

When a perception or belief you've held close begins to fall apart right before your eyes, it's devastating. Awakening to the natural order—Nature's way—can be brutal and traumatic.

Ask yourself this: Are you an extension of Nature, or is Nature an extension of you, or are you one and the same, expressed in an infinitely unique way? Consider your answer, and as you do, notice that weighing Nature—and yourself—in terms of good or bad isn't an equation that works.

Pregnancy and its losses are personal in many ways. But they are also impersonal in that they are not punishment for being bad. A loss like this, as devastating as it is, is a reminder that you are of the natural world, that you belong here. Your loss, your experience, and your grief matter. You matter, too.

"Nature never deceives us; it is we who deceive ourselves."
—Jean-Jacques Rousseau

"One out of four pregnancies ends in miscarriage; this was simply nature's way of saying, 'Not this one, not yet.' As a fertility doctor whom I interviewed once said to me, 'Nature is extraordinarily wasteful when it comes to reproduction—look at all the acorns on the forest floor.'"
—Rebecca Johnson, "Risky Business," featured in *About What Was Lost: 20 Writers on Miscarriage, Healing, and Hope* (Jessica Berger Gross, editor)

Betrayal

Feeling betrayed by God

I thought He was watching out for me.

I wasn't raised in a traditionally religious family, but we celebrated Christian holidays like Easter and Christmas. I had a brief phase of attending church in my early twenties, but I stopped going once the minister asked everyone to pray that it wouldn't rain on the outdoor nativity scene. California was in a drought at the time.

My parents sent me to a private Catholic high school after witnessing drug deals in progress while picking me up from my public junior high. I didn't have to wear a pleated skirt (though I did get detention for my shorts being too short), but I was given a hefty dose of Bible education. It was hard *not* to absorb some of the teachings about God's omnipotence and love. I'm not going to lie—it was comforting to think of someone or something being "in charge" and looking out for me.

"I was pissed at God. I remember my emotions flowing over one day and my husband said, 'You need to go get that out.' At the time, I had two other young children. It's not that easy to just pop off anytime, anywhere with little ones watching your every move. But to this day I'm glad I listened to my husband. I went to our basement and had it out with God—shaking my fist and screaming. God could handle my anger. My faith morphed into something more solidified and tested after that." —Wendy, on her two first-trimester miscarriages

Even though my losses occurred many years after my Catholic school lessons, they brought up a lot of God issues for me. I'd said for years that I didn't really believe in God, but my losses made me aware that I did. Deep down, I did. I'd had this thought in the core of my being that someone (God) was enforcing fairness in the world. I'd been assuming that this power much larger than myself was ensuring everything "made sense."

So, when I lost one pregnancy after another, I was angry. Really angry. Pissed off. Rageful. What happened to this omnipotent God? Was He too busy listening to basketball players praying to Him before their stupid games? What was He *doing*? Why was He making these terrible things happen to me when I'd tried so hard to be a good person? Why was He punishing me when all these other women were having no problems having healthy babies? What was all this nonsense about His "plan"? How in the hell (can I say that?) could I ever have faith in this ridiculous "plan" again?

All my anger meant I did lose faith, but that wasn't a bad thing. I found it again, eventually (See "Finding faith"). I redefined my understanding of my higher power in a way that brought me a lot of peace. Eventually.

Meredith

Betrayal is a powerful impetus for change, deeper meaning, and, as Kim says, redefining your own faith. So often we get stuck in the betrayal, as it were, and the injustice. Betrayal hurts so much. When you put your trust in something and it fails you, it can be devastating. The loss of a pregnancy inflicts the wound of betrayal across the board—body, mind, and spirit—and you begin to question everything you believed in.

As Kim alludes to, there are differences between religion and faith, though they may, in fact, intersect. Religion offers a framework within which to view life's challenges and interpret them according to a set of beliefs. This can help a person in times of loss by providing structure (and scripture) to help make sense of what has been taken away. These defined steps, many that have been passed down from generation to generation and practiced by one's ancestors, can help comfort a grieving person while she tries to make sense of the loss.

"I was sobbing and just asking, 'Why on Earth do I keep getting pregnant if I can't have a kid? Like, what is this? Shut the door. Like, do something. Either shut the door or let me have a kid'... And for the first time, I feel like I actually told God how I felt. And I feel like we're supposed to do that."
—Carrie Underwood, singer, on her three miscarriages

But religion may not be enough, and new ways to access the Divine become necessary. For some, that means going more inward; for others it means finding a safe harbor to weather the storm of doubt in addition to loss.

Julie Mussché, spiritual director at St. Joseph Spiritual Care in Orange, California, says that crises such as these can bring people to their knees both literally and figuratively. Suffering is both a spiritual and psychological process that occurs within the individual—the body—here on earth. Pregnancy loss *is* a crisis of the mind, the body, and the spirit. To be faced with the fact that the religion, faith, or beliefs you relied on are simply not enough can be devastating. Suddenly, you are asking different questions, and the old beliefs don't work. Now you are faced with two endings, and they overlap.

Anger at God or feeling betrayed by God is a crisis of faith—a spiritual crisis. This crisis has its own stages of grief that you're forced to walk even as you mourn the loss of your baby. The betrayal, which feels awful, is the very thing that forces you to explore entirely new emotional territory. Though there are no timelines for this, ultimately, one day, you'll emerge with a new understanding of your unique relationship to something greater than yourself. You may call it God, Nature, or something else. But it will be at a deeper level than you ever imagined.

A word about "God's plan"

When someone says that a traumatic loss is all in "God's plan" or that "God is directing this," it is a simplistic way to shut down a conversation. "Fix-focused," is how Julie Mussché, director of St. Joseph Hospital Center for Spiritual Development, describes it.

Fix-focused can mean a lot of things. Often these fixes come by way of pat answers and expressions that don't make sense except on the surface and as a way to sweep past the moment of discomfort

People do this to assuage their own discomfort. They can't tolerate your pain because it stirs up something in them. They try to manage the other person's pain like a project. They go down the road of trying to fix the pain. But it doesn't work—you are still hurting.

Sadness and despair

Is it normal to be this sad?

I asked myself this often, and now I see the answer was always yes.

In sessions with my therapist, I said things like, "I don't know why I can't get over this. It's not like I lost a living, breathing child." I told her how social media had made me aware of all the suffering in the world, of all these horrible things happening—true atrocities. What right did I have to be THIS SAD over a baby I'd never met? That's when my therapist said something that I think of often: "Kim, tragedies can't be ranked."

It's sad that part of me felt like I wasn't allowed to be devastated. It's not a mystery where I got that message. I felt like my friends and family were thinking, "She needs to move on." The babies weren't real to them like they were to me. And our society, in general, is not very comfortable with grief. We want people to just move on (See section "Grieving in a society that sucks at grief").

"Miscarrying at nine weeks, I didn't feel entitled to the absolute devastation I felt." —Cindy Harkin, featured in the *New York Times* Opinion piece, "You Know Someone Who's Had a Miscarriage" (Lauren Kelley and Alexandra March)

The loss of a baby is extremely painful though. It doesn't matter if the baby was the size of a grain of sand or full-term. It doesn't matter what other people might think, or what society might expect. Yes, there are lots of tragedies in the world. But this is *yours*.

My therapist told me I wasn't doing myself any good by chastising myself for my grief. That was just layering shame on my grief. I dared to take her advice and just let myself be devastated. I had to block out the thoughts in my head like, "But I have such a good life" and "There are so many people who are so much worse off than me." It was only when I broke the dam and allowed myself to feel without inhibition that I could get to the heart of my grief. Getting to the heart is where the healing began.

Meredith

"Is this sadness normal?" is a sweeping question.

The answer is yes, of course it is normal. And natural. Sadness, during grief and mourning, is something we expect to occur.

When you've never encountered this depth of sadness or the traumatic nature of loss, however, it might make you question the intensity of your feelings. The sadness that blankets people during a loss that is tragic to them can feel physically heavy, emotionally confusing, and spiritually distressing. That said, all of this is normal.

"It wasn't until I went to therapy after having postpartum depression after the birth of my daughter that I finally confided to my therapist about my miscarriage. I brushed it over, saying, 'well, I know so many others who had much worse situations.' I remember the therapist stopping me and saying, 'No, your pain is valid. You have every right for that event to have impacted you.' That was comforting, because I often want to downplay certain life events or situations as 'it could always be worse.' But just because my miscarriage may not have been as tragic as another woman's doesn't mean it didn't cause me great pain and grief." —Michaela, after her first-trimester loss

The way each of us processes sadness is extremely personal. Coming from a place of self-care, you will need to determine what you need to do to help you live with the sadness until it slowly, gradually subsides. "I'm really sad right now" is something you will need to get used to saying—to yourself and to other people.

It's also a question that a woman asks herself *on behalf of society*. After the loss of a pregnancy, yes, it is "normal" and it is natural. But as for society, I present another question: What is it about grief that makes it so intolerable to us as a society? We need to take a step back and mindfully explore the negative way we view sadness. We prolong sadness by pressuring ourselves to conceal it. Sadness is a natural part of loss.

Sadness during loss, like when a pregnancy ends, is territory of the heart. You can try to think your way out of this heart space, but you'll always find yourself right back in the same place. Trying to reason with sadness, negotiate with it, or shame it out of existence doesn't work. Even gratitude lists—which in and of themselves are nice—are not the proper antidote to a primal emotion. This is an emotion that, quite simply, needs to be felt and recognized. When allowed this space, sadness this deep typically recedes. So, let it run its course.

Note: If you are asking yourself "Is it normal to be this sad?" because your sadness has intensified or lingered for a prolonged amount of time, it might be depression. See "Dealing with Depression."

Sadness and despair

Crying all the tears . . . or not

From strong and stoic to sobbing.

For the first couple days after my surgery to remove my first ectopic pregnancy, I was fairly stoic. In shock, maybe? With the determination of a military general, I declared the beginning of Operation Move On. I made a list of all the things my husband and I would do instead of having a family. I became fixated on planning a trip to wine country. We could go to Napa. I'd never been to Napa. I pictured myself in fancy tasting rooms, eating delectable meals in quaint farm-to-table restaurants.

Then the tears hit me, suddenly and with a force that terrified me (and my husband). The spigot broke, and I couldn't turn it off.

"To weep is to make less the depth of grief."

—William Shakespeare

There are people, like my husband, who pride themselves on "staying strong." I am of the belief that if you don't cry the tears, they will stay inside you and get moldy. You'll rot, basically. You've gotta get it all out. You've gotta let the snot run down your nose. You've gotta let your eyes get so puffy and squinty that you can barely see straight. You've gotta embrace your ugly crying face. You've gotta trust that the raging river of tears will slow to a trickle at some point, that you won't drown.

I cried a lot after my first-trimester miscarriage, mostly because I really did think I'd "paid my dues" with my ectopic pregnancy and was not expecting another loss. The tears were shock and sadness and residual grieving of my first loss. After losing Miles in the second trimester, I cried for days and days. I came to embody that phrase "burst into tears." Some loved ones said, gently, "It's probably the hormones." And maybe that was some of it (see "The hormones are real"), but I think most of it was just grief.

With my fourth loss, the ectopic pregnancy that occurred after losing Miles, I didn't cry much. I did more yelling and screaming than crying. I was just so frustrated at that point. I felt guilty about the lack of tears, like I wasn't respecting the embryo like I should have been. But then I talked to women on message boards who didn't have the deluge of tears either. Some found solace in a medical point of view, rationalizing that the pregnancy wasn't viable. They were logical, focused on next steps. That's how I was with my fourth loss—I just wanted to resolve the issue, medically, and get back to baseline.

Pregnancy losses are so personal. Tears—the amount of them, the frequency of them—are personal too. Mine were different with each loss, and I think all of them were "normal."

Meredith

Grief, mourning, and all those tears: no apologies accepted.

It's your grief.

Treat it as you would something valuable, something you need to treasure. Owning your difficult emotions is just as important as owning the ones that are more pleasant.

Denying your own suffering actually blocks the life force inside you. It is its connection to this life force that ignites hopefulness that things can and will get back to a new kind of normal. In other words, there is energy beneath your grief. There is a common misperception that it is the other way around, that suffering blocks joy and that we must rush to negate suffering before it begins. But healing doesn't work that way.

Trying to bypass, outthink, or outsmart grief inadvertently prolongs it. It was there before the loss of your baby and it's still there. Nature requires that we take ourselves inside the sadness in order to renew our connection with the joy that is still there but has receded due to loss.

You feel what you feel when you feel it. Messy tears in a hot shower in the middle of the night. A croak into the folds of a pillow as you lay alone midday. A dry-eyed stare out the window at the leafless tree. A furious missive written in your journal cocooned in your car on a lunch break.

When it comes to grief, the concern of making someone else uncomfortable as you navigate your own discomfort is foreign to me. People who are scared of their own grief will react to yours. I view grief's expression as something sacred. It indicates there was something cherished that is now gone. It indicates your capacity to feel and love. To be allowed to witness and support the grieving of another person is actually an honor. Feel free to extend that honor back to yourself.

Finally, think back in time, to when you were younger. What lessons did you learn about sadness? What messages did you receive? Were you taught to associate sadness with feeling sorry for yourself or "playing the victim"? If you were, recognize the shortcomings in what you were taught and what you internalized. Look instead at how you can explore grief in a more evolved manner. The more you try to rush through your grief or sidestep it, the more distorted it becomes. This is what I've observed—and experienced. Simply reminding yourself that the old messaging is outdated, lifting that up to the light, is often enough to make room for better self-care to take root and grow.

Huong

There is science behind tears. Biochemist and "tear expert" William Frey found in one study that emotional tears (those formed in distress or grief) contained more toxic byproducts and stress hormones than tears of irritation. Also, emotional tears contain 24 percent higher albumin protein concentration than irritation tears. This means that crying can remove toxins from our body, reduce our manganese levels, and release oxytocin and endorphins.

In some cultures, such as Japanese culture, people strongly believe in the benefits of tears and have "crying clubs" called *rui-katsu* (meaning, tear-seeking) where people come together to cry. Typically, after crying, our breathing and heart rate decrease, and we enter into a calmer biological and emotional state.

So, please, cry.

"What cannot be said will be wept." —Sappho*

*Though apparently there is some controversy about whether or not she really said this. Thanks for complicating things, internet.

Sadness and despair

Dealing with depression

When the sadness lingers . . .

I've dealt with bouts of depression since I was a teenager, so I was very familiar with the telltale signs of it after my losses. For me, depression is marked by a profound emptiness and hopelessness. Thoughts like "What is the point of life, anyway?" take me down rabbit holes of despair. I feel extremely tired but restless at the same time. I'm cranky and irritable and pessimistic and disinterested in socializing. In other words, a real joy to be around.

My husband met me after I'd gotten my past depression under control (mostly . . . with the help of therapy and antidepressants). He had no experience dealing with Depressed Kim. I'm pretty sure Depressed Kim felt like a stranger to him. I'm pretty sure she scared the shit out of him. It was only recently that he confessed he was afraid he'd never get his wife back.

I was concerned too. I knew firsthand how heavy and difficult depression could be. One benefit of my history was that it was easy for me to identify what was happening and get my butt straight to therapy. For women who don't have that history, it may be difficult to recognize or articulate the problem. And, even with recognition, some women may not consider therapy (because of stigma or cost or lack of experience with accessing it). I have a feeling many women resign themselves to just "waiting it out," which may work (eventually), but it doesn't have to be that hard. For me, losing a baby was hard enough; I wanted all the help I could get in the aftermath.

"It's important to understand that this depression is not a sign of mental illness. It is the appropriate response to a great loss."—Elisabeth Kübler-Ross and David Kessler, *On Grief and Grieving*

My therapist helped me realize that this depression wasn't like my past episodes. This depression was a natural reaction to loss, part of my grief process. I've realized depression is not always something to be feared. It doesn't mean you've "lost it." It doesn't mean you're a mental case. It may just be a necessary phase as you mourn your baby. And if it lasts longer than "a phase," there is so much help out there (see "Getting professional help").

What the studies tell us

- Bereaved mothers have **four times** higher odds of depressive symptoms compared to nonbereaved parents. (*Journal of Women's Health*, 2016)
- Depression has been shown to affect up to 20 percent of women following a miscarriage. (*BMC Psychiatry*, 2018)
- 10 percent to 15 percent of women who miscarry reach the clinical threshold for a major depressive disorder in the months after the loss. (*Archives of Women's Mental Health*, 2017)
- Sometimes it lingers: Women may experience depressive symptoms up to nine months after a loss. (*American Journal of Obstetrics & Gynecology*, 2019)
- Sometimes there is a delay: Some women may not show depressive symptoms until three to six months after their miscarriage. (American Society for Reproductive Medicine, 2010)

Meredith

Is it depression?

There is a time to consider asking "Is it normal to be this sad?" That is when you've seen no improvement in your mood or if your sadness increases. Your mental health affects your ability to cope with grief. After you lose a pregnancy, there are many variables to consider. Be mindful of the biological effects of pregnancy on mental health—the surge and decline of hormones. The plummet in estrogen and progesterone and the spike in prolactin after a women gives birth—or loses a pregnancy—affect how she feels both mentally and physically (See "The hormones are real").

The signs of grief can look a lot like the signs of depression, but depression is different. Grief can exacerbate depression. But grief also responds to being processed, felt, and explored. Depression, on the other hand, blunts that ability. With grief alone, we can still find joy in everyday things. With depression, that is much harder and often impossible to do.

Depression manifests differently for different people. While doctors and therapists follow certain guidelines to diagnose depression, how it affects a person is very individual. For some, it is masked by anxiety—workaholism, for example. An inability to concentrate can accompany depression. Feelings of exhaustion, sadness, disinterest, and diminished pleasure in life, as well as insomnia or the inability to sleep, physical agitation, or pervasive fatigue are different (and seemingly contradictory) signs of depression, and, as the illness worsens, recurring thoughts of wanting to die (as opposed to the fear of dying) may emerge.

Assess your stress

There are questionnaires available to assess the stress you are under and if you are showing signs of depression. Please see the Patient Health Questionnaire-9 and the Patient Stress Questionnaire in the "Questionnaires and screeners" section at the end of this book.

Note: These questionnaires do not in any way replace the guidance of a trained mental health professional. See "Getting professional help" for tips on finding someone to help you talk through your responses to the questionnaires.

Sadness that has movement—tears, periods of anger, moments of calm, some ability to concentrate, ability to articulate needs and identify the cause of your sadness even when it is tormenting you painfully—typically suggests you are processing, grieving, mourning. Basically, you are moving through the pain.

Sadness that continues to torment you indefinitely is not meant to be part of grief. Are you scared something bad will happen beyond what is considered a natural reaction to loss? Is the heaviness winning? Are nightmares or flashbacks or obsessions happening? Is life harder than it ever was?

The loss of a pregnancy is a traumatic event, one that can trigger the onset or recurrence of depression. If symptoms don't improve, if you cannot concentrate or stop crying, and if no matter what you do the sadness is insurmountable, you need help. Talk to your physician, who may refer you to a psychiatrist. With the correct professionals, you can discuss a course of treatment that will help you in both the short- and long-term.

Depression can make you feel like nothing will help. Defy that belief, no matter how difficult it is to do. Tell someone you trust. Call your doctor or a therapist. Help is available (See "Getting professional help"). You are not alone.

If you are having thoughts of harming yourself...

Please get help.

See "Getting professional help" for tips on finding someone in your area who can help you. Or if you are in crisis right now, please dial 911 or call one of the helplines below. If you are outside the US, please go online to find a helpline in your country.

Research shows that suicide risk increased in women during the year following a stillbirth, miscarriage, or termination of a pregnancy. There is nothing "strange" about your devastation, but you need to get help. That is why we've placed this information here.

Suicide Prevention Lifeline
suicidepreventionlifeline.org
1-800-273-TALK (8255) / TTY: 1-800-799-4889

24-hour, toll-free, confidential suicide prevention hotline available to anyone in suicidal crisis or emotional distress. Your call is routed to the nearest crisis center in the national network of more than 150 crisis centers.

SAMHSA's National Helpline
samhsa.gov/find-help/national-helpline
1-800-662-HELP (4357) / TTY: 1-800-487-4889

Also known as the Treatment Referral Routing Service, this helpline provides 24-hour free and confidential treatment referral and information about mental and/or substance use disorders, prevention, and recovery in English and Spanish.

SAMHSA provides suicide prevention information and other helpful resources to behavioral health professionals, the general public, and people at risk.

SAMHSA's National Suicide Prevention Lifeline is available at 1-800-273-TALK (8255).

Anxiety and posttraumatic stress

Feeling a loss of control

And realizing I had so little to begin with.

Throughout my life, I've done all I can to control as much as I can. I am a lover of control, a devotee. I am a list-maker, a planner, a calculator, an analyzer. So, when "things just happen," it really rattles me. Yes, I was upset about each of my pregnancy losses because of the loss of the babies and the dreams they represented. On another level though, these experiences so deeply affected me because they shattered whatever illusions of control I'd had, illusions I'd been leaning on for thirty-five years.

My losses made it *impossible* for me to continue believing I had any real control over things. Before they happened, my life had gone according to plan, for the most part. Any hiccups were easily explained by choices I'd made: I did X, so Y happened. There was no simple equation for my pregnancies though; there is no rhyme or reason when babies die.

"Although coming to terms with randomness is frightening, it can be liberating. It can free us from irrational fears and unfounded self-blame. And recognizing that we have only ourselves and each other to rely on empowers and motivates us." —Ralph Lewis, MD, *Psychology Today*

Part of healing from my losses has been coming to terms with how little control I have. Sometimes this is terrifying, and I find myself feeling anxious and vulnerable to all kinds of other things going wrong (and I need to take several deep breaths or go for a run or talk to my mom or pet my cat to feel a sense of calm again); other times, it feels like a blissful letting go, the biggest exhale. I have to think this is not just about losing a baby. This struggle between control and surrender is part of the human condition.

We do have control over certain things, but we rarely have total control over outcomes. When the outcome we desire is a baby, the suffering with a loss can be almost unbearable.

"Taking charge" or "having control" or "assuming ownership" of what we can is, to me, more a spiritual process than a psychological one. Spiritual concepts are difficult to quantify; everything about them is individual, and the results, as it were, really can't be measured.

But in this context, when a baby dies or there is a miscarriage, and once the trauma has sunken in, the answers to questions like "why" and "how come" that medicine has not sufficiently answered will still be waiting for the right answer. Only you will be able to fill in those blanks. Someday. Maybe.

Loss can be devastating. It leaves us feeling gutted and betrayed. The only way through it is to surrender to that reality. Lay it down. Let it go. It takes strength to put all that work into something with no guarantee your heart will meet its desire. It takes courage to give yourself over to that truth.

"I think that this is what changes you:
the realization that the worst can happen to you."

—Alexa Bigwarfe, *Sunshine After the Storm: A Survival Guide for the Grieving Mother*

Practicing mindfulness is one way to help ease the anxiety of not being able to predict or manipulate the future or answer the question of why (See page 125 for exercises to help you practice mindfulness). In time, you may come to accept that not having control is, in fact, not an unnatural state of being.

Let your mind imagine what's dear to you. And trust that sometimes you will get what you want, sometimes you will get something you hadn't imagined, and sometimes you will continue to ask why. Soon, maybe, you will be OK not knowing.

Anxiety and posttraumatic stress

I'm worried about more
bad things happening

If it happened once . . .

When my losses undermined my sense of control, I was left with a lot of fear and anxiety. I started thinking, "If that happened, what else could happen?" I found myself worrying about things I hadn't worried much (or at all) about before—my husband getting in a car accident, my mom dying of cancer, our dog drowning in the pool. Whenever a loved one's name popped up on my phone, I was convinced they were calling to tell me about some kind of emergency or catastrophe or accident—something horrible. I was afraid to go out of town and leave my pets (my these-will-have-to-do children) with sitters. We'd done this so many times before, but now I was terrified of all the things that could go wrong.

"No one ever told me that grief felt so like fear." —C. S. Lewis, *A Grief Observed*

My losses had exposed my vulnerability to tragedy, and the effect was that I was constantly bracing for impact. For me, this feeling of helplessness, powerlessness, fragility, and fear was one of the most jarring aftershocks of my losses. I'd lost not just my babies but a lot of innocence and optimism. I found myself going through life with a sense of dread, holding my breath in anticipation of what would happen next.

With time, my fears have translated to gratitude. I'm grateful for my health, for the resilience of my marriage, for my daughter. I no longer take any moment of health and happiness for granted. Knowing that any security I feel could be gone in an instant, I've learned to cherish all the good days and trust that I am strong enough to endure the bad ones.

"It made me fearful about connecting with people and fearful to really experience LOVE, afraid that loving too much and having good things in your life can only end up hurting WAY too much ... I also started having irrational fears about something bad happening to my husband or loved ones (constantly checking on them all the time to be sure they were safe)."
—Jessica, on her second-trimester loss

Meredith

All this worry has a name: anxiety. Usually, as shock and denial lessen, anxiety increases as we feel flooded with the reality of that which we can't control. It may be low grade anxiety or hypervigilance, or vague worry that something else bad is going to happen that might not even have to do with pregnancy. In addition to this being part of the grief process, I view anxiety as a kind of signpost, an indication that inside you something else is waiting its turn— sadness, perhaps anger, and deeper than you may have ever felt before in your life.

Even though anxiety is typically associated with fear, it can also hide anger we don't feel entitled to feel. Anger is intimidating—it feels wild and unruly, especially when it's been repressed. Anxiety is something more "palatable" in our society, especially for women. Those of us who have been taught that anger is a flaw may feel ashamed when we're mad and try to hold it in. If you've ever held in your anger, you know that, especially in the long-term (and even in the short-term), it doesn't work. Now you're angry and resentful for not being able to express what is natural.

"Anxiety, for me, was cruel and overbearing. It crept into every part of my day and caused me to be scared of even my phone ringing or a knock at the front door." —Elle Wright, *Ask Me His Name: Learning to Live and Laugh Again After the Loss of My Baby*

What the studies tell us

- In the largest study so far to assess the psychological impact of early-stage pregnancy loss, approximately one in four women suffered moderate to severe anxiety one month after a pregnancy loss. (*American Journal of Obstetrics & Gynecology*, 2019)
- In that same study, one in six women still suffered moderate to severe anxiety nine months after their loss. (*American Journal of Obstetrics & Gynecology*, 2019)

When anxiety spikes after pregnancy loss, keep the medical in mind too.

Prolonged anxiety may indicate several things worthy of exploration, for example:

1. Something physical might need to be addressed. This is not uncommon after medical trauma.
2. You may be fighting with yourself regarding acceptance of your emotions. Talking to a therapist or attending a grief group can help.
3. Depression might be a factor. Depression can mask itself as anxiety.
4. Anxiety can appear in different ways—overworking, not sleeping, obsessing, overeating or not eating (change in eating patterns).

Recognize that anxiety about the unknown is part of this. Doing so can help when anxiety threatens to overtake you. Become the watcher of your anxiety. This is known as mindfulness and provides space for your emotion to be expressed, to be witnessed, and, finally, to dissipate. See "Practicing mindfulness" on the next page for meditative exercises that may help you.

Is anxiety affecting your life?

Please see the **Generalized Anxiety Disorder 7-item Scale** to get a better sense of how anxiety may be affecting your life.

Remember: Questionnaires like this do not in any way replace the guidance of a trained mental health professional. See "Getting professional help" for tips on finding someone to help you talk through your responses to the questionnaires.

Practicing mindfulness

Mindfulness—focused attention on the present moment or what is right in front of you at this moment—alleviates stress. Meditation can help encourage mindfulness. Learning to quiet your mind might aid in reducing anxious thoughts. This could lead to lasting benefits to mental and physical health.

Simple exercises to bring you back to yourself:

EXERCISE 1
- Notice what is right in front of you—do nothing except see it.
- Breathe. In, out, in, out.
- Notice what is right in front of you and breathe.

EXERCISE 2
- Concentrate on your body; focus on wherever you land.
- Breathe.
- Notice that part of your body and breathe.

EXERCISE 3
- Find a simple activity like pulling weeds, making tea, getting the mail.
- Breathe.
- Notice how your body moves as you complete this activity and breathe.

EXERCISE 4
- Whatever you are doing, pay attention to that.
- Experience that experience.
- Breathe.

There is no need to assess or rate your experience. All you need to do is practice it and get used to taking the time to practice it.

It may seem like a silly exercise, but it is a powerful one for many of my clients as they shift from being a "victim" of their incessant thoughts to remembering that they are in control and can choose to believe or not believe a thought.

Identify your "fear monster"

One activity I use with clients is to have them draw a picture of their "fear monster" and give it a name (one client calls theirs "Mean Momo"). From there, clients can engage in a short dialogue with their fear monster by saying, "Look. I know you're here because you want to protect me. But all your worries and anxious thoughts are scaring me and the baby. How about this: I give you ten minutes a day to show up and tell me all about your fears and worries, but after that, you have to go away so I can focus on enjoying this pregnancy and also my life."

Anxiety and posttraumatic stress

Why am I obsessed with death?

Probably because losing my baby was one of my first close encounters with it.

One of the main reasons I started seeing a grief therapist was because I kept obsessing about death. I started reading books about death—*When Breath Becomes Air, Being Mortal, After This.* On my work commute, I kept fantasizing about driving my car off this one overpass. It wasn't that I *wanted* to; it was just that I kept thinking about how it could happen, how my car would careen through the waist-high retaining wall and crash into the lanes of the freeway below. In my fantasies, I could see pieces of concrete falling with my car. I could see the field of brake lights of the cars below. I could hear the crunch of metal, the smell of burning, my own screaming.

In the film *Return to Zero*, the character of Maggie (played by Minnie Driver) has lost her son at thirty-eight weeks. At a family dinner, as everyone is discussing what they are thankful for, she says, bitterly, "I'm thankful that today I can see life for what it really is, to know that just beneath the surface, just under the radar, is death. And every day we wake up and we run from it as fast as we can, but it's coming. Maybe not today, maybe not next week, but when it does, this, all this, it doesn't matter."

This, I think, is part of the depression that comes with the loss of a baby. It's such a startling loss, a loss nobody expects, despite statistics. When my world was upturned by that loss, I came face-to-face with death in a very real and personal way. Seeing how a baby could die just like that led me to question everything I'd come to trust about how the world works.

I'm still somewhat obsessed with death, but in a more reverential way. Knowing that life is fragile keeps me grounded and grateful. My relationship with death has enabled me to appreciate life in a way I never did before.

"[People] want to hear that I had a bad obstetrician, or that I took something you are not supposed to take, or didn't take something that you are. They want to hear that I neglected to get an ultrasound, or that I have some kind of rare blood disorder that can be fixed with the right medicine or surgery or iPhone app. They want to know what they have to eat to keep from being me . . .

They want to believe that everything happens for a reason. Some people need to believe this to indemnify themselves against miscarriage or misfortune in general. Some people need to believe it so they can say, 'You'll get pregnant again and everything will work out fine.' Because they want to comfort me. *But in a strange way, I am comforted by the truth: Death comes for us. You may get 10 minutes on this earth, or you may get 80 years, but nobody gets out alive. Accepting this rule gives me a funny flicker of peace.*"

—Ariel Levy, *The Rules Do Not Apply*

Meredith

I used to work in a hospital that published a daily employee newsletter including the number of babies born the day before. This was the best part of the newsletter, though right below it was another tally that announced not the beginning of life but the end.

On the most symbolic level, babies represent beginnings. They represent all the possibility, the hope for goodness, sweetness, curiosity, love. I used to visit the maternity ward during my break (it was allowed back then). The face of a sleeping baby holds something infinite and eternal and makes us feel like everything is going to be OK. Babies do hold the future. Unless suddenly, that future is gone.

While death can occupy thoughts, especially with a traumatic loss such as this, I'd invite you to experiment with viewing it more symbolically, going beyond the loss of the fantasy of parenthood. Are you neglecting a part of yourself? Something vital that needs support—your support—to take root and grow? Perhaps it is faith, or reflection, or contemplation.

Finding these lost and neglected and as yet undiscovered parts of yourself can open and change you—another new and unexpected beginning.

Is it complicated grief?

Complicated grief is intense grief that lasts longer than one year. It may be characterized by catastrophic thoughts. According to the Center for Complicated Grief at Columbia University: "The person is riddled with fear about their own survival and ruminates over bad things happening in the future, though there be no evidence that support such. Such thoughts are persistent and interfere with daily life."

If this sounds like you, talk to a therapist to help identify and manage your grief (See "Getting professional help").

Anxiety and posttraumatic stress

Posttraumatic stress:

It's a thing

An agonizing thing.

My first loss—an ectopic pregnancy that ended abruptly with emergency surgery—shocked me. When that loss was followed by others, my shock compounded.

After each of my losses, I had trouble sleeping. Then I'd wake up in the morning thinking, "Maybe it was just a nightmare." Then I'd have to come to the slow realization, over the course of a few painful moments, that it wasn't. When part of my psyche refused to exit denial, I had to relive the whole ordeal all over again in order to return to reality.

After we lost Miles, I kept hearing the doctor say, "I'm not seeing a heart-beat" and "I'm so sorry, Kimberly." I kept seeing the final ultrasound photo of my son, when he was still alive. He looked like an alien, his head turned to me, the black circles of his eyes seemingly saying, "Help! I'm in trouble." Now, years later, this photo is still imprinted on my brain. It still gives me nightmares.

It was my mom who said, "I think you have some PTSD." I always thought posttraumatic stress disorder (PTSD) was for soldiers coming back from war. I didn't think it applied to me. But the more I talked to other women and the more I read (in books and online), I realized that, yes, post-traumatic stress and even PTSD is a very real thing for women dealing with the loss of a baby.

Note: Posttraumatic stress and posttraumatic stress disorder (PTSD) are two different things. See Meredith's explanation.

... And it might be a thing for a while

The other day, I had an appointment with a new dermatologist. When I looked at the address, I didn't think much of it, but as I approached the area, I started to feel my stomach tighten. When the directions on my phone led me to the parking lot, I felt a distinct sadness come over me. The dermatologist's office was in the same building where I'd had my D&E (dilation and evacuation) after losing Miles at seventeen weeks. I didn't have a breakdown or anything, but I *felt* the sorrow in my body. It was still there.

When I went in to the appointment, I had to fill out all the new patient paperwork. I got to the question about past surgeries and listed my salpingectomy (the surgery I had to remove my fallopian tube after my first ectopic pregnancy) and my D&E. I had my appointment and went on my way, but I couldn't shake an "off" feeling the rest of the day.

Also recently, I developed a cyst on the back of my knee, and the doctor recommended an ultrasound. Just the sound of him rolling in the machine and seeing the familiar tube of gel made me anxious. As he moved the wand around my knee and sighed, my heart raced. I braced myself for being told something awful was wrong. I'm assuming I'll always feel this way during an ultrasound. "Is everything OK?" I asked, unnerved by his silence. "Yep, just taking some measurements," he said.

I feel physical symptoms of posttraumatic stress in medical situations like these. My heart races, my palms get sweaty. My discomfort probably isn't obvious to others, but I feel it, and I know why it's there. To cope with it, I close my eyes, take a few breaths, and think about the babies I lost—not in a sad way, but in a commemorative way. These situations remind me of the pain I still carry within, and I have compassion for that pain.

I've come to accept that the body doesn't forget. My body will always associate certain medical situations with impending danger—and rightfully so. I'm OK with that. My goal isn't for my past experiences to have no impact on me. My goal is to come to peace with their impact.

Meredith

The loss of a baby in the womb, a miscarriage, and stillbirth are all significant traumas. Every person will respond to them differently. Your words, how your body behaves as it heals, how you move through your recovery, and the ways the experience has reshaped you are unique to you.

Posttraumatic stress is a reaction that occurs after the trauma itself is over. It's like vapor that rises from the trauma itself. It is reasonable to assume that these vapors or echoes form during the trauma. But they are held until later and are expressed, sometimes randomly, sometimes consistently, after the actual event is over.

During different parts of the traumatic event, your survival instincts kick in. We often refer to fight or flight, but people adapt to acute stress in other ways too. Getting devastating news or enduring a painful event might make one person freeze to the point where speaking, let alone moving, is not possible. Another person may faint but quickly recover.

These temporary responses help you get through the actual event—not finding a heartbeat or miscarrying alone at home, for instance. At this same instant that you are fighting (or fleeing) for survival, more emotion (fear, terror, rage, anger, or helplessness) gets deposited in the unconscious, where it sits and sits and sits until the energy it has built reaches a boiling point. Then come the vapors mentioned above—the symptoms of posttraumatic stress.

In other words, the "thing that happened" might have stopped, but the stress continues. The stress can look different from person to person.

Your trauma is the event; the reverberation—thoughts, feelings, flashbacks, fears—is the posttraumatic stress.

While the intensity of the posttraumatic stress can vary, it often feels like the traumatic event is reoccurring. This hopefully diminishes over time and resolves to a point where the reverberations are manageable and do not disrupt daily life.

Posttraumatic stress disorder (PTSD) is different. With PTSD, these reverberations do not resolve. PTSD requires more than grief work and mourning to treat it; it requires therapy, possibly medication, and, in some cases, brief hospitalization.

With PTSD, the trauma has become lodged in the psyche and replays erratically, unpredictably, and disruptively as though on repeat. It is a disabling condition. Many women who have suffered pregnancy loss may *appear* to meet many of the criteria of PTSD—and to some extent, their partners do as well. But that does not mean that they have PTSD.

Posttraumatic stress is very real. But in time, the intensity lessens. It responds to therapy, support, mourning, and grief work, whatever shape that takes.

PTSD, on the other hand, is progressive and worsens without appropriate therapeutic intervention. Very specific intervention is required to help, and some treatments like EMDR and CBT have proved helpful.

Posttraumatic Stress Disorder (PTSD)

These are some of the criteria used to diagnose PTSD.

Living through the trauma in **_one_ _or more_** of the following way(s):

1. Directly experiencing the trauma
2. Witnessing, in person, the event(s) as it occurred to others
3. Learning that the traumatic event occurred to a close family member or friend. In cases of actual or threatened death of a family member or friend, the events must have been violent or accidental. (The latter, typically, would describe most pregnancy losses.)
4. Experiencing repeated or extreme exposure to aversive details of the traumatic event in person. (This could apply to partners as well.)

Re-experiencing the trauma in **_one_ _or more_** of the following way(s):

1. Unwanted, involuntary, intrusive, and upsetting memories of the trauma, which the person has little or no control of
2. Nightmares and dreams that relate to the traumatic event
3. Flashbacks
4. Psychological distress, rumination, and anxiety related to the trauma; fear that it is happening again; the experience that it is happening again—these reactions are very intense and do not subside
5. Reactions in the body (jumpiness, shaking, chills, or sweats, for example) to anything that reminds the person of the trauma, or has symbolic significance related to the trauma

Avoiding memories of the trauma in one or more of the following way(s):

1. Trying to avoid or block out the trauma-related thoughts or feelings
2. Avoidance of external reminders that trigger thoughts, feelings, and memories that are closely associated with the trauma

Distress related to thoughts and mood that have worsened after the trauma in two or more ways:

1. Inability to recall key features of the trauma, overly negative thoughts and assumptions about oneself or the world; exaggerated

self-blame or blaming others (though it may not feel exaggerated to you); isolation, negativity, and little interest in activities; difficulty maintaining positivity or experiencing it
2. More reactions that began or worsened after the trauma in two or more ways
3. Irritability, aggression, risky or destructive behavior, hypervigilance or heightened startle reaction, difficulty concentrating or sleeping

Other problems can also look like PTSD but are not PTSD. Not all symptoms that occur in individuals exposed to an extreme stressor should necessarily be attributed to PTSD or called PTSD.

Huong

People want to make sense of things. Making sense of something traumatic doesn't make it right and less painful. But we are all trying to understand the world and find rules we can abide by. After a trauma, we can get stuck in negative feedback loops in our brains. One way to get unstuck is through Cognitive Processing Therapy (CPT).

Are you struggling with PTSD?

Please see the **PTSD Checklist** in the "Questionnaires and screeners" section at the end of this book.

Note: If you've had previous traumas in your life, you may be more prone to experiencing PTSD. **The Life Events Checklist** at the end of this book can help you identify previous traumas.

Remember: Questionnaires like these do not in any way replace the guidance of a trained mental health professional. See "Getting professional help" for tips on finding someone to help you talk through your responses to the questionnaires.

CPT is considered the "gold standard" for treating symptoms of PTSD and is used in the Veterans Administration (VA). The goal of CPT is to free clients of their stuck points, which are conflicting beliefs or strong negative beliefs that create unpleasant emotions and problematic or unhealthy behavior after a traumatic event. Stuck points can be formed in two different ways following a trauma:

1. Stuck points may be conflicts between prior beliefs and beliefs after a traumatic experience. For example, one of your previous beliefs could be, "I can take care of myself and my body." Therefore, if you experienced a pregnancy loss, your new belief could be, "I lost my baby, I cannot protect myself (and my baby), and I am to be blamed." Unfortunately, if you cannot change your previous beliefs to accept what has happened to you, you may start questioning your role in the situation and find yourself "stuck" in a cycle of self-blame.

2. Another way a stuck point can be formed is if you have prior negative beliefs that seem to be confirmed or are reinforced by the event. For example, if a prior belief was "good things never happen to me" or "it is dangerous to be happy; I always have to be on guard for the other shoe to drop," then a pregnancy loss can reinforce that belief.

What the studies tell us

- For women who experienced miscarriage or stillbirth, disruptions of core beliefs can lead to grief and symptoms of posttraumatic stress. (*Psychological Trauma*, 2017)
- In the largest study so far to assess the psychological impact of early-stage pregnancy loss, approximately one in four women suffered posttraumatic stress one month after a pregnancy loss. (*American Journal of Obstetrics & Gynecology*, 2019)
- In a smaller study, 45 percent of women reported symptoms of PTSD three months after their miscarriage. (*BMJ Open*, 2016)
- It can linger: An average of nine months after a loss, bereaved women showed remarkably high and persistent levels of distress, measured by symptoms of depression and PTSD (*Journal of Women's Health*, 2016).
- Bereaved mothers have **seven times** higher odds of PTSD symptoms compared to nonbereaved parents. (*Journal of Women's Health*, 2016)

Unfortunately, if you come to see the pregnancy loss as further proof that joy is illusory, then you will believe this thought even more strongly. If you are stuck here, you may have strong emotional reactions that interfere with your ability to believe in good things happening to you.

Ask yourself what your beliefs are and consider what stuck points you may have. A therapist can help you get "unstuck" (See "Getting professional help").

"Some researchers argue that the definition of trauma should be expanded to include the psychological and emotional response to not only physical threats, but threats to deeply held expectations of life."

—Regina Townsend, "The Lasting Trauma of Infertility," the *New York Times*

Understanding your grief process

What is the "process" anyway?

The "process" of grieving varies from person to person. Many of us want to believe there are specific steps or a to-do list with grieving, and there just aren't. However, it can be helpful to review the stages of grief (which you may have heard of), as well as some common terms related to grief and grieving.

The five stages of grief

Elisabeth Kübler-Ross was a Swiss-American psychiatrist who first introduced the world to her model of grief based on her experience with terminally ill patients. In her seminal book, *On Death and Dying* (1969), she described the five stages as a series of emotions experienced by terminally ill patients *before* death.

However, the stages were later used to describe the potential grieving process for those who have lost loves ones. According to Kübler-Ross, these stages are *not* meant to represent a linear and predictable progression.

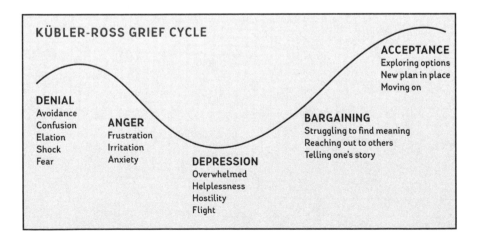

KÜBLER-ROSS GRIEF CYCLE

ACCEPTANCE
Exploring options
New plan in place
Moving on

DENIAL
Avoidance
Confusion
Elation
Shock
Fear

ANGER
Frustration
Irritation
Anxiety

DEPRESSION
Overwhelmed
Helplessness
Hostility
Flight

BARGAINING
Struggling to find meaning
Reaching out to others
Telling one's story

The meanings of loss

The terms grief, mourning, and bereavement have slightly different meanings:

- **Grief** is a person's emotional response to loss.
- **Mourning** is an outward expression of that grief, including cultural and religious customs surrounding death. It is also the process of adapting to life after loss.
- **Bereavement** is a period of grief and mourning after a loss.
- **Anticipatory Grief** is a response to an expected loss.
- **Complicated Grief** is severe, prolonged (more than twelve months) grieving, during which a person becomes preoccupied with the loss to the extent that it dominates their life. Approximately 10-15 percent of bereaved people experience complicated grief.
- **Ambiguous Loss** is characterized by lack of closure or clear understanding.

Remember, these are just labels to try to encapsulate a cluster of symptoms and feelings for groups of individuals. The purpose is to make us feel as though we are part of a group (aka not alone), but sometimes it can have the opposite effect if we do not believe we meet the full criteria.

The fact is this, no matter what you call it, you are in pain, and that requires attention and love.

Adapted from *Grief Reaction* by Saba Mughal; Yusra Azhar; Waqas J. Siddiqui. StatPearls Publishing.

There are some critics of, and limitations to, this model, so I would encourage you to proceed cautiously and to use this as a general framework to refer to, not as an exact blueprint or map for your unique experience.

The five stages include:

1. **Denial.** Denial is a coping tool to help us survive the loss and also to pace our feelings of grief. It is our brain's way of protecting us by letting in only as much as we can handle. In the case of pregnancy loss, it can look something like, "The doctor is wrong and made a mistake."
2. **Anger.** Anger is an emotion in reaction to perceived injustice in your life or the world. It is also a necessary emotion for healing. Some have been taught to express anger and enjoy demonstrating anger since it can feel

powerful and energizing. Others have been taught to repress it and are afraid of feeling anger because it can feel overwhelming. But underneath all of the anger is pain. It is often easier to blame others and be angry at others than to sit with the pain ourselves. We may ask questions like, "Where is God in this?" "Why is God punishing me?" "Why doesn't my partner understand?" "Why isn't my partner grieving with me?" "Why does [friend's name] get to have kids and I don't?"

3. **Bargaining.** This is a stage where we begin to twist and turn our minds and wonder about the "what ifs," the "if only . . . " and the "woulda, coulda, shoulda." Some may even begin to bargain with the pain and make promises like, "If you can take this pain away. I promise I will . . . ," or "If I can get pregnant again, I promise I will . . . "

4. **Depression.** After we spend some time bargaining, we may begin to become present with our emotions, and then the grief and sadness enter the picture. Please remind yourself that just because you may be experiencing the depression phase does not mean you have clinical depression (See "Dealing with depression"). Sadness and grief are normal responses to loss.

5. **Acceptance.** It is important to remember that accepting something does not mean that it was "right" or "justified." To accept something means to accept the reality of your pregnancy loss and to accept the pain. It is living with the "new norm" and knowing that this pregnancy loss will be a part of you but it does not have to define you.

In 2019, Kübler-Ross's colleague, David Kessler, added a sixth stage: Meaning. See "Finding meaning" to learn more about this.

Kim

The story of the mother orca

In the summer of 2018, I was obsessed with the story of a mother orca mourning her dead baby. The calf was born on July 24, then died within hours of its birth. As the body sank into the water, the mother repeatedly pushed it up, keeping it afloat for at least three days as she and her pod kept moving.

Ken Balcomb, the founder of the Center for Whale Research, was quoted by CNN saying: "They know the calf is dead. I think this is a grieving or a ceremonial thing done by the mother. She doesn't want to let go. She's probably lost two other calves since her first offspring eight years ago."

"The way that parents respond to a perinatal loss may range from little response to highly intense, long-lasting grief. Grief after such losses may be intensified when the loss experience is highly incongruent with a parent's expectations, and the parent is unable to act to reduce this incongruence."
—*The American Journal of Maternal Child Nursing*, 2019

When this was happening, I'd wake up every morning to check the news for any reports on the mother orca. I felt for her. I cried for her. After seventeen days, she finally let go of her calf. All of us who have lost babies know that letting go of them physically is one thing, but I'm not sure if we ever fully let go in our hearts. I'm not sure we'd want to.

Perinatal grief

Perinatal grief is a specific and unique label for those who experience active grief, difficulty coping, and despair due to the social and psychological impact of pregnancy loss.

The Perinatal Grief Scale, developed in 1989 and used throughout the world, utilizes thirty-three questions to help categorize a person's grief. The categorization is based on answers to questions regarding thoughts and feelings about the loss of the baby.

I encourage my clients not to focus so much on the labels and not to diagnose themselves. But if you are curious about the scale, see "Questionnaires and screeners" at the end of this book. Based on your answers, you may find it helpful to further explore your feelings of loss with a therapist or in a support group. See "Getting professional help."

Meredith

The similarities and differences between the species—whale and human— are striking in the outward expression of grief. Striking and sad because the human is both expected to grieve but not make others uncomfortable in the process.

I think we are drawn to this story because we recognize the bond between a mother and baby, a parent and child. We observe something so natural, the longing for closeness and the torturous grief when that is denied. In life,

Nature's plan would be for the mother to protect and teach her young. In her baby's death, I am imagining, her instincts are trying to organize the empty space where what remains is yearning.

Yes, of course, whales and humans differ. But while the animal kingdom can be a cruel place, the psychic mourning shown by this mother orca appears incredibly wise, even self-affirming and soul-affirming. And her pod supports her instincts and needs. When she is ready, and only then, she lets go.

How long is this going to last?

As long as it needs to.

"The question isn't: When will I stop grieving? The question is: How do you keep on living? And I believe the answer is: You accept your sadness. You sink into it." Mira Ptacin, *Poor Your Soul*

"How long is this going to last?" my husband asked one day as we sat across from our grief therapist in her office. He was even more intolerant of the vague and uncertain grieving process than I was. In retrospect, it was just hard for him to see me suffering so much. The therapist said what I expected she'd say: "There's no exact timeframe. It's different for everyone." But then she offered my husband (and me) what we needed—a little bit of structure. She said, "Most couples I see start to experience some healing after six months to a year."

Meredith: As it is difficult for a partner to see you suffering, it is probably difficult for you to see your partner struggling as well. There is a natural desire to not see someone we love suffer, and this goes for you as well. This adds a different kind of stress as you try to sort through your own pain, a pull between taking care of yourself and caring about your partner's well-being too.

In our case, we put our energy toward trying to get pregnant again less than six months after each loss, and just trying again helped ease some pain (though it was also stressful; see "Should we try again?"). Because we had multiple losses, the grief compounded for us. So it's hard to give an accurate timeline of our healing. It's probably different for everyone, like the therapist said. I'm guessing the therapist only gave us a timeframe as a sort of mental life preserver, knowing the "six months to a year" might not apply to us.

In the weeks following each of my losses, when the shock and pain was so raw and real, I didn't know how I would survive. I became obsessed with "getting through" the grief process. I was desperate to feel better, to return to being the competent, collected person I'd always been. In the midst of grief, I was anything but collected. I was hysterical. I felt like a wild animal.

Meredith: Emotions will surge and fall. Don't mute your feelings from yourself by medicating them away (though, if depression persists, see a psychiatrist for evaluation to determine if medication could help). Be gentle with yourself. Expect tears at inopportune times or all the time for a while. Grief is so specific to the individual—to you.

The "Ball and the Box" analogy (Lauren Herschel)

In 2018, Lauren Herschel went viral for her "The Ball and the Box" analogy for grief. The idea is that when you first have a loss, you are easily brought to tears. You can't go five minutes without crying or screaming or feeling like you will/want to die. Your grief is this huge ball in a box, and every time that ball hits a button in the box (which is often, because it's huge), you feel the loss intensely. Over time, the ball gets smaller. It's still there, but because it's smaller, it doesn't hit the button as often. You can go longer periods without feeling the weight of your sadness.

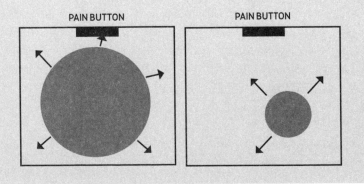

What I've learned is that there is no quick, easy way to "do grieving." There are no specific steps you can follow. Even the five stages (denial, anger, bargaining, depression, and acceptance) aren't *steps*, and it's common to fluctuate between stages ("And for my next trick, I will go from anger to acceptance in sixty seconds!").

Meredith: Emotions can come in batches. In other words, it's common to experience acceptance simultaneously with experiencing anger, for example. This can further add to the inner turmoil. And, for many, the space inside depression can last the longest. Just as there is walking pneumonia, I have observed a kind of walking depression during the loss of a loved one. One woman may want to start trying again quickly; another may take more time to feel ready. For some, taking action as soon as possible feels right; for others it doesn't. Both are OK.

It's been more than three years since my last loss. I still carry grief. I still cry at times, but those episodes are fewer and farther between. Maybe this is because I went on to have my daughter, or maybe that's just how healing works.

I've come to see grief as like that feeling of foreboding nausea during a bad stomach bug, when you think you might actually die. But then, somehow, you don't die. You feel better momentarily until the next wave hits. But this, unlike a stomach bug, goes on for days. Weeks. Months. There is no way around it. It cannot be overcome or ignored. There is no shortcut, no checklist, no progress markers. There is nothing you can do to be better at it. All you can do is be patient. Endure.

Meredith: If the intensity of the pain does not subside, or if the depression lingers, seek the support of a licensed therapist. The posttraumatic stress might be a bit too much to process on your own. But you know what? That's natural too. Grief is dynamic; it changes, but we do too.

Don't feel rushed to show how you're dealing "appropriately" and grieving "well," says spiritual development counselor Julie Mussché.

Grieving is not performance art. It is not a show.

If you are questioning yourself, wondering "Why is this taking so long?" or "Am I doing this right?" please know there is no "right." Utilizing a Buddhist mindfulness meditation lens, I often describe the pregnancy loss as the "first arrow" of pain; the "second arrow" of pain, which further worsens the initial pain of the first arrow, is questioning the validity of our pain, wondering if we are "crazy," and thinking there is something wrong with us because we can't seem to move on fast enough to please those around us.

"The only way out is through."

—Elisabeth Kübler-Ross and David Kessler, *On Grief and Grieving*

Riding the grief rollercoaster

Hold on to your hats and glasses.

Grief is a weird thing. It's a process, and not a linear one. There are ups and downs and lots of loops. I really wanted it to be simpler, more clear-cut. I wanted to be able to check off items on a Grief To-Do List. I wanted to "conquer" one stage and move on to the next. It just doesn't work like that.

There were days I woke up feeling OK-ish, and I thought, "Great! This is progress! Things are on the upswing!" Then, the very next day (or even later the same day), I'd be back to wanting to hide under a rock and cry. My mood, like the weather in places I hope to never live (I'm Californian, born and bred), could turn on a dime.

"Some days you'll feel as free as a bird, other days you'll feel like you're wearing boots full of concrete."

—Georgie, who had a stillborn daughter (Ella) and two first-trimester miscarriages

If anything, this rollercoaster taught me not to get too attached to any one mood, whether good or bad. The only predictable thing about moods is that they pass. Every day is different. My to-do list became this: Wake up, check in with myself, react accordingly.

On the bad days, critical voices in my head scolded me when I was feeling down again—*You were feeling fine yesterday, what's wrong with you?* I tried to be kind and patient with myself. I've learned that impatience with a bad mood just makes it worse.

I tried to appreciate the good days for what they were instead of living in fear that they wouldn't last. I treated the good days as proof that I would survive. I tried to trust that, over time, the OK-ish days would outnumber the crappy ones.

Huong

Something I like to tell my clients is to consider the *both* and the *and*. As humans, we are capable of managing and navigating multiple conflicting emotions. You can be *both* grateful that you are alive *and* angry about the pregnancy loss. You can be *both* relieved *and* sad, *both* at peace *and* struggling.

Also, it's worth noting that human beings are capable of experiencing thirty-four thousand different emotions! That is a lot of emotion to manage, especially when you're riding the grief rollercoaster and already experiencing different emotions simultaneously.

"It's so curious: one can resist tears and 'behave' very well in the hardest hours of grief. But then someone makes you a friendly sign behind a window, or one notices that a flower that was in bud only yesterday has suddenly blossomed, or a letter slips from a drawer . . . and everything collapses."
—Colette

I talk to my clients about the difference between an emotion and a feeling, and this difference may help you with your grief process. In psychology speak, emotions are neurological reactions to an emotional stimulus. In regular speak, emotions are our body's natural reactions to seeing something, like when your face softens and you smile when you see a cute puppy (if you like dogs!).

On the other hand, feelings are more of the conscious experience of emotional reactions. Another way to understand this is your feeling is the label you put on the emotion you experience. So in the above example, your feeling when seeing a cute dog could be joy, happiness, pleasure, and/or excitement.

When my clients are begging to get off the rollercoaster, I find that the Feeling Wheel (developed by Gloria Wilcox) helps them understand and label their feelings. The wheel has six core feelings: mad, scared, joyful, powerful, peaceful, and sad. A secondary ring of words helps narrow those feelings down. A third, outer ring gets even more specific. In all, there are seventy-two adjectives to link to your feelings. Science shows that when we can pinpoint and label our emotions, we are sending a message to our brain, "I got this. I know what we are feeling. We are safe. Don't worry."

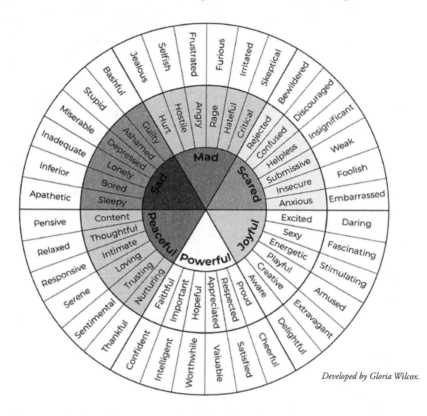

Developed by Gloria Wilcox.

As you ride the rollercoaster, this wheel can help you better identify your emotions beyond just, "I feel bad." You can use the wheel in conversations with your therapist, when writing in your journal, and/or when talking to a friend or your partner. In doing so, you begin to process the feeling, gain awareness of its impact, and, from there, decide what to do with it (like keep it, throw it away, internalize it, discuss it further, or something else).

"They call it grief but it feels like insanity." —Mira Ptacin, *Poor Your Soul*

Your emotions are likely to change day to day as you grieve, so use the wheel to connect with yourself and pinpoint what's going on inside. This will help you feel compassion for yourself and help you gain confidence on your grief journey.

If English is not your first language

Research has shown that for some non-native English speakers, their first language is their emotional language, whereas English is the intellectualized language. I encourage my bicultural and bilingual clients to express their emotions in whatever language they feel most comfortable. It's the best way to get to the heart of their pain. I am fluent in Spanish, so my Spanish-speaking clients are always grateful that I understand the slight nuances between *dolor, angustia, tristeza,* and *perdida.* (These are different words for pain, sadness, and loss.)

Grief in other languages

Yūgen (Japanese): A profound, mysterious sense of the beauty of the universe—and the sad beauty of human suffering

Uffda (Swedish): A sympathetic word to be used when someone else is in pain. It combines "Ouch for you" and "Oh, I'm sorry you hurt yourself."

Saudade (Portuguese): A melancholic longing or nostalgia for a person, place, or thing that is far away from you

Dor (Romanian): The feeling of longing/craving/yearning for someone or something, combined with sadness

Meredith

As you've reviewed, there are "stages" of grief, but that does not mean grief is a linear process with a set timeframe. Each person travels the path of grief in their own way. The process is individual for the individual and can change day to day. Instead of being distressed by this, relax into the knowledge that, once again, there is no one specific way to grieve, mourn, or recover.

For example, after having a miscarriage, you may transition very early into deep sadness about the baby, still be in shock about how fast everything unfolded, and angry at your partner for not listening to you. Mixed into these stages are feelings of guilt—*did I do something wrong?* These stages, like the feelings attached to them, are not linear. In fact, they might be more circular as you get closer and closer to the depth of your grief.

You'll circle around your loss until you reach a point where you notice that, instead of feeling spent and exhausted from all this processing, you begin to feel stronger and more whole.

It will happen.

Physical signs of grief

There's the broken heart and so much more.

Several times during my grieving, I told my husband, "I think I'm coming down with something." I felt such overwhelming fatigue and an upset stomach. I braced myself for the onset of illness. But nothing came. It wasn't a virus; it was grief.

I carry a lot of emotion in my stomach. As the writer John Powell says regarding emotion, "My stomach keeps score." When grieving, I felt literally "full" of emotion. This translated to waves of nausea, bloating, and wonky appetite (or lack thereof). I lost weight, which is always what happens to me in times of stress. Some people gain; I lose. Fun fact: The Germans have a term, *kummerspeck* (literally translated to "grief bacon" or "sorrow fat"), to describe the weight people gain after a loss.

The overwhelming fatigue was my body's way of saying, "Lie down. Rest." My limbs felt like they weighed a thousand pounds each. I had so little energy that even walking to the bathroom felt like a journey (and this was just months after I'd run a marathon). At night, I found myself staring at the ceiling, unable to sleep, which didn't make sense given the fatigue, but the whole process of grief doesn't make sense.

What's interesting is the ways the physical signs of grief resurface. Every year since losing Miles, I get stomach aches in April, which is when we lost him. There are certain times of the year when my body just feels heavy. Whenever I stop and think about it, I realize it aligns with one of my losses. The body remembers, even when we've willed ourselves to carry on.

Meredith

Grief inhabits the body in a multitude of ways.

There is evidence that grief increases inflammation in the body. Grief-related stress can lead to high blood pressure, tachycardia (a high resting heart rate), and increased levels of cortisol (commonly known as the stress hormone). Too much cortisol can affect your body in undesired ways including, for example, causing fatigue, difficulty concentrating, irritability, and headaches. Other physical symptoms of grief include chest tightness and choking, shortness of breath, abdominal distress, decreased muscle power, and lethargy.

Grief has been proven to exacerbate pain in older adults, and though there is not a study that specifically addresses it yet, there is little reason to imagine it doesn't do the same in most of us, regardless of age.

Grief can have other effects on the body, too, effects that aren't necessarily found in the medical literature. But having met hundreds of patients over the years, I can say that symptoms like these are common after a loss:

Constant stomach ache; a feeling of emptiness and hunger but with no desire to eat; feelings of being tired but unable to sleep; exhaustion from crying; irritability and agitation, though nothing immediately irritating or agitating is going on; quick to temper, quick to burst into tears; impatience; numbness; staring into space; walking around the house aimlessly; waking up early; wanting to sleep all the time; not wanting to go to bed; hypervigilance; startling easily; difficulty concentrating; constant movement; mild aches and pains; headaches; sinus headache; crying during sleep; nail biting after not having bitten nails for decades; breakouts from stress; dizziness; rash; inability to tolerate certain foods, particularly if the person who died liked that food—triggering sadness; dry mouth and eyes from crying; increased body odor (possibly from a change in hormonal activity or from anxiety); forgetting to eat; inability to concentrate; moving more slowly; trouble balancing; diarrhea; chest tightness; heart palpitations; a feeling of fogginess. The list goes on.

All these symptoms eventually subsided as the individuals worked through their mourning period. We cannot know if the symptoms were due to grief, but I can tell you that to the individual, they were associated with the grief. Consult a doctor as needed, especially if symptoms linger.

Yes, there is such a thing as a broken heart.
Takosubo Cardiomyopathy (Broken Heart Syndrome) is a weakening of the left ventricle caused by severe emotional or physical stress such as loss of a loved one, sudden illness, a serious accident, or a natural disaster. It almost exclusively occurs in women and resolves within a month.

Adapted from *Grief Reaction* by Saba Mughal; Yusra Azhar; Waqas J. Siddiqui. StatPearls Publishing.

Grieving in a society that sucks at grief

Feeling pressure to "move on"

Can everyone just give me a second?

When I went back to work after my first loss, one of my coworkers came into my office and said, "You need to take vitamin B12 to get out of your depression." I wanted to say, "Actually, I think depression is pretty appropriate for what I've just been through."

A friend said to me, "Let me know when you're ready to grab a drink." I wanted to say, "And until then, what? Don't bother you?" Another friend: "You have to push yourself, even if you don't feel like it." Push myself? I'd just lost a baby. The impatience of my friends made me anxious. I felt no allowance for my sadness. I know they just hated seeing me suffer. They wanted me to be the Kim they knew, the Kim with the witty jokes and easy laugh. I get it. But I needed them to understand that I couldn't be her by sheer will alone. You can't will your way past grief.

"Rather than embracing a grieving mother, often we silence her.
Rather than acknowledge a loss that will impact her for the rest of her life,
we tell her to move on, to get over it."
—Alexa Bigwarfe, *Sunshine After the Storm: A Survival Guide for the Grieving Mother*

People seem to think that grief is this thing that must be "cured." It's not respected for what it is—a process, a valid, necessary process. Grief is not meant to be cured; it's meant to be endured.

The reason I think people want grief to be curable is because they are so uncomfortable with it. When I was grieving, I felt the discomfort of people around me—in the sweat of my palms, the heaviness in my stomach. I know some of the discomfort was rooted in people feeling bad for me and hating that they couldn't do anything to make it better. But I think there's a deeper level to the discomfort, too—to see someone suffering after a loss is to acknowledge that *losses happen* and that all of us will have them at some point. Nobody wants to be reminded of the suffering that will befall them. They want to think it's possible to escape somehow.

"We are a grief-illiterate society. We are also a society that wants to 'fix' everything. When someone is grieving, they aren't broken. They don't need to be fixed. They need someone to sit with them in their pain and to witness their grief." —David Kessler, author and founder of Grief.com

I talked in depth with a friend who had just lost his wife about how weird our culture is about grief. We are just not raised to be comfortable with death or loss. Other cultures embrace these things as parts of life, but we don't do that here. We hide our pain more than share it. Just look at the highlight reels people post on social media. My friend sent me a piece from the *Huffington Post* ("Stifled Grief: How the West Has It Wrong" by Michelle Steinke-Baumgard) that articulated the thoughts in my head better than I could:

" . . . We are a culture of emotionally stunted individuals who are scared of our mortality and have mastered the concept of stuffing our pain. Western society has created a neat little 'grief box' where we place the grieving and wait for them to emerge fixed and whole again. The grief box is small and compact, and it comes full of expectations that range from time frames to physical appearance. Everyone who has been pushed into the grief box understands its confining limitations, but all of our collective voices together can't seem to change the intense indignation of a society too emotionally stifled to speak the truth. It's become easier to hide our emotional depth than to reveal our vulnerability and risk harsh judgment. When asked if we are alright, it's simpler to say yes and fake a smile than to be honest and show genuine human emotion."

Our society is all about forging ahead, overcoming adversity, rising above, putting one foot in front of the other, and on and on. The grief process is slow and delicate, though; there is no "forging." It requires patience—for both the griever and the people around them.

When I got the message that I needed to focus on moving ahead, putting the sadness behind me, I felt like nobody understood how much pain I was in. Surely they wouldn't push me to move on if they understood. I started to feel like I should just keep my sorrow to myself instead of sharing it. If I shared it, that would be admitting that I was failing at "moving on." I thought people would be let down or irritated.

I have to think some of the silence around pregnancy loss is related to this—people going through it feel devastated, then ashamed of their own devastation in the face of a society encouraging them to "get over it" (See "If it's so common, why do I feel so alone?"). I wish people would just acknowledge the significance of the loss and the depth of the pain, and allow people to take their time with their grief. Maybe I should create a T-shirt: "Grieving in progress. Sorry-not-sorry if it makes you uncomfortable."

Meredith

You can't cure grief. It's part of being human. When you are the one who is sad, though, you see all around you evidence of what a difficult time people have with sadness.

Some people have distress intolerance. You don't have to love distress, but having a tolerance for it is crucial in dealing with it. Distress intolerance is the inability to do that. A person can have a difficult time experiencing sad or unpleasant emotions themselves or seeing them in another person—this happens to everyone from time to time. But intense emotions intensify their intolerance, and they want to get as far away as possible. Sadness is not the only emotion that triggers anxiety in people with distress intolerance; anger and fear do as well.

"We're naturally programmed to celebrate and rejoice in all things associated with the perfect birth—a happy baby, a content mother—so when your baby dies everyone's thrown off kilter ... The bottom line is no one really knows how to treat death, so they stumble through conversations with awkward pauses and uncomfortable words and all the while you just want to shout, 'My baby has just died, stop talking so loudly and leave me alone!'"

—Georgie, who had a stillborn daughter (Ella) and two first-trimester miscarriages

A person who has distress intolerance to a lesser degree might be the person who tries to talk you out of your sadness. Their mission is to cheer you up—or so it seems. It is more a reaction to keep the emotion you're experiencing at bay—and away from them.

"He is not something I want to move on from, he is our son;
and I most certainly will never 'move on' from being his mother."
—Elle Wright, *Ask Me His Name: Learning to Live and Laugh Again After the Loss of My Baby*

If you encounter someone who is trying to talk you out of feeling a certain way, even guised in upbeat chatter and banter, this person is likely not going to be able to really "be there" for you in your sadness. Their impulse to avoid the emotion has already kicked in. You may feel rejected, and it can feel personal, though their reaction has little to do with you personally. This can hurt, too, especially when it happens with a friend.

Feeling distressed or upset may be unbearable to this person, but up until now, you didn't realize it. Just because they have an issue with it does not mean your distress is abnormal. Recognize the difference between your need to grieve and their difficulty with difficult emotions. Turn to others if you need to talk and let it out.

Huong

There is something called disenfranchised grief that can happen with types of loss that are not so readily recognized or supported by society. These may include the death of an ex-spouse as well as non-fatal losses like divorce, the end of a friendship, losing a job, infertility—and, yes, pregnancy loss.

The word "disenfranchise" means "to deprive someone of a right or privilege." Unfortunately, many of my clients often feel they are being deprived of their right to grieve their pregnancy loss as a meaningful loss. People around them not only gloss over the loss but also pressure them to move on quickly. This can leave the griever feeling very alone.

Part of you may think, "Who cares what society says? This loss is real to me." But it's not always easy to fully embrace that when you are getting subtle messages that you do not have a right to your grief or that you are doing something wrong. After a pregnancy loss, you're likely already feeling fragile, so messages like these can be hard to shake off.

"The grief that results after a stillbirth or neonatal death has been described as complex and unique at least in part because of a lack of acceptance or legitimization of the grieving process by society." —*BMC Pregnancy Childbirth*

While we can't change society's grief rules overnight, we do see that the norms and expectations around grief change over time, largely because grievers (like you and those around you) continue to express their rights to their feelings. In a way, you can think of your grieving as helping others who are looking for examples of "how to do this."

Owning your experience and your feelings can lead to a great amount of personal growth that will extend far beyond this time of your life.

"All grief needs to be blessed. In order to be blessed, it must be heard. Someone must be present, someone who is willing to hold it by listening without judgment or comparison." —Dr. Lani Leary

All the unhelpful things people say

They want to make it better; you just feel worse.

Through each of my losses, I kept a running list in my phone of all the annoying, insensitive, hurtful, judgy, or just plain weird things people said to me in attempts at comfort. At the time, most of these things angered me. I deeply resented any implication that I shouldn't be that sad, that I should move on. I *wanted* to be sad. My grief was honoring the love for my babies. When people dismissed my right to sadness, it felt like they were dismissing my babies.

Now, with some distance, I can see that most of the things people said to me were a reflection of them, not me. They were unwilling (or unable) to just sit with me in my grief. It was just too uncomfortable for them. That's a shame, for all of us, collectively. I wish we were more tolerant of grief, in all its ickiness.

I hope this list helps you feel less alone—and maybe brings a laugh or two.

"It's common for people to believe that 'everything happens for a reason' and that things are 'meant to be.' The need to feel in control contributes greatly to our propensity to believe that the universe is governed by a higher power with a higher purpose." —Ralph Lewis, MD, *Psychology Today*

The unhelpful thing someone said	My imagined response	Let's unpack this
"At least you could get pregnant."	"And then I endured a horrible tragedy. Lucky me!"	This is like saying to someone who crashes their car, "At least you know how to drive." It's dismissive of the actual painful event. Here's the thing: I *was* lucky to get pregnant—each time, despite the losses and pain. But in the aftermath of my losses, I wasn't in the mood to contemplate my alleged good fortune, and I was super annoyed with people who suggested I just bypass my grief and count my lucky stars. I was sad and angry, and I just wanted to be allowed to feel that way for a while, without the pressure to get over it (and get pregnant again).
"There will be another one."	"Uh, OK. Can we talk about *this* one?"	Again, dismissive. I wanted acknowledgment for the loss of *this* pregnancy, not encouragement for future ones I didn't even know if I wanted.
"Just keep trying. One of them will stick."	"*Stick?* This isn't like throwing darts at a wall. We're talking about creating a life here."	I wanted acknowledgment of the mental and physical investment that happens with each pregnancy, each life created.
"My friend's aunt had, like, eight miscarriages and then had three children."	"Good for her. I guess I'll keep my fingers crossed through my own failures!"	I know success stories should be inspiring, but they just made me feel like I was failing again and again. Maybe I wasn't trying hard enough? Maybe I was missing some piece of the puzzle? Maybe I just needed to be patient? In any case, I didn't want to hear about friends-of-friends-of-friends or far-flung relatives.

The unhelpful thing someone said	My imagined response	Let's unpack this
"You can always adopt."	"Right, because that has zero risk of complication or heartbreak."	I heard this a lot, probably because I had multiple losses and people got tired of saying, "Just try again!" It infuriated me to hear this for two reasons. First, it's not like adoption is this easy walk in the park. People can be on adoption lists for *years*. An adoption may fall through at the last minute, potentially even when the adoptive parents have already arrived at the hospital to meet their newborn baby. Adoption is not easy. It takes a lot of grit, determination, patience, and often money. Second, the push to adopt made me feel like I was selfish for wanting a child that was biologically mine. My husband and I did consider adoption. We even contacted a few agencies. One agency told us that they would not work with us if we were still attempting to have a biological child. They wanted couples who were dedicated to adoption. I understood that. I would have had to go through a whole other grieving process before I would have been ready to adopt; I would have had to mourn the fact that I couldn't have a biological child. It is *not* selfish to want a biological child. The desire for it is very human; in the most basic sense, it's what keeps the species alive.
"Trust me, having kids isn't all it's cracked up to be."	"Oh, really? It can be challenging? I hadn't heard. It's a good thing you got to have the experience so you could warn me."	This is like telling a blind person, "You're not missing much. Trees and the sky aren't that cool." Many would surely love to see for themselves.
"Do you know why it happened?"	"Are you just aiming to satisfy your own curiosity or what?	I get why people ask this. They want there to be a reason, something easy to understand (so they can avoid a similar fate, or at least avoid having to realize that things happen without a reason all the time). But any inquiries along these lines felt really invasive. And the implication that there *is* a "why" kind of inherently blames the woman.

The unhelpful thing someone said	My imagined response	Let's unpack this
"There was probably something wrong with the baby."	"OK, so I should feel fine then?"	Most doctors will tell you that the vast majority of miscarriages are due to chromosomal abnormalities. That's good information to know, but it's not inherently consoling. When people said this to me, I felt like they were implying that I should get over my losses because they were "just a fluke of nature," not a big deal. But, see, even if a loss *is* "a fluke of nature," it's still a loss. Attached to that "fluke of nature" were a lot of dreams and hopes and expectations.
"I mean, you wouldn't have wanted an unhealthy baby."	"So I should be grateful this is happening to me?"	To me the underlying message of these phrases is, "Move right along now, no need to wallow!" Wallowing should be allowed with any loss. End of story.
"Maybe it's for the best."	"How would you, or anyone, know that?"	I don't see how losing a baby could ever be "for the best." It's true that I learned a lot from my losses and, eventually, I had my daughter. But that doesn't cancel out the heartache of each loss I experienced. Losses are awful—physically, emotionally. Each of mine put me smack in the middle of a personal existential crisis. Any implication that this was "for the best" just infuriated me.
"I didn't even know you wanted kids."	"Well, I did. So, thanks?"	I was one of those people who was known to be on the fence about having kids, so after my first loss, I couldn't help but wonder if my initial lack of enthusiasm for motherhood was to blame. That's when my friend said this particular unhelpful thing. It was almost like she was saying I wasn't allowed to be upset because I hadn't been aspiring to be a mother since my toddler years.
"Time heals all."	"In that case, can someone put me in a coma for however long you think is necessary? Thanks."	I've come to believe time heals *some* (See "How long is this going to last?"). But it's not just the passage of days that helps; it's the experiencing of emotions over the course of those days. It's embracing the suck.

The unhelpful thing someone said	My imagined response	Let's unpack this
"Everything happens for a reason."	"When I punch you in the face, that will be for a reason too."	When we witness another's sadness, we want there to be a reason for it. We tell ourselves there is a reason for it. It's too unsettling for many of us to accept that we live amongst chaos, where things *just happen*, without a reason. But what could possibly be the reason for a baby dying? There isn't one, not really. I created my own meanings in time (See "Finding meaning"). It didn't happen nearly as quickly as others would have liked, and that's OK.
"It just wasn't meant to be."	"Good to know! I'll just move right on then."	Sometimes when people said this, I thought, "Maybe they're right." But that didn't help me *feel* any better. I still felt angry and gypped and sad and empty. Was trusting in "meant to be" supposed to relieve all those bad feelings? Why couldn't anyone say something to help me with those? People should save "meant to be" for wedding vows, and even then, use sparingly.
"It's God's plan." "Trust in God's plan." "God must have needed another angel."	"If that's the case, I'm not sure how I feel about God. Thanks for adding a crisis of faith to my plate!"	When people said these things, I felt like they wanted me to respond with, "Phew, if it's His plan, then cool. I'm good." But I wasn't good. And I wanted people to care about *that*, not about God.
"It is SO common."	"Maybe so, but I'm still hurting in my own unique way."	I didn't want to be lumped into a group of other women, part of a statistic. I was very possessive of my pain. My losses meant so much to me in a deeply personal way. Even when someone tells me she lost a baby, I don't launch into everything I've learned on my journey. It's not about me; it's about her. When someone loses a baby, she is consumed with her own experience and emotions (and rightfully so). People need to allow for that.

The unhelpful thing someone said	My imagined response	Let's unpack this
"At least it happened early." "At least you didn't get too attached."	"It may have been early, but I still got attached—whoops!"	Fact: There is no "at least" with pregnancy loss. It hurts, no matter how early. With each of my pregnancies, I got attached, even when I told myself not to. It just happened, and I don't regret it.
"It could be worse."	"Um, all right. I guess my sadness means I'm self-absorbed and lack perspective?"	What I hear with this phrase is, "You need to get over yourself." This particular "consolation" carries with it a guilt trip. Because that's what a woman needs after losing a baby—a guilt trip. As my therapist told me, "Tragedies can't be ranked." We only have our own experiences and our own emotional reactions to them. There's no sense comparing. David Kessler, founder of Grief.com, says, "The worst grief is always yours." So, yeah, it could be worse; it could always be worse. That doesn't make losing a baby any less painful.
"It'll happen when the time is right."	"It'll happen? Careful with the promises, my friend! Also, I guess I chose the 'wrong' time—silly me!"	People's optimism and overconfidence in the face of my losses really bugged me. Did they not realize what I'd been through? Did they not care? I felt like adding "when the time is right" was their way to soften their promise that "it'll happen." So, if I lost yet another baby, they would just shrug and say, "Guess it still wasn't the right time."
"Everything will be OK."	"Um, even if that's true, can we just talk about how it sucks *now*? My time-traveling skills need work, and I am still in the present."	Logically, I knew everything would probably be OK, just like I know that it will probably rain in winter in California. But logic is not part of grief. When you're in a summer drought, the promise of rain months away is not comforting. You want someone to sit with you and acknowledge that it's fucking hot.

The unhelpful thing someone said	My imagined response	Let's unpack this
"How ARE you?"	"How do you think I am?"	On the surface, it seems like this is a very harmless question. It shows the person is curious how you're feeling, right? But, somehow, when I got this question, I got irritated and overwhelmed. First, this question suggests that I could be feeling anything but awful after losing a baby. The answer should be painfully obvious. Second, I was never sure how much the person really wanted to know. Were they genuinely interested in my pain, in the range of emotions I was dealing with? Probably not. Most of the time, I just said, awkwardly, "OK" and walked away with the icky feeling that comes with shallow social interactions. In *Option B: Facing Adversity, Building Resilience, and Finding Joy*, Sheryl Sandberg talks about how a better question is "How are you TODAY?" This is far less daunting, and it acknowledges the fact that someone grieving is dealing with a lot of different emotions.
"I totally know how you feel."	"Do you though?"	A couple people said this to me—one was referring to the pain she was feeling after the loss of her cat; the other was referring to an early miscarriage she'd had years ago, before going on to have four children. I just wasn't able to connect, and I resented attempts to lump my babies—my unique babies—into a generic category of "other losses."
"You'll come out of this stronger."	"Maybe. But I feel like a total disaster NOW."	Fact: I *have* come out stronger after my losses, but that happened in my time, on my terms. Being told it would happen, at some unspecified time, did not help while I was in the midst of grieving. First of all, it felt like a lie. My losses decimated me; I could not at all envision how I would survive, let alone come back *stronger*. Second, it made me feel oddly guilty for feeling so weak, like I was letting down all these cheerleaders who were so convinced of my strength.
"You're so brave!"	[Looks over shoulder] "Are you talking to me?"	I got this a lot—because we had multiple losses and kept trying. I never felt brave. I was scared shitless. Being told I was brave just made me feel like a fraud, or like nobody really "got" me or what I was going through.

"The 'at least you could get pregnant' or 'it'll happen again' drove me nuts. Like I could just discard the previous pregnancy and go through a drive-thru and order up a new baby." —Michaela, on her first-trimester loss

"When we gradually started sharing our sad news, friends and family urged us in different well-meaning ways not to dwell on it. 'Keep trying. You'll get pregnant again,' they'd say, as if then this loss wouldn't matter. But it did matter. It still does."

—Matthew Thorburn, "Why We Write: A Life Imagined," *Poets & Writers*

Meredith

People will have opinions, and they will likely share them with you whether you want to hear them or not.

Remember that their opinions do not define your reality, your loss, and your future.

Rather than showing support, seemingly upbeat catchphrases can actually be dismissive and a way of blocking further conversation. It may catch you off guard.

Kim refers to being possessive of her pain, but I think there is something else—you may be protective of your pain as well. It is a valuable resource, after all, something that has opened up your capacity to love. Wanting to shield your pain (and yourself) from further prodding, judgment, and pressure to stifle it makes perfect sense.

Mourning doesn't have a specific end date. You may always feel a twinge of sadness for the pregnancy or pregnancies you lost even as decades pass. A woman I know in her eighties told me of the four miscarriages she endured before their son (a friend of mine) was born; she still spoke of the lost babies wistfully.

The challenge of all the unhelpful things people say lies in your ability to continually remind yourself of what your loss means to you at every level—what you lost and what you found or gained as a result.

Huong

Brené Brown has spoken extensively on empathy versus sympathy. She makes the distinction that empathy is feeling *with* people: "In order to connect with you, I have to connect with a part of myself that knows that feeling." For some people, this is simply too scary. When they dole out platitudes or say other unhelpful things, it is because of that fear.

When people say things that *sound* positive, it's confusing when you *feel* angry or irritated in response. *They're just trying to help me see the bright side*, you think (followed by guilt about your own anger). It's a fact that numerous research studies have shown the benefits of gratitude and a positive mindset. Rick Hanson, PhD, is a world-renowned expert on happiness, and he talks about how our brains are Velcro for negativity and Teflon for positivity, so it's important to notice the things we have in our lives that are good.

"There's a fine line between helping someone feel less daunted, and belittling their very real, warranted fear and anger with 'you'll be fine.'"
—Dr. Kelsey Crowe and Emily McDowell, *There is No Good Card for This: What to Say and Do When Life is Scary, Awful, and Unfair to People You Love*

However, that does not mean we need to "turn that frown upside down" or to accept "at least . . . ". There is a new term for those who wish to retain a positive outlook and force that outlook onto others: "toxic positivity."

An example of toxic positivity would be, "This will make you stronger." A more helpful alternative would be, "This is hard. You've done hard things before, and I believe in you." Another example of toxic positivity would be, "See the good in everything," which could be reframed as, "It's probably really hard or near impossible to see any good in this situation. We'll make sense of it later."

Or maybe nothing needs to be said at all. Here's a story I like to share about the power of just being there.

The Broken Doll by Dan Clark

From Chicken Soup for the Mother's Soul

One day my youngest daughter was late coming home from school. I was both annoyed and worried. When she came through the door, I demanded in my upset tone that she explain why she was late.

She said, "Mommy I was walking home with Julie, and halfway home,

Julie dropped her doll and it broke into lots of little pieces."

"Oh, honey," I replied, "you were late because you helped Julie pick up the pieces of her doll to put them back together."

In her young and innocent voice, my daughter said, "No, Mommy. I didn't know how to fix the doll. I just stayed to help Julie cry."

I see this in my practice all the time. What most of us want in life is a safe space to feel our feelings and to be seen by another. True support is allowing others to cry, wail, or throw a temper tantrum (and a pillow or two)—all without any judgment.

Sometimes, I am at a loss for words as I sit across from a client. They look at me with anticipation—half hoping I will find the silver bullet of words but also half expecting me to mess up and confirm the belief they are alone. I don't like to dole out platitudes. I sit there, in the yuckiness of the pain, and I reflect to my clients what I am feeling in the room—confusion, sadness, whatever it is. Most of the time they are relieved to know that even an "expert" doesn't quite know what to say at all times. As Brené Brown says, "I don't even know what to say right now. I'm just so glad you told me."

When people say nothing at all

It feels like they don't care.

What's worse: when people say the wrong thing, or when people say nothing at all? For me, the silence was probably worse. When people said the wrong things, at least they were making an effort. When they were silent, it felt like they didn't give a shit.

After I lost Miles, I sent an email to certain coworkers about what had happened, because I knew I wouldn't want to explain it in person on my first day back at the office. So, when I came back and nobody said anything to me, I was really hurt.

"I see people as they approach me, trying to make up their minds whether they'll say something about it or not. I hate if they do, and if they don't."
—C. S. Lewis, *A Grief Observed*

I'm sure I gave off a vibe that said *Don't talk to me*, but I wish people had pushed past that to at least send an email or leave a note on my desk. I didn't want pity; I just wanted acknowledgment of my loss. I wanted Miles to be real.

There were lots of pregnant women at my office while I was busy losing babies. They were especially silent, distant. Did they just feel awkward around me? Or was it more sinister than that? Did they think my misfortune was contagious? In general, I felt that way around everyone—like I was this representative of tragedy and I made them uncomfortable. I got vibes of "I'm so glad I'm not you" and "That happened to you, but it would never happen to me." I felt like a leper at times. It was isolating, lonely.

With some distance, I've decided that the reasons for silence are probably simple—people fear doing or saying the wrong thing. Essentially, they don't want to fuck up, and I can have some compassion for that. It's not their fault; in a society that doesn't embrace grieving, it's hard to know what to say.

Meredith

Your loss has triggered something beyond the other person's understanding. When this happens, even people who care about you will blurt out things, or say nothing, to bring the interaction to a new level of awkward. It is perfectly fine to say: "You know what? That's not helping me right now." Or, "I'm not going to talk to you about this right now." Or, "I just realized I don't want to say anything else."

"Don't ignore the obvious. Silence is worse than anything . . . People think, 'She'll be upset if I say something,' but it's actually the opposite. By discussing it, you're validating the experience and honoring the grief . . . It's about holding space for the emotional experience around grief and trauma."

—Dr. Ivy Margulies, clinical psychologist specializing in pregnancy and infant loss, in an interview with "Good Morning America"

If you, too, have trouble with grief and sadness, then allowing yourself the space to simply feel is a huge step. Another's less-than-supportive reply (intentional or not) can amplify your pain; it vaguely reminds you of how you feel inside. In other words, on some level it mirrors your discomfort. This is simply good information, to be dealt with at another time. Right now, you are getting acquainted with your own grief, which is where the healing, the growth, and the deeper understanding begins.

You may not respond to another person in mourning with the same reply. In fact you may be supportive and kind, but somewhere inside is a pocket of discomfort that is getting hooked and prodded by the other person's less-than-ideal reply.

I have worked extensively in hospitals and with the dying, and at times I have been at a loss for what to say when face-to-face with another's primal vulnerability at the end of life. Why? Because that vulnerability touches a part of my own.

The same can happen to you. In fact, it happens to most everyone.

Given that, the question becomes, do you want to explore that space inside you? Give yourself room to say yes. Then, get curious about yourself. That said, there is no need to continue to subject yourself to insensitive things other people say or do. Excuse yourself. Take care of you.

"You're thankful for the kind things people say,
you forgive the dumb things, but you're crushed by the silence."
—Nora McInerney, *It's Okay to Laugh (Crying Is Cool Too)*

The Pity Face

You know—the furrowed brows,
the jutted-out bottom lip, the sad eyes.

I. Can't. Stand. Pity.

Well, I should clarify. I was happy to throw my own private pity party—a real rager, to which my husband RSVP'd "no, thank you"—but I did not want others feeling sorry for me.

What I wanted was acknowledgment that my baby had died and that I was in pain. I wanted some compassion. I wanted empathy. There is a difference between pity and empathy. Empathy makes me feel loved, held. Pity makes me feel pathetic and hopeless. When someone says, "Oh, you poor thing!" they are just reflecting my own sad circumstances back at me, which just makes me feel worse. Pity leaves me feeling terribly alone, like I'm stuck on this island of grief while the rest of the world dances on cruise ships passing me by.

Meredith: In such a vulnerable state, you are more susceptible to absorbing someone else's fear than you would be under normal circumstances. It's important to acknowledge that pregnancy loss is awful, but it does not make you "pitiful."

There are a couple people in my life who gave me the Pity Face, and I wanted so badly to say, "Please don't feel sorry for me. It feels like you're implying I can't get through this." But I didn't say that. I am the queen of being tongue-tied in these types of situations. If you encounter the Pity Face, feel free to use that line though. I'd love to hear how it goes.

Meredith: When I've encountered the Pity Face, I have felt someone was implying "it's such a pity you were so unlucky and unfortunate to have created this in your life." I think that's another facet of the belief people have that you somehow brought on the unthinkable by thinking or believing, or not believing enough. Nothing could be further from true.

What I wish people would say

Feel free to stick a bookmark here and
give this to a loved one.

I admit, it's hard. When I asked people who have been through this what they wanted to hear after their losses, many said that a simple and genuine "I'm sorry" did the trick. For me, personally, "I'm sorry" didn't cut it. It felt like pity (see previous entry for my feelings on that).

"My one bit of advice to people is pick up the phone, send a text—send a bloody pigeon if you have to. Just a 'I'm so sorry to hear. I am here for you.' That's all. Failing that, just throw some emoji hearts their way in a message; even that is better than silence." —Elle Wright, *Ask Me His Name: Learning to Live and Laugh Again After the Loss of My Baby*

All I wanted to hear was *"That really sucks. I hate that you have to go through this. Do you want to talk about it? I'm here."* That's it. Don't try to fix it, don't try to minimize it. Just admit that it blows. Let me know that grief is OK, that there's no rush to move on. Sit with me in the not-OKness instead of trying to skip over it and launch me into a future where everything is OK. When I say "sit with me," it doesn't have to be physically, though it's always nice to offer that (if I decline, it doesn't mean that was the wrong thing to say; I'm grateful for the offer, just not ready). "Sit with" is just acceptance of someone's pain, acknowledgment of it, honoring of it.

Tips for friends and family members

- Say *something*, even if it's just, "I don't know what to say."
- Listen, listen, listen.
- Try to resist the urge to fix their pain; you likely cannot, and any suggestion you can implies that their pain must not be that bad.
- Resist the easy platitudes ("Everything happens for a reason," "Maybe it's for the best," and the like). You will feel them on the tip of your tongue—resist!
- Avoid any phrase that starts with "at least" ("At least you could get pregnant" or "At least it happened early"). There is no bright side to pregnancy loss, sorry.
- Avoid any phrase that includes "just" ("You guys should just try again" or "Maybe you should just adopt"). These phrases imply that there is a simple solution to the person's pain. Pregnancy loss and its aftermath are rarely simple.
- Check in—text, email, phone call, in person, whatever the person seems to need. If you don't know, ask. Or start small—a text or email—and go from there.
- Don't worry about "messing up." If your intentions are good and you are genuine in your care, you will not "mess up."

Meredith

It is so OK to ask for what you need. It's OK to tell people the way in which you'd like them to acknowledge your loss and your feelings. This is particularly true in the early stages of mourning, when shock can have a numbing, otherworldly effect. "I don't know what I need right now, but what you said is not helping" works. It doesn't make you weird. It doesn't make you less competent. It doesn't mean you're inherently aimless, though you might feel adrift right now. You are figuring this out in *your* way. And that is the only way that matters. I'm not talking about micromanaging word choice, but rather about trusting that you know yourself enough to know what you need. Ask that people listen to your language, both verbal and nonverbal. It's OK to say, "I want you to be here, but please, let's not talk about what happened." Lean on people you can trust. If you can't get the words out to others, let them be your voice.

Do's and don'ts of how to help someone through pregnancy loss

Don't say, "You can try again."
Do say, "It's OK if you talk, and it's OK if you don't."

Don't hurry people off the path of grief.
Do say, "I'm here to listen when you're ready. I'll check in with you on a regular basis."

Don't tell them they've cried enough for today.
Do sit with them as they mourn the loss and try to make sense of something that makes no sense.

Don't say, "This is God's plan. If you're meant to be a parent, it will happen."
Do say, "I'm as confused as you are. I'm here as you sort through it." Hold up a proverbial light (through gentle support, sincere caring, and lots of hugs—but only if that person likes hugs!).

Don't be afraid to acknowledge the loss. Guess what? She's already upset.
Do say the baby's name if one has been given.

Don't say, "Tell me what you want me to do."
Do tell her that you'd like to bake bread for her/entertain her kids for the afternoon/take her for a walk on the beach—whatever you think she might like.

Don't let her isolate.
Do respect her request for short-term privacy. Leave meals at the door, text often, and write notes.

Don't avoid eye contact.
Do look the person in the eye and witness their pain and show them you care, you understand, and you want to support them.

"Be specific about what you need—and what you don't. In a perfect world, your close friends would know what you'd need at any given moment. But they probably don't have a clue. Help them out. They want to be useful."
—Rebecca Soffer and Gabrielle Birkner, *Modern Loss: Candid Conversations about Grief. Beginners Welcome.*

Connecting with
your baby

Who was my baby?

So much of my grieving was for the future
I had imagined for my babies (and for me).

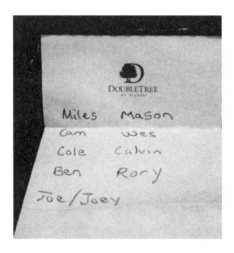

This is a list of names my husband and I dared to imagine for our son. When we passed the first trimester, we thought we were safe to start thinking about names. We chose Miles. I carried Miles for seventeen weeks. Saying goodbye to him was saying goodbye to a future I had started to envision. Would he be a soccer lover, like his dad? Would he be a reader, like me? Would he be tall (my genes) or short (my husband's genes)? Would he be sensitive and quiet, or loud and gregarious? I had been entertaining fantasies related to all of these questions from the moment we found out we were having a boy (we found out early because I had every blood test known to man). I still wonder who Miles would have been, but the wondering doesn't make me sad (or sadder). I think some people believe that thinking about him and who he could have been is just exacerbating pain. But, no. Thinking about him is a way of honoring him. It's been part of healing for me.

If I were meeting *you* for coffee, I would ask you the questions I like to receive:

Who was your baby?

What was your baby's name?

How did you picture his or her personality?

What activities did you daydream about doing together?

What part of parenthood were you most looking forward to?

What part of parenthood scared you?

<hr/>

"It is the incompleteness that I struggle with. It is missing someone I never knew, but whom I wanted desperately to be a part of my life." —Kari Smalkoski, "Untranslation," featured in *What God Is Honored Here? Writings on Miscarriage and Infant Loss by and for Native Women and Women of Color* (Shannon Gibney and Kao Kalia Yang, editors)

Meredith

Even the briefest connection is still a connection, and these exercises create space to commune with your child, with your unfilled role as a parent *of this child*. Exercises like this also open a door that allows you to mourn that part of you as a parent who did not get to live in a day-to-day relationship with your baby.

Suggestion: Designate a journal for these exercises. Carry your journal with you so you have it as thoughts arise. It's very common for grief to catch us off guard, when we are going about the usual routine of our days, or even during a time of immense joy when it's least expected (See "When grief sneaks up on you"). Whether going through the motions of everyday life or doing something out of the ordinary, the natural emotions are embedded within. Providing a space for them to land (your journal, notepad, or audio app on your phone) allows you to meet and honor them in your own way.

<hr/>

"Embryos are not people, and yet, I have missed the people those embryos never became every day since I lost them." —Dania Rajendra, "Binding Signs," featured in *What God Is Honored Here? Writings on Miscarriage and Infant Loss by and for Native Women and Women of Color* (Shannon Gibney and Kao Kalia Yang, editors)

A little ceremony goes a long way

It was important for me to honor my babies in a semiformal way.

After my first loss, my mom suggested Chris and I do something to honor our baby. At first, I thought this was silly. I mean, I didn't lose a "real" baby. She said she'd read online that some people plant flowers or a tree, some wear a certain piece of in-memoriam jewelry, some get a tattoo. "It's good for closure," she said. How could I need closure for a baby I barely knew? But, I did. I'd had a very real connection to the embryo that was growing inside me. And I wanted—needed—to honor that embryo, to acknowledge his or her life, however brief it was.

"I bought stuffed animals for them. And wrote letters."

—Wendy, on her two first-trimester miscarriages

My husband and I took a bouquet of roses a friend had sent us during my recovery and went to the beach. We plucked the petals from the bouquet and scattered them across the sand and in the ocean. Then we spoke aloud to the baby we'd lost. I'm not much of a hippie type of person—I have never attended a drum circle, I do not dance about my feelings, I have never burned sage. And my husband is the polar opposite of that type of person. So I was worried this petal-scattering mini-ceremony would feel contrived, but it didn't. It helped. It solidified the loss as something *real*.

I thought about getting a tattoo as well but figured my surgery scars serve the purpose a tattoo would. I look at them all the time. They remind me of the journey I've taken to have my daughter. I remember when they were fresh, and I thought, "There's no way these are going to fade." But they have. Nobody but me would probably notice them now, and I'm so grateful to notice them.

> ### Ideas for honoring your baby
>
> - Create something—knit, quilt, needlework, draw, paint, sculpt.
> - Wear or make a piece of jewelry.
> - Write about your baby.
> - Write *to* your baby (See "Writing to my baby").
> - Plant a memorial tree or garden.
> - Frame an ultrasound photo, if you have one.
> - Create a fundraiser, or donate to a charity or organization dedicated to pregnancy and infant loss support (See Appendix for a list of charities and organizations).

Meredith

It can be so healing to make real your child and your role as parent and, at the same time, mourn the passing of both. Take seriously your need to validate the life that began and ended. It was a life, however short.

When you consider a ceremony, feel free to think creatively. A ceremony can be anything that speaks to you. It could be a morning meditation, a candle lit at dusk, or a prayer before bed. You might do these once or more often. You might pick a day of the week or the month, or even the due date.

If you choose a ritual, keep things fluid. Rituals are processes that help us honor someone or something important. In this case, the ritual is to honor your feelings about the baby or the pregnancy you lost. Therefore, let the ritual speak to you so that you, in turn, can speak to your baby. Because you are changing and growing and evolving, allow your rituals to do the same. If something stops feeling right, follow your instincts and do something else. If doing something regularly no longer feels necessary because you've found enough resolution and feel that the baby you lost is part of you, then let go of the need for a ritual as well. You can always start up again if you feel the need. Trust yourself.

I like looking to other cultures to see how they honor babies lost during pregnancy. In traditional Japanese culture, the deity Jizo is the guardian and protector of children, especially those who have died before their parents, as in the case of pregnancy loss. Parents often engage in *mizuko kuyo*, which is a Buddhist ritual to mourn pregnancy loss and involves adorning Jizo with deeply personal meaning, such as writing the child's name on a piece of paper and placing it under the figure. It is also common to burn incense, light candles, and leave offerings of food or flowers.

Funerals and cremations

If you gave birth to a baby who passed away shortly after birth, or if your baby was stillborn, you may want to plan a service to affirm your child's life in addition to what is legally mandated in terms of burial or cremation.

Religion, culture, family, and personal beliefs can help provide a framework for ways to think about how to approach a service, burial, unveiling of a gravestone, and memorial. You may find these traditions useful to follow, or you may use them as a blueprint to create something meaningful for you. Despite how we may feel, most religions and cultures espouse the belief that grief is not meant to be carried alone. There will be family and friends who want the opportunity to honor your baby as much as you do.

"We planted a tree in memory of Ella, and we scattered her ashes in two rivers, one in Africa, one in England. Water is life, and we wanted for her to forever be moving along rivers that mean a lot to us."

—Georgie, who had a stillborn daughter (Ella) and two first-trimester miscarriages

Writing to my baby

It helped me.

I resisted connecting with my son, Miles, for weeks—months—after losing him. Then, on his would-have-been birth date, I wrote to him. And I put the letter in a Ziploc baggie, rolled it up, and stuffed it into the neck of an empty wine bottle.

My idea was to throw the bottle in the ocean, to let Miles float free in the waves. I thought of how cool it would be if someone across the world found the bottle, if his existence could be acknowledged by a stranger. That stranger would think of him for a moment. They would acknowledge him.

This was the letter:

September 11, 2016

Dear Miles,

I call you Miles, even though there were a few other names in the running. Miles was always our favorite.

Today is your due date, the day you were supposed to join us as a living, breathing, crying, hungry little human. It's hard to believe. My belly is flat. Nobody can tell by looking at me that I am supposed to have a baby today. There are people who knew I was pregnant with you, who even knew your due date, but they've forgotten because remembering is too painful. Please know that I will always remember you. And I'll always remember what today was supposed to be.

Everyone cringed when we said 9/11 was your due date. Not the best day to be born, I guess. Bad juju or whatever. But thirteen is my favorite number, and I love black cats, so I've always turned my nose up at superstition.

But then we lost you, and I was left to question everything I ever believed.

We were so ready for you. Your dad read books about being a father. He met with architects and obsessed over plans to renovate the house, to make room for you. Your dad coaches soccer—six- and seven-year-old boys. He would have loved to coach you—in soccer, in life.

I daydreamed about breastfeeding you, reading to you, teaching you, cooking for you (and with you. Your dad is domestic that way, always doing the dishes and laundry. I wanted you to be like that, to be someone's future ideal mate). I will miss seeing you smile and giggle, play with the dogs, take your first steps, make your first friends. I will always wonder who you would have been—serious and ambitious and intense like your dad and me? Or the opposite of that, bestowing upon us some karmic lessons; in other words, giving us a run for our money? All we really know is that you would have had dark brown hair and blue eyes—because we both do.

I don't know if I'll get pregnant again. I hope so. If I do, will it be with you? Will you come back? Or will it be another soul's turn? If there's one thing I've learned, it's that the future is unknown. There is little certainty, and even less control. I trust that you know we love you. I trust that you're still part of our lives, and always will be. If you don't come back, maybe you will help select the soul who does—your sibling. Or maybe you will gently remind your dad and me that the love we have for each other means we are blessed enough.

I'm grateful for the four-and-a-half months I carried you. When we lost you, I never thought I would say that. I was angry—at you for leaving, at myself for not keeping you safe. But, now, five months have passed and I can say I'm truly grateful for the time I had you. Those months were the most terrifying and magical months of my life so far. You opened me up, made me vulnerable in a way that I hadn't been before. I won't be the same again, thanks to you. And that's a good thing.

I love you, little boy. I am finding peace, and I hope you are, too.

Love,
Your mom

Chris and I took the bottle to the beach, which had become our place of ceremony for our losses. I threw the bottle into the waves . . . and then it came right back to us. After another attempt, with the same result, Chris said, "I'm going to have to swim it out there." So, off he went, determined, lips pressed together, eyes big and wild. I watched until he nearly disappeared, his head just a dot on the horizon. He came back, cold, shivering, covered in goosebumps. I hugged him.

A few minutes later, the bottle was back.

Chris is stubborn—so stubborn. But on this day, he was especially persistent. In his eyes I saw the kind of persistence that comes from acute pain. He insisted on swimming out again, farther this time. He did.

And the bottle returned. Again.

I could almost hear Miles laughing at us, his ridiculous parents. We ended up taking the bottle home. When we moved, it moved with us. It now sits on our kitchen counter. I'll keep it always.

I've had to learn to live
with this: we
didn't see you, didn't
meet you, only
knew you
were there a little while
and then you weren't.
it's this question
I've kept
coming back to
all year: how
can I love you
without
ever knowing you?
and there's no
answer, finally,
none at all—
but I still do.

—Matthew Thorburn, *Dear Almost*

Huong

With Cognitive Processing Therapy (CPT; see page 134), part of the treatment includes writing a narrative about the traumatic experience from start to finish. Some researchers are starting to investigate if narrative writing helps with PTSD.

It's been shown that writing with pen or pencil to paper has greater benefits than typing. The process of writing allows the brain to start to process the trauma and the events (since we typically write slower than we type). Try keeping a journal and writing about what happened to you. Or write a letter to your baby, as Kim did. You might find your own words very healing.

Meredith: If words do not come easily, you might want to draw, paint, or collage. Snip words or sentence fragments from magazines, then piece them into sentences, short poems, or lists. Glue these sentiments into a journal or frame them. Using your hands while concentrating on the art can bring emotions into awareness, sometimes very quickly, without the need to "work" so hard. This helps you process and heal.

Where is my baby now?

I wondered this. I still do.

Some women are very clinical about the loss of a baby, comforting themselves by saying things like "It wasn't a viable pregnancy" or "It's for the best." I thought I would be one of these women, but I wasn't.

With each of my losses, I pondered the baby's soul, which "old me" would have considered "out there." I wondered if the baby was effectively "dead," forever gone, or if he or she would return in another pregnancy. After losing Miles, I even consulted a psychic, who assured me that he "just wasn't ready for the world" and was happy "on the other side." Of course, I have no idea if this is true (nobody could possibly know this), but it did make me feel better.

"I really think I will see the baby again. I believe in Heaven and reuniting with loved ones, and I really do believe I will see him or her."

—Michaela, after her first-trimester loss

It's hard not having absolute answers. I can't KNOW what happened to the little souls I harbored. What I've done is create a narrative that feels good and right for me. I like to think that the babies I lost are "on the other side" and that they are linked to my husband, my daughter, and me forever. I like to think that they are at peace, that they are looking over my family. I like to think that I will "meet" them when it is my turn to be "on the other side." That's my narrative. Yours might be totally different. There is no right or wrong with matters this close to the heart.

Reiki Master Julie Russell explains that what we think of as "the other side" is simply unembodied energy. This means that the spirit of your baby is forever alive. That you are forever connected.

If this energy needs a space to ground, let it be inside you. Let your heart hold it as opposed to your hands. Your heart will never forget the connection you share. You are the only person on earth who can recall that feeling of that precious life inside you. It is still stored there, only in a new space that is eternal.

"I wonder, not for the first or second or third time—where did they go? My babies. Where are they? I feel desperate to find them, like I've lost my keys and if I look hard enough, digging down in the cushions of the couch or underneath the coffee table or through the clutter on my dresser, I'll find them. They're there, waiting for me. Somewhere. I just have to find them."

—Colleen Oakley, *You Were There Too* (in this novel, the main character, Mia, endures multiple miscarriages)

"The
Universe
is made of
stories, not of atoms."

—Muriel Rukeyser, poet and political activist

Tracking a pregnancy
that is no more

This was another way I connected with my baby.

In the months after each of my losses, there were many moments when I looked down at my stomach and thought, "It should be out to here by now." I imagined the bump, the pregnancy symptoms. Every time I drank a beer or went for an especially challenging run or took a scalding-hot bath, I thought, "If things had worked out, I wouldn't be doing this right now."

They say when people lose a limb, they feel like it's still there, a phenomenon called phantom limb syndrome. I definitely experienced phantom pregnancy syndrome. It's not that I believed I was still pregnant (though I did have fantasies that this was the case), but I tracked my life as if I were, wondering what would have been different, how I would have been feeling. For me, this was a way of connecting with the baby I'd lost, grieving what could have been and wasn't.

Meredith

Have you ever heard the term "parallel universe"? It's defined in quantum mechanics as a universe theorized as existing alongside our own, although undetectable. Scientists and engineers use this term, but it's also applicable here, with the loss of your pregnancy.

In addition to this being a way of connecting with the baby that you've lost, it's also a way of connecting with that part of yourself that didn't get a full opportunity to emerge. There is a longing, not only for that baby, but for that woman who didn't get the opportunity to grow and "become." Perhaps on a certain plane, however distant it seems, that relationship lives. Perhaps that plane is right inside you, in your heart.

Allow this to bring you comfort. That baby lives in a space that doesn't require words. You hold them that way. They are part of you, always. Alive in your heart.

Connecting with
your partner

Grieving differently

One size does not fit all.

The day after losing our first baby, while I was in bed woozy from the pain pills they'd given me after the emergency surgery to remove my "out of place" embryo, my husband, Chris, went to a hockey game with his brother. During the week, instead of working from home like he usually would, he left for "client meetings" that I'm not sure were real. The truth of it: He couldn't stand being around me. "Being in this house raises my blood pressure," he'd said. So he just . . . left.

When I expressed frustration about this to a friend who had lost a baby at ten weeks, she said, "When I had my miscarriage, my husband went to Vegas."

"We experienced the loss and grieved completely differently. I went straight to the rebound, wanted to get back up quickly and move on. Clearly that wasn't going to work for you. I didn't want to feel vulnerable, but I realize now that I unintentionally distanced myself. You needed someone to endure the pain with you." —Chris (my husband)

In the film *Return to Zero*, a successful couple named Aaron and Maggie lose their son at thirty-eight weeks, then grow distant from each other. Aaron has an affair, and they contemplate divorce. When I watched it, I was in awe of how the writer/director (Sean Hanish) got the emotion so *right*. Then I learned it was based on his real-life experience.

When I woke up from surgery after losing Miles at seventeen weeks, Chris was at my bedside looking terribly uncomfortable. He started rambling about something he'd been discussing on the phone with his boss in the waiting room, trying to distract me (and/or himself) from the blood gushing out of me as I sat up in the hospital bed ("Don't worry, that's normal," the nurse said). Chris continued rambling on our whole drive home. Three losses in and I'd finally pegged (not accepted, but identified) his grieving style: Avoidance. I wanted to talk and process and feel; he wanted absolutely none of that.

"My approach to dealing with our losses was consistent with how I deal with most challenging situations. I like to switch into action, look for solutions, try to make things better." —Chris (my husband)

The disconnect between partners after losing a baby is a real thing. Typically, one half of a couple is the "fixer," the one focused on problem-solving. They pride themselves on being strong and having a stiff upper lip. For them, the loss of a baby feels like a failure they can't fix, which is deeply unsettling and frustrating for them. Many immerse themselves in activities because being productive restores their sense of worth. They have a strong need to counter the feelings of helplessness and feel competent and in control.

The previous paragraph fits my husband to a tee.

During our losses, Chris distracted himself with various projects. He took up mountain biking, plotting out different routes through the local hills, highlighting maps and leaving them all over the house. He crashed one day and came through the door with his head bleeding. He needed stitches. There are scars.

He went on long runs. He volunteered to collect signatures for local causes that had never mattered to him before. He became obsessed with cleaning—one day I found him in the backyard, scrubbing the *cement*. At one point, he signed up for a disaster preparedness course. He would research things online like, "Can you drink pool water in an emergency?" It was like our experiences made him feel vulnerable to myriad things going wrong. He had to do what he could to prepare for the worst.

"I was worried that you would be a different person. I didn't want to believe a permanent scar would be left behind that would alter our future."
—Chris (my husband)

We had to renovate Chris's mom's house to get it ready to sell, and that became his focus, a second job in addition to his full-time job. With any spare moments, he obsessively researched random things—the best wireless headphones, the best home security cameras. We found out rats were slinking around outside at night, eating the cat food, so he came up with "trap strategies." He left no time for sitting with his feelings.

"I was sad to see you struggling. I probably should have focused more of my energy on being attentive and supportive of you." —Chris (my husband)

To me, it appeared that Chris wasn't grieving at all—he was clearly too busy for that. I resented his stoicism. He appeared cold, unfeeling, like he didn't really care about our losses. He seemed so . . . over it. I mean, how was he able to just jump into all these other projects? I knew he had to be struggling in his own way, but he appeared "fine," which just left me feeling alone in my suffering.

Like many who lose a baby, I needed to sit with my feelings. I needed to talk about them. This was hard on our marriage, because my need to talk and share alleviated pain for me, but it was a burden for him. He *hated* seeing me cry. He thought I was dwelling on it, getting lost in my thoughts, making no effort to "move on." Once, he said, "I think you need to stop talking so much about the pregnancies." In other words, *Shut the hell up, woman!* I felt like he didn't understand me at all. I pictured us on different sides of a vast canyon, him yelling, "Come here. Come to the bright side." But I was so trapped in clouds and darkness, I couldn't even see him.

I realize now that Chris and I were both afraid for our marriage while we were grieving. He was afraid that I would never get over our losses; I was afraid that he did not really care about our babies . . . or about me. At one point, he said something in passing that explained so much: "You're my rock. I don't know what to do when you're crumbling." I wish we'd just acknowledged our fears and comforted each other through those fears instead of resenting our differences in grieving. It would have made for a much less bumpy road.

Meredith

Even those who are relatively *good* in stressful situations can be propelled backwards emotionally after a loss. You know your partner loves you. So when your partner seems to you to be doing everything wrong, what's going on?

In times of stress, people may default to earlier coping strategies. This is shocking to a partner who knew their significant other as kind, capable, and available. Suddenly, it's the opposite. They are avoiding you and don't want to hear the medical details or witness the physical pain you are in. The more this happens, the more contentious your relationship gets. You want to talk; they don't.

That alone seems unfair. After all, it's your body that has held life, shared life, and lost the life it helped create. No one on earth, not even your partner, can know this bond but you.

Avoidance, shutting down, finding someone to blame, and leaving are coping mechanisms—distractions, actually—that ultimately don't alleviate the suffering. The person may not even be aware of what they're doing. The grief, however, remains.

Your loss is, by Nature itself, different than your partner's. Your intimacy with the life once growing inside is interwoven with your grieving and, ultimately, your healing. You deserve to have someone who can be there for you. But, because you do not have the power to change them, you will need to widen your view of your loved one and begin to find ways that open doors to them.

"Grieving is personal, and within a marriage, it's really easy to assume you know *exactly* how the other person feels, the words and actions they'll choose in the face of loss. Except you don't, not 100 percent. Not even when it comes to your spouse or long-term partner."

—Julia Dellitt, "3 Marriage Lessons I Learned After My Miscarriage," TheEverymom.com

Let's start at the beginning

When we are little, we rely on our caretakers to guide us through our pain. Parents and other caretakers help us understand and mediate feelings of hurt, loneliness, and fear. This lays the groundwork for how we navigate feelings in general throughout life.

Trauma as an adult can take us back to childhood, when we were still learning how to hold and manage our feelings. When you are in a relationship with someone else, this is happening to both of you at the exact same time.

Even for someone who has been fortunate to have support for their emotional development early in life, trauma can be rough, and perhaps even tougher to witness in a partner. Everything is multiplied, and, depending on personality, the way each individual deals with pain might conflict with the other.

Looking in the mirror

All the pain a loved one is going through is like watching a movie. And in seeing that movie, the person can be reminded of their own helplessness and how frightening that is. Maybe, inadvertently, you silently judge each other for your grief reactions. Maybe you've lost your greatest supporter because your partner is trying to make sense of their sadness. This adds additional pressure when a person feels they are not doing it right. Someone who sees themselves as a fixer will be especially dismayed to not be able to live up to their ideal.

The stress of losing a baby brings all that to the surface.

Couples are impacted in so many ways.

Your relationship is really about communication, the heard and unheard messages that travel back and forth, the physical closeness or distance, the manner in which you give, take, and share.

The loss may bring you closer. But sometimes sharing the pain hurts more. Being aware of tiny cracks in your communication early can help. Some of these cracks might have been there before but, without the pain of loss, seemed manageable.

Consider all the ways you communicate:

- Touch that is nonsexual: Do you still hug or lean in to each other? What about holding hands or just walking close by when you are out?
- Nonverbal communication: Do you still make eye contact, or reach across the table and squeeze hands? What about a wink or a smile? Some little gesture, just between the two of you?
- Sexual touch: Intercourse is only part of sexual touch and arousal. Sensuality in a couple is most sustainable when there is mutual trust and it is safe to be vulnerable. When sex becomes the focus—whether

that is wanting or not wanting to have it—something about the emotional life of the relationship is being overlooked and will benefit from attention.

- Verbal communication: How do you learn to talk about the loss, and how do you honor each person's need at any given moment, particularly when the loss is new and the wound is raw? Though you are in a partnership, separate people will have separate processes and different words to cope with grief.

You both want to be cared for and nurtured in the way that speaks to each of you. In this state of mourning, there is also the desire that your mourning processes and reactions mirror each other. Somehow it can feel harder to not experience the pain together in the same way.

"Grief moves like an amoeba and shows up when you least expect it, or will ghost you when you assume it's due to arrive. When it does hit, the ways in which people respond are as varied as the trajectories of their grief, and this disparity often causes resentment between the partners."
—Mira Ptacin, "How to Stay Married After Losing a Baby," the *New York Times*

"Sometimes I wondered if we were experiencing the same loss. The following months saw us frequently walking through isolated hells, two loving parents separately grieving the loss of our baby girl, bereft and desperately nostalgic for a future that would never be."
—Mattie J. Bekink, "The Promise," featured in *Modern Loss: Candid Conversations about Grief. Beginners Welcome.* (Rebecca Soffer and Gabrielle Birkner, editors)

You can see how complicated this is, because the hurt is not only of today with your loss but of conditioning and patterns that were established before the pair of you ever knew each other.

So, what can you do?

- Realize this happens in every relationship—and can get exacerbated after a trauma.
- Be prepared to see facets of your partner and yourself that you were not prepared for—some you may not like, others you might welcome.
- You may be aggravated with your partner for how they deal with loss

and feel that they cannot know what you are experiencing since they didn't go through it. Likewise, your partner may feel left out, or like they can't express how vulnerable they feel since they didn't experience the physical loss as well.

- Find a means by which to communicate. If you can't look into one another's eyes, perhaps you can sit side by side and stare out the window. If that is too hard, perhaps you can speak in the dark to lessen vulnerability in the short-term.
- Stay away from black/white and right/wrong; try to talk as best you can, even if you can't agree right away; and keep the conversations going.
- Understand that the issues getting in the way now were likely there before, but everything comes to the surface when a loss like this occurs.
- Recognize that issues don't need to be fixed NOW or resolved THIS INSTANT unless they are life-threatening.
- Focus less on specifics and more on patterns. Things don't need to be perfect, but they do need to work in the new normal of your loss. Once you've got a groove, you can refine the details—together.

"You've been united in the creation of the baby but now the grief is a solitary process." —Julie Mussché, spiritual development counselor

We know not everyone going through a pregnancy loss has a partner or is in a heterosexual relationship, and we have entries for you.

Please see:

- When you don't have a partner
- Thoughts for LGBTQ+ couples

Huong

There is a term for the disconnect between partners that can happen after pregnancy loss—**incongruent grief.** Researchers attribute this to "the significantly earlier and more intense attachment to the unborn baby by the expectant mother compared with the prospective father. While attempting to be supportive, husbands sometimes betray impatience and irritation over their wives' prolonged grieving. Fathers wonder when and if their wives will ever 'get over it' . . . "

Sometimes, it helps my clients to know that this type of thing has been researched, that there is science to help understand what feels so strange and off-balance in their households.

Understanding your Other Half

They've got a lot going on too.

In retrospect, I didn't give much thought to my husband, Chris, in the midst of our losses. I was pretty consumed with myself and my own pain. When I did think of him, my thoughts were usually resentful. I was the one who felt like a train wreck (mentally and physically). I was the one who felt more of a connection to the babies, which he himself confirmed. At best, I was distracted and dismissive of him, and at worst, I was mean.

With time and distance (and therapy), I've come to see that Chris was struggling too—struggling with the losses, and struggling to support me. These are just a few of the things I've learned about what the other half goes through.

They probably feel helpless.

Chris is a classic fixer, and there is no easy "fix" to the grief that accompanies pregnancy loss (or any grief for that matter). Chris is like Captain Problem-Solver, so to have this problem (my pain) that he couldn't solve was very unsettling for him.

"Yeah, it wasn't fun for me to have to experience a problem that I couldn't help solve." —Chris (my husband)

What the studies tell us

Studies of the psychosocial effects of stillbirth on fathers show common themes:

- Grief suppression (avoidance)
- Employment difficulties and financial debt
- Increased substance abuse
  (*BMC Pregnancy Childbirth*, 2016)

Following a stillbirth, fathers "experienced significant levels of anxiety and posttraumatic stress disorder" (*The British Journal of Psychiatry*, 2018).

They probably need some direction.

A grief therapist we saw together suggested that I ask Chris explicitly for what I needed from him. She said that giving him something clear that he could do for me would help him feel more helpful. So, that night, as we sat on the couch watching something dumb on TV, I said, "Can you please put your hand on my leg?" I felt totally absurd giving such robotic instructions, but it worked. He felt less helpless, and I felt more supported.

"I really had no idea how to support you. Some days you seemed so upset, and I interpreted that my presence wasn't helping. When I'm upset about something, most of the time I just want some space, but that clearly isn't the best way to help you. When I created a little temporary distance between us, that seemed to make it worse." —Chris (my husband)

They probably feel sad (and scared) too.

I'll never forget how excited Chris was when he found out I was pregnant the first time. His eyes lit up. Instantly, he became a man on a mission: fatherhood. When the pregnancy turned out to be ectopic and I was rushed to surgery, he was terrified. Just as that experience stole some of my innocence and faith, it stole his too. With my subsequent pregnancies, I didn't see his eyes light up like they did that first time. He was scared. His mission had changed. He was no longer thinking so much about fatherhood; he was bracing for tragedy (and, sadly, we would have more of it).

"I felt like that had become my role—to be prepared for the next thing. I now knew how fragile pregnancy could be, and it was stressful to scrutinize every little thing along the way. I suppressed any daydreaming about my future as a dad and tempered my expectations." —Chris (my husband)

They probably feel the need to "stay strong."

When Hilaria Baldwin publicly shared her first miscarriage, her husband (Alec Baldwin) was quoted as saying, "My wife's happiness is my prime concern." Recently, I talked to Craig, husband of my friend, Jessica, who had a second-trimester miscarriage (and is quoted throughout this book). He echoed this same sentiment: "I think it probably takes time for men to come to terms with the loss, because they feel their first responsibility is to their wife."

When I pressed further, asking about how he "stuffed down" his own emotions, he made me aware that I had presented this "stuffing down" as a bad thing when, in his mind, it was necessary and beneficial for the relationship: "When a wife is at her most frail, does she want the man to be at his most vulnerable point as well? If so, will the relationship get stronger in the arms of empathy or drown in the sea of instability?"

"Similar to Craig, I thought that representing myself as a steady partner that could put aside my own needs would have a calming, comforting effect on you. I realize now that I was only punctuating the differences in how we were grieving and probably making you feel lonelier."—Chris (my husband)

Maybe he's right—maybe the relationship does benefit from one person "staying strong." But I think a dose of vulnerability is helpful too. I wanted to know Chris felt some of the pain I felt, that I wasn't alone. In general, though, I know that Chris, like many men, just doesn't feel comfortable with that vulnerability. As Craig told me: "From day one, we are told not to cry on the playground because it shows weakness. Repressing sad or fearful emotions has been instilled in us from the earliest age. We consider ourselves strongest when we can show our protective abilities and overcome our fears and sadness."

"We are also battered by the waves of emotion that come with loss, but we are meant to be the rock, steadfast and unflinching too—the strong silent type."
—Keyan Milanian, journalist who suffered five miscarriages with his wife, Amy Swales

They probably feel lonely.

In 2015, Mark Zuckerberg wrote on Facebook about the three miscarriages he and his wife (Priscilla Chang) had suffered: "You start making plans, and then they're gone. It's a lonely experience." I'm embarrassed to say it was a lightbulb moment for me, like *Oh, men are hurting too?!*

I'm guessing Chris felt lonely during our losses because he'd lost me, or at least the version of me he'd known. I was in Grief Land, and I guess he was, too, but his seemed miles away from mine.

"The rules of pregnancy seem designed to maximize the feeling of male helplessness . . . It feels a little like walking a mile standing right alongside someone who's trying to carry a mattress by themselves. It's not that it's so heavy. And you know they're capable of it. But it's unwieldy and awkward, and frickin' hard. And it sure would be easier if you were allowed to take the other end and help a little. But you can't." —Danny Schmidt, "Miscarriage: We Need a Better Word," StillStandingMag.com

They probably feel like your punching bag.

In the midst of my second loss (my seemingly never-ending miscarriage), I told Chris to pick up a couple pregnancy tests at the Dollar Store so I could see if I was still registering as pregnant. I was hopeful that my pregnancy hormones had dropped enough to not register. Spoiler alert: they hadn't. It would take another week or so of bleeding and waiting.

Because Chris is a man and is not good with purchasing instructions, he bought two expensive tests at the grocery store. I was furious with him.

"Why did you spend thirty dollars on tests for a failed baby?" I yelled at him.

"I remember this, going to the store for those tests. Again, I thought I was helping, and I screwed up. Or that's how it felt." —Chris (my husband)

My anger was way out of proportion and obviously represented so much more than the stupid pregnancy tests. I was angry at the fact that it was my body having to go through this. I was angry at his aloofness. I was angry at how "fine" he seemed. And I lashed out. A lot. He didn't fight back. I think he accepted himself as the receptacle for all my rage because he knew someone had to fill that role. This, I see now, is real love.

"'Shall I get you a cup of tea?' Tom asked, at a loss. He was a practical man: give him a sensitive technical instrument, and he could maintain it; something broken, and he could mend it, meditatively, efficiently. But confronted with his grieving wife, he felt useless."—ML Stedman, *The Light Between Oceans* (in this novel, the main characters, Tom and Isabel, suffer two miscarriages and a stillbirth)

That said, I don't think it's OK that I treated him the way I did. I wish I'd had more presence of mind to see my actions for what they were, to explain them to him, to apologize when necessary. I've explained and apologized since (and he has done the same, for his own moments of being less than his best self). Grief is just hard on a couple. It's a bitch.

"We went to our separate corners for a while. You're my one constant, I lean on you a lot, and that became a lot more apparent to me through this experience. I wondered if things would ever be the same."
—Chris (my husband)

"A partner could exhibit a more anxious presentation, or it could be a more withdrawn presentation. It's 'I have to be strong for my partner. I shouldn't show my feelings.' All the while, internally, they're really struggling and maybe not even recognizing it . . .

There's such a focus on mom and baby, but we're trying to be more inclusive. Everyone who is taking care of someone needs to be taking care of themselves, too." —Dr. Shara Brofman, licensed clinical psychologist, to *Washington Post*

"Christopher just seemed stupid, and I watched for him to make mistakes. His only one was in not being able to lose as much as I had, and I was mean and raw and didn't feel the generous arc of love, the wish to protect him."

—Susanna Sonnenberg, "Twins," featured in *About What Was Lost: 20 Writers on Miscarriage, Healing, and Hope* (Jessica Berger Gross, editor)

Can my relationship
survive this?

*The better question: Do I want my
relationship to survive this?*

I really was not sure how our marriage would stay intact after so much loss. I was just so *angry* at Chris—angry that he didn't appear to share my pain, angry that he couldn't just sit with me and cry, angry that he was able to just go about his life as if nothing had happened. He was angry with me too—angry that I couldn't "get it together," angry that I was "dwelling," angry that I couldn't seem to move forward and be happy with our life together, as I'd been before we ventured into trying to have a family.

"It kind of shook us both and took us into a place that was really dark and difficult." —Mariah Carey, on the loss of her first pregnancy with husband Nick Cannon

It's a lot on a couple—loss, grief. It was only recently that Chris and I talked formally about how we'd grieved, separately while together. He said, "What should I have done differently?" and I said, "Nothing. You had to do exactly what you had to do." What we could have done differently, as a couple, was respect each other's ways of grieving, instead of stewing in resentment, frustrated with the other person for not doing it our way. We could have been more compassionate with each other and with ourselves. Grief is the ultimate "the only way out is through" experience; it would have helped to accept it instead of fighting it (and each other) every step of the way.

Survival strategies for couples

Here is what worked for us:

- We shared our resentments and frustrations—not always eloquently, and sometimes only in the presence of a therapist.
- Oh yes, we saw a therapist, and I highly recommend this, even if your husband hates it as much as mine did (and still does!).
- I did a lot of research into how people grieve differently in an attempt to have compassion for my husband's approach.
- Once I realized I was being kind of self-absorbed (understandably, I might add), I tried to put myself in my husband's shoes to understand why he was frustrated with my way of grieving. Then I articulated for him what was probably in his own head but he didn't want to say, like "I know it bothers you when I cry, but . . ."
- I did my best to remember that this loss happened to both of us, even though it often felt like it just happened to me.
- My husband kept reminding me of the big picture. He does not get stuck in the present—for better or worse. He sees everything as a phase. When I dared to express worry about our marriage, he countered those worries.
- I focused on forgiveness. People are not their best selves when grieving. Stress is hard for any couple, and grieving is very stressful. I tried to remember that we are human, doing the best we can.

Now, years later, I can say that what my husband and I went through made us stronger as a couple. I know that sounds cliché, and you may be rolling your eyes, but it's the truth. It's been liberating for us to see what we are capable of surviving together. It's given us a confidence in our relationship. That has helped me cope with the sense of vulnerability to tragedy that came up for me after our losses.

"After all those miscarriages . . . I never felt like we'd just lost a baby. I always felt like we'd lost a little piece of our marriage too." —Hannah Beckerman, *If Only I Could Tell You* (in this novel, the characters of Daniel and Lily endure multiple miscarriages)

A partnership is perhaps the most intimate way you get to know yourself. It holds up a perpetual mirror for both of you. After a trauma you will each be shaken in different ways. You've each suffered a loss. But what that loss means to you, and how you suffer and grieve it, will be inherently different.

This difference can be a scary prospect, especially when you both want and need each other for support. Research shows that miscarriage is hard on relationships whether you're married or not. Fathers, and likely any partner who views it as their responsibility to provide emotional support for their partner and family, are often inclined to keep feelings to themselves. But by pushing away grief and suppressing it, they inadvertently risk other issues like anxiety and depression.

"We were determined to not lose each other in our grief. That required learning to respect our different processes and give each other the space to weather our own storms. It was not easy."

—Mattie J. Bekink, "The Promise," featured in *Modern Loss: Candid Conversations about Grief. Beginners Welcome.* (Rebecca Soffer and Gabrielle Birkner, editors)

Learning ways to talk, and not only about the loss, can help strengthen or, perhaps, rebuild your relationship.

This might mean re-learning how to share *and* listen without trying to fix a problem, at least not in that very moment. The goal is to regain closeness, and that is done little by little—sometimes quickly, sometimes slowly. The act of sharing when you are afraid to, listening when it's hard to, and finding room for both people to get at least some of what they need takes courage. You will feel vulnerable. Struggling and watching your partner struggle is not easy. But your willingness to be vulnerable will pay off as you regain trust in your partner and yourself.

So much about good communication comes down to empathy—being open and trying your best to understand what your partner is feeling. Imagine what it must be like to be in their shoes. Empathy is about tolerance, kindness, and remaining present (as opposed to cutting off). It's about choosing your words carefully to convey a willingness to be present and knowing that healing and becoming closer than you ever were is possible—all of which mean good news for the life of a relationship.

The F Word: Forgiveness

The word *forgiveness* has a lot of baggage. When you've been hurt, you may wish you could let that slight or that betrayal go. But the harder you try, the more it bothers you.

Forgiving does not mean forgetting how your partner behaved, or even the effects of the pain, but it can allow you to remember the incident without being at the mercy of your own anger, pain, or anxiety about it.

If you are having a hard time forgiving but wish you could find a way to begin to let go, try to think in terms of acceptance instead. In other words, accept that the incident happened, the relationship happened, the pain happened. Make that your focus instead of forgiveness. It might be too early to think about letting go, and that is OK.

Acceptance (like forgiveness) doesn't mean you have to like, love, want, or approve of what your partner did or said, but it does signal (to yourself) that you acknowledge that it happened. By acknowledging it, you become open to healing from it rather than solely reacting to it.

Huong

According to psychologists Drs. John and Julie Gottman, creators of the Gottman method of couple's therapy, there is a magical "six hours a week" together to promote closeness and bonding. These six hours include partings (e.g., asking about what is happening in your partner's day before saying goodbye), reunions (e.g., sharing a hug or kiss that lasts at least six seconds upon arrival at home), showing appreciation and admiration (e.g., trying to notice the small things your partner does that you appreciate), affection (e.g., embracing each other before falling asleep), date night once a week (complete with open-ended questions), and a state of the union meeting (one hour per week to discuss any areas of concern). However, for those who need to work up to the magical six hours, I encourage them to consider starting with rituals first.

After a trauma, a couple can experience disconnection and isolation within their relationship. It is important to be mindful of this potential rupture and to create opportunities for closeness and support. (The Gottman Institute and method also highlight the importance of rituals as a way of increasing connection in a relationship. These are called rituals of connection).

Rituals create a sense of safety because they are planned and expected, and that structure is needed following an unexpected loss and trauma. So, for example, if a couple wanted to develop a ritual in response to the pregnancy loss, it could be journaling together once a week, writing short messages to their unborn child, or reading a chapter of a book on pregnancy loss. Other rituals for connection that do not directly involve the pregnancy loss but that could foster reconnection could include setting aside five minutes to have coffee together in the morning, or going for a short walk in the evening after dinner.

Therapy for couples

EFT: Emotional Focused Therapy (EFT) is a short-term form of therapy that focuses on adult relationships and attachment/bonding. The therapist and clients look at patterns in the relationship and take steps to create a more secure bond and develop more trust to move the relationship in a healthier, more positive direction.

The Gottman Method: This method is derived from research and practice with more than three thousand couples of all types and can be applied at any stage of life to restore healthy functioning to distressed couples, whether stuck in chronic conflict or engaging in other destructive patterns. Therapy is based on a couple's patterns of interacting, and partners learn and implement relationship-building and problem-solving skills together.

Another strategy to foster connection and intimacy is by understanding each other's love languages. According to Dr. Gary Chapman, author of the book *The Five Love Languages*, there are five different love languages:

1. Physical Touch
2. Receiving Gifts
3. Words of Affirmation
4. Quality Time
5. Acts of Service

Perhaps you and your partner share the same top two love languages. Hooray! Perhaps it is easy to demonstrate love if you both love quality time sitting on the couch and cuddling (physical touch). However, what if you and your partner do not have the same love languages? Was there tension before the pregnancy loss? Is it common for you to wonder, "Does my partner really love me?"

"I do not believe a child loss is what causes divorce; I believe judgment of each other's grief causes divorce." —David Kessler, "Unlocking Us" podcast with Brené Brown

---

Your love languages were most likely expressed and solidified before a pregnancy loss, but the differences may be more acutely painful following a pregnancy loss. For example, one female client shared with me her frustration that her top love language is "words of affirmation" whereas her partner's top love language is "acts of service." Although she rationally knows that her partner is demonstrating love when he washes the dishes and takes out the trash, it is still painful not to hear any words of affirmation, especially following a pregnancy loss.

> **What the studies tell us**
>
> According to a study that followed 7,700 pregnant couples for 15 years:
>
> - Those who experienced miscarriage were *22 percent* more likely to break up than couples who hadn't.
> - The percentage was even higher for couples who experienced stillbirth.
> - Most couples who broke up did so within one-and-a-half to three years after losing a baby.
> - The increased risk of divorce and separation could still be seen up to a decade after the loss.
>
> *(Pediatrics, 2010)*

I encourage my clients to be direct in their needs but also to temper their expectations. Often following a pregnancy loss, each partner is trying to cope and will naturally tend to gravitate toward their strengths and the things they are already doing well in the relationship.

Chapman also co-authored a book with Candy McVicar, a grieving mother who leads a support group for grieving parents. That book, *The Five Love Languages for Grieving Parents: Holding on to Love After You've Lost a Baby,* highlights the complex feelings that come from the grief process, how to understand your partner's unique grieving needs, and how to support them and use the five love languages through grief.

Intimacy after a loss

Yes, I'm talking about sex.

Since we had decided we wanted a family, sex had been about procreation more than recreation. It took on this grand purpose. Having sex after a loss just reminded me of that. On a deeper level, I had come to equate sex with loss.

I assume there are some women who crave sex after a loss. They want the closeness, the comfort. I was not one of these women. I was so drained emotionally and physically after each of my losses that I just had no interest in sex. Like, at all.

I'm sure there were hormonal changes going on to explain some of my disinterest. But it was more than that. For a while after each loss, I didn't want to get pregnant again. I was afraid. That fear translated to complete refusal to have sex. And that translated to distance between Chris and I during a time when we already felt distant from each other.

"To me, sex is a good indicator that our relationship is generally on track. The longer it went on, the more palpable that void became and the more insecure I felt. There aren't too many better ways to put me in a bad mood than by making me feel like I'm failing or inadequate." —Chris (my husband)

I'm guessing most men would be frustrated by a sex strike. Chris is not the kind of guy to push this issue; he was very patient and respectful. But I know he missed me. Many men see sex as a source of support and relief. And I was denying him that.

I don't really know the answer to this. So much of grieving together is about accepting each other's differences. Coming back together (emotionally and sexually) takes a lot of patience and persistence. Eventually, we settled back into each other, but it felt uncomfortable at first. I'd be lying if I said it didn't.

" . . . there was nothing I wanted less than to be touched or even looked at. I refused to accept his back rubs. Occasionally, we held hands. Some find affection to be therapeutic; human touch made me feel nauseated. Grief is rude and relentless." —Mira Ptacin, "How to Stay Married After Losing a Baby," the *New York Times*

Meredith

While established research can tell you when it is physically safe to return to sex after a pregnancy loss, there is no such data that points to when you will be emotionally ready to resume sex again.

The physical toll of miscarriage can leave your body fragile even if you are healthy and well. This extends to your emotional readiness to return to sex too. Even thinking about sex may trigger acute sadness for the pregnancy you lost, and your desire to protect yourself from the renewal of pain will kick in. This explains why returning to sex may be difficult.

"Miscarriage does a number on your sex life. For men it was, 'When can I go back to her? I miss her.' For women, it was, 'If I never have sex again, I'll die a happy woman." —Kristen M. Swanson, RN, PhD, dean of the College of Nursing at Seattle University

Huong

In my work with both heterosexual and gay couples, intimacy after loss is often a tenuous topic to broach. It should be noted that the definition of intimacy for some couples could also include non-sexual touching or non-penetrative intercourse. Therefore, a couple can begin to develop emotional intimacy and some light physical intimacy before engaging in sexual intercourse after a loss.

There is often the misconception that the non-gestational partner is pressuring the gestational partner into sex and intimacy following pregnancy loss. However, in some cases, it is the gestational partner who is more ready following a loss.

What the studies tell us

- 32 percent of women felt more distant from their husbands interpersonally one year post-miscarriage.
- 39 percent of women felt more distant sexually.
  (*Psychosomatic Medicine*, 2003)

According to psychologist and reproductive health specialist Dr. Jessica Zucker, there is no "one size fits all answer" to the question of returning to sex after a miscarriage. Zucker described one client who was ready to have sex after a stillbirth right away, because that was her way of "reclaiming" her body and feeling "in control." However, in my practice, I have seen some women who are feeling "too raw and vulnerable" to engage in sex. Many feel disconnected from their bodies. One client described it as, "It feels wrong to feel pleasure out of a body part that just expelled my child."

For some non-gestational partners, they have described feeling "disconnected" following a pregnancy loss. One partner stated, "I feel like my wife isn't really there with me. Her body is there but her mind is elsewhere. I feel like she's worried about so many things, and it's hard to feel into it when she gets that way." On the other hand, some couples report experiencing increased intimacy and closeness after re-engaging in sex.

In addition to negotiating feelings around sex itself, the couple needs to discuss if they will use any contraception, especially if the goal is to try to avoid pregnancy again. Also, it may be helpful to have a conversation about positions due to any potential pain or emotional triggers, and it may be helpful to discuss that some tears may be shed during the first few sexual encounters. Lastly, *the focus should be on connection instead of reaching orgasm.*

My main recommendation for couples is to communicate their needs, desires, and expectations for re-engaging in penetrative sex. Some couples are hesitant to have these types of conversations because they believe it "kills the mood," but some couples later report that while the conversation was hard to initiate, it allowed for vulnerability, openness, and closeness, which created the perfect environment for mental and physical foreplay.

Kristen M. Swanson, RN, PhD, dean of the College of Nursing at Seattle University, "advises couples to consciously separate 'sex for fun and sex for function.' The first is to enjoy being intimate; the second is with the plan of becoming pregnant." —Elizabeth Leis-Newman, "Miscarriage and Loss," American Psychological Association

When your partner can't give you the support you need

Getting outside support helped my marriage, not hurt it.

I've always rolled my eyes at women who say things (usually on social media) like, "My husband is my best friend, my partner in crime, my lover, my everything." I've never liked the idea of this one person being "everything." I have rich friendships with women that my husband will never be able to compete with. Within those friendships, I have friends who are good for deep discussions of life's meaning and others who are good for gossip and laughter (and wine). My sister, my parents—those relationships are so unique, so specific, so full of a kind of love that doesn't compare to any other. To me, this collection of people is "my everything."

Meredith: "My husband is my everything" is one of those double-edged-sword kind of statements. It is wonderful to feel so close to your beloved. Yet there is a fine line between being dependent versus interdependent. The former is akin to "two halves make a whole"; the latter is more about two wholes make a better partnership.

Of course, it's not so much about competition but about friends enriching our lives. Studies have found that friendships are not only enriching and meaningful, but they promote wellness and help us live longer.

When it became obvious to me, right after our first loss, that Chris and I were grieving very differently, I started to turn to friends and family (my mom and sister, specifically) for emotional support. My therapist encouraged me to appreciate the ways Chris was supporting me (for example, he was keeping our day-to-day life running smoothly, cleaning obsessively, trying to maintain some sense of order in our chaos). I was disappointed that we weren't connecting as well emotionally, but grief is a very personal thing, and I came to accept (slowly) that we were just . . . different.

Meredith: In many relationships, opposites do attract. And even if you and your partner share similar personality traits, you are separate human beings with different pasts, perspectives, and needs (see "Grieving differently").

Seeking support outside of Chris wasn't giving up on our marriage; it was taking pressure off our marriage. Once I got that support, my anger at Chris diminished. My needs were met—not always by him, but they were met. And that saved us. The tension in our house dissipated. The whole experience gave me a clearer understanding of what is in his wheelhouse (and what is not) as my partner. Do I wish he was more of an emotional guy? Sometimes. But I know if he was, he would probably be lacking in some other area. I love him for who he is, and I know full well that there will be times throughout our life together when I will need the support of others. In a way, I'm grateful that I figured this out early in our marriage. It's shifted what we expect from each other and clarified what we need. Loss has a tendency to do that—shift, clarify.

Meredith: To think that any one person can meet all of your needs puts severe limitations on you and that one person. You would have to taper your interests, and so would they, to ensure you "align" on everything. Nobody wants (or needs) that!

When you don't have a partner

It might be lonely. Or liberating. Or both.

When you lose a pregnancy but don't have a partner, you will likely have the space to grieve in your own way without needing to mind the feelings of another person. This is more common if you've used a sperm donor to become pregnant or adopted embryos on your own. There is an expansiveness you might cherish, an attunement to your own mourning, with no interruptions, so to speak, from someone else. That is one of the benefits.

Kim: I know this is awful, and I'm cringing as I'm about to type it, but there were many times during grieving when I thought, *This would be so much easier if Chris just wasn't here.* I daydreamed about renting a little condo by the beach for myself, just so I could get away from the tension in our house (a tension born of the differences in our grieving styles). Sorting through my own feelings after our losses was a full-time job. Sometimes it felt overwhelming to also have to deal with our relationship (the disconnect, the disappointments, the distance).

Or, you may wish you had someone to share your pain with, someone who wanted this baby as much as you did. You may feel more or less alone in this, despite your independence and ability to manage by yourself. Yes, your life is still good. And perhaps you prefer it to be solo despite the pain you feel today, but it's important to be mindful not to misinterpret independence for isolation. Keep close the family and friends you trust.

If a relationship with the person you thought was going to co-parent has ended, for whatever reason, the breakup can echo and therefore accentuate the loss of your pregnancy. Even if you're the one who broke it off, it can still trigger feelings of abandonment. The loss of a pregnancy, or the stillbirth of a baby, can exacerbate the pain of being left and feeling alone (again, even if you were the one who ended it).

Recognize that not having a partner carries its own unique characteristics as you mourn. These are not better or worse than having a partner, but they will be different.

Kim: There is a blogger I follow whose boyfriend left her during her pregnancy with their son. So, while dealing with all the usual postpartum stuff (hormones, sleep deprivation, emotions on high), she was also dealing with grief over the loss of her relationship. When I heard this story, I was grateful that her son was healthy. I thought about how hard it would have been if her pregnancy had had complications, or if she had lost the baby. Then what? Would she have blamed the loss on the stress of the breakup? How would she separate the grief of the breakup from the grief of losing her baby? Does one have to separate these? How do you recover when it's all mixed together, one big grief stew?

Even though Chris drove me crazy at times while we were grieving, I was always grateful for the stability and security of having him. I feared for our marriage at times, but I knew on some level that we would survive. That confidence in our togetherness allowed me the space to grieve how I needed to, ugly tears and all.

Thoughts for LGBTQ+ couples

*So much of loss is universal, but there
are some things to consider if you identify
as part of the LGBTQ+ community.*

Witnessing and honoring the loss of another is one way we can help grievers
make sense of their pain. However, when it come to queer losses, there is
much silence around the experience. In "Queering Reproductive Loss:
Exploring Grief and Memorialization," Elizabeth Peel and Christa Craven
explore the extent of such silence: "Queer losses are often overlooked (or
perhaps avoided) in most academic and popular books on LGBTQ+ reproduction, and queer experiences remain absent from most self-help books
on recovering from reproductive loss." Furthermore, lack of support before
the pregnancy loss and subsequent lack of support after the pregnancy loss
may compound and complicate grief and pain. I mentioned earlier that in
my practice, I use a concept called intersectionality to look at each person's
multiple identities and how they overlap. The overlap (for example, "I am a
lesbian" and "I was raised Catholic" and "I lost a baby") can create additional
layers of grief and trauma.

A pregnancy loss is especially compounded when family and friends have
not been supportive and when they even try to justify the loss with a religious slant: "This wasn't natural. This isn't what [insert God or other religious figure] intended." A pregnancy loss often triggers shame in women,
which may unleash any history of previous trauma and shame due to their
sexual orientation and gender identity. They may have thoughts like, "Maybe
I lost this baby because I'm in an 'unnatural' relationship." While the most
common grief responses cut across all gender identities and sexual orientations, it can be especially painful for a queer couple due to their "place" and

"designation" in society.

For some couples, having a child was either consciously or subconsciously an entryway to be included and accepted as a "family unit" and to belong to the "parent club." Some couples tell me that pregnancy loss alienates and isolates them even further.

Lesbian Couples

For some lesbian couples that experience pregnancy loss, numerous other factors may complicate their grieving process. Some of my clients tell me they had to "jump through more hoops" to get pregnant, and so the pain is exponential. These can include physical, emotional, and financial hoops, which make the grief process harder since pregnancy requires *much* dialogue and planning (often much more than for heterosexual couples).

Lesbian couples will have to consider who will carry the child, where they will obtain sperm (whether from a friend, a sperm bank, a family member), the costs of IVF and other medical bills, the physical pain of injecting oneself with hormones and undergoing painful procedures, potentially dealing with ignorant medical providers who do not allow the same-sex partner into the room and make derogatory/hetero-normative comments (like "Where is your husband?"), and parental leave concerns (some companies do not offer maternal leave to the non-gestational partner).

Heather Love cautions in *Feeling Backward* that queer losses are frequently hard to identify or mourn since many aspects of historical gay culture are associated with the pain and shame of being in the closet and hidden away from the public eye. The subject of reproductive loss—the personal, and sometimes communal, experiences of miscarriage, infant death, and failed adoptions—has often been a silent burden for LGBTQ+ parents, one frequently intensified by fears of homophobia and heterosexism.

Furthermore, lesbian couples may encounter difficulty with the medical community who may not understand their loss or also have their own biases and judgments about a lesbian couple and pregnancy loss. The discrimination and lack of understanding may be less pervasive in big cities and more informed communities. However, in smaller rural towns, this is a big concern in that medical providers are not trained in working with the LGBTQ+ community and even small comments like "Where is your husband?" can be triggering for someone (especially during a tense period such as pregnancy loss). I have even heard stories of medical providers not allowing the non-gestational partner into the room to say goodbye to the fetus/baby.

Unfortunately, even for those who did not feel they experienced homophobia during their loss, their *fear* of homophobia frequently kept them from accessing resources such as local loss support groups, which other researchers have shown to be helpful to many heterosexual couples.

In 2007, Danuta Wojnar published the first empirical study on lesbian couples' experiences of pregnancy loss. This small qualitative study drew on interviews with ten white lesbian couples in the United States, all of whom had planned their pregnancies. (She notes that about 50 percent of heterosexuals' pregnancies are unplanned.) Wojnar found that, unlike some heterosexual mothers, lesbian mothers frequently bonded with their unborn child early in pregnancy.

Joanne Cacciatore and Zulma Raffo later published a study on "same-gender (homosexual) bereaved parents" in the journal *Social Work* in 2011. Through interviews with six white lesbian parents, they explore the intersection of what they term "stigmatized relationships" and "stigmatized deaths." Bereaved lesbian mothers experience a double disenfranchisement; not only do they experience a dearth of support for their experiences with loss, but they may also avoid support services that require them to explain or justify their family. For all six participants, the authors noted that "ritual and remembrance—including things from hand molds to memorial services—appeared to play a key role in the integration of loss [into their lives as the 'new normal']."

The limited research on lesbian and bisexual women's experiences with pregnancy loss is overshadowed by the lack of research on pregnancy loss for gay and bisexual men pursuing adoption or surrogacy, or the pregnancy losses of transgender and other queer parents. The minimal resources available offer little support for grieving pregnancy losses, nor memorializing these experiences in ways that acknowledge and support queer identities and communities.

The importance of memorializing loss is even more important in the LGBTQ+ community because historically, "so much of our experiences get invisibilized" (as stated by one individual in "Queering Reproductive Loss: Exploring Grief and Memorialization" by Elizabeth Peel and Christa Craven). One lesbian female said, "There are ways in which the queer community has had to find ways to make our experiences valid or to ritualize things or to make them just as important as straight experiences."

Partner Pain

In lesbian couples, it is common for the non-gestational partner to feel guilty that she did not carry the baby. There are also situations where each partner takes turns having a child, and therefore it is even more painful if one partner had a full-term pregnancy and the other experienced a pregnancy loss.

There is also the added misbelief that if one female partner experiences a pregnancy loss then the other female partner can "take over," as if they are passing a baton between the two of them in a relay race. This may not be feasible for many reasons—medical or psychological reasons, or gender identity reasons (for example, the partner could be an assigned female at birth but identifies as trans masculine).

In terms of how the couple handles the pregnancy loss, Wojnar has found that the non-gestational partner has a similar response to a man in a heterosexual partnership following the miscarriage. "The response tends to be, 'I lost her and I don't know how to get her back,'" says Dr. Kristen Swanson, dean of the college of nursing at Seattle University.

I also see these reactions in my practice for the non-gestational partner. No matter how they identify on the gender identity spectrum, there is a sense that they are "pushed away" following a pregnancy loss due to the gestational partner believing that the non-gestational partner cannot share in the same level of grief because they were not carrying the baby. There is a sense in the non-gestational partner of hopelessness and frustration ("I don't know what to say or do" and "Everything I seem to say or do is wrong") and also potential underlying guilt that is hard to admit ("I didn't carry the baby so the impact is less for me" or "I can't feel as much as my partner because I wasn't the one carrying the baby").

Non-gestational parents (eg, gay parents, two male-identified individuals) and pregnancy loss for a surrogate

For some gay couples who work with a surrogate to achieve their goal of a family, there may already be a sense of distance from their surrogate. Therefore, what is the experience of loss like for them? For some clients, they noted feeling isolated in their grief, especially as non-gestational parents. Also, they felt that their losses and grief were not acknowledged. Furthermore, some gay couples feel pressured to try surrogacy or reproductive technology again without having time to grieve.

According to the Australian Psychological Society's Information Sheet on LGBT pregnancy loss, "The difficulties of conceiving (e.g., via donor sperm, surrogacy arrangement) mean that a significant amount of planning, hope, anticipation, negotiation, time, and money is likely to have gone into conceiving, which raises the stakes of the pregnancy, and can create multiple losses if the pregnancy is lost."

"You try to trick yourself into not getting excited because you know anything can happen at any time . . . You keep telling yourself that and trying not to get your hopes up, but you're always going to have those thoughts in the back of your brain where you're already planning out their lives."

—Lance Bass, singer, after suffering multiple miscarriages via surrogate

Transgender Parents

Transgender is an umbrella term for individuals who do not identify with their assigned sex at birth (ASAB). A transgender man is a person who identifies as male but whose sex may have been designated female at birth. As such, transgender (trans) men are commonly born with reproductive anatomy that allows them to become pregnant and give birth. In a landmark Australian 2018 study, researchers interviewed twenty-five transgender men about their experiences with pregnancy. The overarching themes were of loneliness and acknowledgement of the difficulty in choosing to become parents in a world that was designed to exclude them. This study aside, there continues to be a lack of research on the experiences of pregnancy loss in transgender men.

Justin Brandt, an assistant clinical professor in the Department of Obstetrics, Gynecology and Reproductive Sciences at Rutgers Robert Wood Johnson Medical School, is another pioneer in the transgender male pregnancy world. His study examined health-care research on transgender men who become pregnant at or after age thirty-five to determine their medical and mental health needs. He stated, "Despite the increased visibility of transgender people—there are about 1.4 million who have transitioned in the United States—medical providers are largely unprepared to care for them and most have had limited educational opportunities."

According to the largest survey of transgender folks published by the National Center for Transgender Equality in 2015, nearly 40 percent of its twenty-eight thousand respondents reported attempting suicide, which is nearly nine times the national average. That risk can be increased in transgender men with the unwanted physical changes resulting from pregnancy, according to Brandt. He stated, "The process of transitioning is long and arduous, and pregnancy, which is regarded as a feminine condition, forces these men to almost fully transition back to their sex assigned at birth, which can worsen gender dysphoria." Overall, transgender men who become pregnant are at increased risk for depression and experience difficulty getting medical care due to a lack of knowledge among health-care providers, a Rutgers study reports.

In general, there is a lack of peer-reviewed research on pregnancy loss among transgender males. One small study of transgender men and gender-variant gestational parents (that is, people who bear a child) found that a miscarriage was "emotionally devastating." Pregnancy loss may be specifically distressing and isolating for transgender men and gender-variant people, given that pregnancy is typically associated with cis-gender women. It has also been suggested that men and gender-variant people who undertake pregnancies may view the pregnancy as giving a "purpose" to their reproductive organs, and that pregnancy loss can further contribute to a sense of unhappiness or dysphoria about specific body parts.

In some ways, though, transgender men and gender-variant people may feel that losing a pregnancy connects them to something bigger. Hazel Pickett, a transgender pregnant male, shared his experience of pregnancy loss with the Huffington Post: "It is a bond of pain that is born across all gender identities, connecting us in an understanding I wish we didn't have. Through this process, I found a community of love and acceptance, because it didn't matter how I identified."

Connecting with others

Joining the Pregnancy
Loss Club

There are so many of us here. Welcome.

As much as I wanted to hibernate after my losses (See "I just want to hide from the world"), I realized that there was so much support out there (and I didn't even need to leave my house to get it—bonus).

There are lots of bad things about the internet and social media, but there are pros too. Online forums and message boards allow you to talk in real time to others dealing with pregnancy loss. Facebook groups, Instagram communities, blogs, essays—it's all out there. You will quickly realize that you are not alone. And the others in the club are just as eager to connect as you are.

Meredith: The comfort you find in the community you discover may be unexpectedly huge, depending on how you describe the others you've met, connected with, and befriended. While these connections can't (nor could, should, or would) replace your baby, the connection to others who *already* understand, without the exchange of words, is nurturing and restorative to a sufferer. The exact details of their loss won't match yours, nor do they need to. It's the emotional resonance that matters.

As some time passed, I opened up on social media and began connecting with people, including friends who had suffered through their own losses in silence, friends of friends, and complete strangers. I met so many women, many of whom are quoted throughout this book. It goes without saying that it's terrible if you have to join the Pregnancy Loss Club, but the tiny consolation is that the club is full of so many smart, witty, hilarious, genuine, authentic, compassionate women. Those women made me feel understood. They validated my feelings. They made me laugh when I swore I'd never laugh again. They got it in a way that other people in my life (even my husband) did not get it.

Meredith: This is not the same as approval. They don't become your expert but rather a co-traveler on this part of the journey, helping you hold the pain. Validation is akin to being witnessed, and it is truly a gift. We know it when we receive it. There is nothing as valuable.

This isn't to say that you have to be Ms. Extrovert. I am EXTREMELY introverted. I need a lot of personal time to process things. I engaged with social media and browsed the internet just enough to feel some support, then I disconnected when it got to be too much. I also had to wait a good few weeks to even engage at all. It was all too raw at first. Everyone is different, obviously. You don't have to be the social butterfly of the club. You can be a silent member. Just know there are millions of others like you.

"... It really helped me when I had a miscarriage to talk to other women and hear that they'd been through it, too. It's one thing to hear the statistics but it's another to put faces to the numbers so you stop feeling like it's your fault. I think that's one of the reasons women don't tell people when they've had a miscarriage—they think it's their fault." —Ali Wong, comedian, in an interview with the *Guardian*

"Paradoxically in your aloneness you were actually in a community with women you couldn't see or hear but whose knowledge of loss lay as deep in their organs as their/your babies once did." —Shannon Gibney and Kao Kalia Yang, "Reclaiming Life," in *What God Is Honored Here? Writings on Miscarriage and Infant Loss by and for Native Women and Women of Color*

"I finally felt as though I had found my tribe ... All of us had had such different experiences, but all with the same final outcome: our babies weren't here." —Elle Wright, *Ask Me His Name: Learning to Live and Laugh Again After the Loss of My Baby*

"Sharing not only let me come to terms with what was real, but it also allowed me to connect with such healing support from so many women wanting to talk about their own miscarriages. We processed our losses together, realized we are not alone, and put this whole experience in the context of a life that is not always benevolent."

—Hilaria Baldwin, author/yoga instructor, "There's No Right Way to Deal with a Miscarriage," Glamour.com

Kim

Navigating social media

Appreciate the pros; be mindful of the cons.

After my second loss, I blocked all my Facebook "friends" who were pregnant or had babies. I instructed Facebook to "show me less posts like this" when I saw a photo of someone's toddler being cute in a way that only the parents could appreciate. I couldn't relate to the excitement of my peers. Their families, their lives, were just beginning while I kept dealing with loss.

There are pros to social media (connection, outreach, support), but there are lots of cons too. For me, social media was nice once some time had passed. But right after my losses, I couldn't handle it. There were pregnancies and babies everywhere—digital landmines, highlight reels that made me feel left out, envious, angry, and so depressed. Even posts that had nothing to do with pregnancies or babies still upset me. I just hated seeing how the world was moving on, how everyone seemed to have something to celebrate, or if they weren't celebrating something, their lives were simple enough that they had time to take photos of burritos and sunsets.

Pregnancy announcements were hardest of all for me. Shortly after my first loss, I was perusing Facebook when I saw an acquaintance announce her pregnancy at eight weeks. This annoyed me. I resented people who had the luxury of naïveté, the bliss of ignorance, no reason to believe anything could go wrong. I made the masochistic choice to read the long post that went along with the ultrasound image. In that post, this woman revealed that her and her husband had been drug addicts and met in rehab. She said, "This baby goes to show that if you work hard and pray, you will be rewarded."

I almost punched a hole through my computer screen.

Was she saying I didn't work hard enough or pray hard enough? Was she saying I was punished for a reason? I restrained myself from sending her

233

a message with that question. I knew she'd just reply with something about "God's plan," and I probably would punch that hole through my computer screen.

Posts like that *still* get to me, but I don't have the same angry response. Mostly, I lament how I never got to be that naïve, happy-go-lucky pregnant person. I grieve that opportunity.

"If you are in your thirties and a woman, you are going to be bombarded by anything baby-related, especially online. It can be overwhelming and make you wish you were back in the eighties, when you could get away with not knowing everyone was pregnant or people caring if you were or weren't."

—Michaela, after her first-trimester loss

"Even now (with two brilliant children of my own), I inwardly recoil from Facebook when a friend's scan photo of a twenty-week-old baby pops up."

—Georgie, who had a stillborn daughter (Ella) and two first-trimester miscarriages

When I was in my third trimester with my daughter, I decided to start sharing more of my story on social media. I had been wanting to, but I kept thinking that talking about it would jinx my current pregnancy. So I waited and waited, until I got to a point of realizing that I would never feel "ready," not in the sense of feeling confident I could share without bringing on more loss. I started to see that my belief in this idea of "jinxing" things was another attempt at control—*if I just don't talk about it, it won't happen again.* I had to accept that loss could always be around the corner, and I felt the need to share my story for others who had made their own turns and run smack into it.

Meredith

Social media has become its own character in stories of pregnancy, a character that's here to stay. It's kind of cool, but it has its associated burdens too. While news outlets report the news or tell a human-interest story based on a woman's experience, once the report is done, it's done. Or, it used to be that way. Not so with Facebook, Instagram, YouTube, or Twitter, as well as all those personal blogs. They are wonderful, and they can be fraught. Proceed with joy—and caution.

Suddenly, private conversations and photographs are public. Exchanges that might seem innocuous to you can become flashpoints, kicking up emotion out there that affects you, and not all of it will be supportive.

It can become an invasion of your privacy even if you did invite others to share.

What the studies tell us

An analysis of nearly 300,000 Twitter postings on miscarriages and preterm births showed that:

- Grief and annoyance were the most commonly expressed emotions within miscarriage self-disclosures.
- Miscarriage disclosures by celebrities led to disclosures by other women who had similar experiences.

(*Paediatric and Perinatal Epidemiology*, 2020)

More and more women are announcing miscarriage on Twitter, for example, and research finds that such a community can be useful in helping women feel less alone. That is good. However, it's important that you own your story first. This means processing your emotion, your pain, and the meaning you give it, in your time. Posting too soon can unwittingly give ownership to the collective voice versus the individual. It might be tempting to post, but in the long run, will you be ready for what anonymous readers will say? If you are, great. If not, hold off.

And more questions remain that only you can answer. Do you want to post every piece of your journey for readers to view and comment on before you've had a chance to own your story first? If you are going to process a private event in public, assume that everything you post publicly will live online forever. Prepare yourself for comments you don't like and that hurt. This adds another layer to an already complex process filled with issues of privacy and confidentiality.

So my advice would be this: Don't post before you've given yourself adequate time to feel grounded in your own story, suffering and all. If you post too soon, others' comments may be a constant source of distraction that may interfere with your healing.

A word about #blessed

I see #blessed a lot. People view #blessed, for themselves or others, in a range of ways. I've spoken to people who espouse varying interpretations. But when #blessed lands in your lap (or in your social media feed) following loss, when the last thing you are feeling is #blessed, it might help to unpack what you experience, suspect, and know and to validate how you feel.

What #blessed is used for

People use it to describe a state of being uncannily lucky or happy. To describe a state of grace or chosen-ness. To express that the belief they've chosen for themselves is the correct belief. To remind themselves to turn their lives over to a power greater than themselves. To illustrate belonging in a specific group that interprets things "correctly." To identify that they've been to hell and back and survived. As a humblebrag. As a placeholder for #morespecial. As a placeholder for #icannotbelievethisworkedout.

Bottom line: #blessed is a loaded synonym for any number of experiences people feel compelled to announce.

Why #blessed polarizes

The last thing anyone wants when they are down is the suggestion that they are #notblessed upon reading someone else's #blessed alert. Unfortunately, that is what #blessed can convey, especially when we are #vulnerable. I know, I know, we are not supposed to gauge our happiness against another's, or compare our insides to another's outsides. And while those are both true, the other truth is that we are human and thus, our depth is shaped by exploring these points of pain and navigating what they mean to each of us—to you, alone. So, when #blessed is trending in your orbit and you're feeling anything but, try to remind yourself that the meaning you place on #blessed is most important.

What #blessed means to you

#blessed may be something you once loved to post, but now it feels insufficient to describe this facet of life that is forcing a pressure on you to grow and dig deep. You may someday be thankful for this journey for how it changed and deepened you, but today? No.

Maybe it stings because you hold the belief that someone else (not you) did something right. Maybe you worry that there is a secret to their #blessedness and, well, you're not privy to it. Maybe someone told you that just because you're sad doesn't mean they can't be happy (not nice!).

How to think about #blessed to ease your suffering

- Understand that, on some level, you are also grieving the loss of the relationship you wanted to have with #blessed.
- Allow room inside yourself to honor the experience you are living; move as deeply as you can into your experience alone.
- Their #blessed bears no meaning on your experience, and your experience does not want to be summarized with a hashtag alone—nor does it deserve to be.
- Consider that your interpretation of #blessed is too narrow; you can find your own meaning for it, or not use it at all.
- Your reaction to this hashtag tells you something you didn't realize— that you need to separate yourself from the ghosts of social media that seem to "know" what pregnancy is about.

How friendships can change

*Mine did—some temporarily,
some permanently.*

It was as simple as this for me: my losses changed me in profound ways, and some of those changes affected my relationships with friends (and family members).

I had (and still have) a number of friends who are single or who have a partner but are childless (most by choice, a couple by circumstance). During my losses, I really felt like my single and childless-by-choice friends didn't "get it." In their defense, how could they get it? They had yet to set a foot on the path I was on, a path to motherhood (or so I hoped). They tried to console me, but I think the depth of my loss was hard for them to grasp. So I distanced myself.

I had a couple friends who were childless because they had suffered their own losses or were struggling with infertility. I became closer to these friends—confiding, sharing, commiserating, supporting, validating. I latched on to those who would help me feel less alone, those who would understand the complexity of my feelings. Many acquaintances became good friends (and remain so) because of the bond we created during that time. And I made brand new friends, mostly through social media.

I chose distance with friends and family members who were pregnant (See "Dealing with other people having babies"). It was just too hard for me. I felt resentful, then guilty for feeling resentful. I couldn't tolerate all that when I was in the initial stages of grieving.

I let go of many casual friendships that revolved around chitchat, gossip, and happy hours. I wasn't up for any of that, and they didn't seem up for going beneath the surface to find out how I was *really* doing.

In time, some friendships faded, but I circled back to most of the friends I'd pushed away. There didn't appear to be any animosity; all was forgiven or forgotten. There are so many phases in life, and I think true friends understand this.

Meredith

Even the most loyal of friendships cannot meet every need you have. True friendships will withstand periods of absence. Loss will challenge your deeply held ideas about what friends are, what they do, and how they should behave. In the process, you'll learn something about your own needs and tolerance levels. And, possibly, about what you've been putting up with that you no longer need to. You are allowed to draw boundaries around yourself and explore new relationships that nurture where you are today. A solid friend(ship) understands and wants this. New life that flows into an existing friendship can nourish and help the relationship between two people get richer and stronger, even after periods of being apart.

"I saw that there were two kinds of people: those who had come into contact with death and those who had been spared contact with death. Obviously it was only a matter of time until the latter joined the former, but in the meantime how clueless and shallow and silly the spared-contact-with-death seemed!" —Elisa Albert, "David," featured in *Modern Loss: Candid Conversations about Grief. Beginners Welcome.* (Rebecca Soffer and Gabrielle Birkner, editors)

Getting professional help

I needed it. You might too.

I hadn't been to see my therapist in several months when I experienced my first pregnancy loss. I still remember calling her, leaving her a voice mail. I remember my voice was shaky. I said something like, "I'm wondering if I can come in. Something kind of . . . traumatic . . . happened to me." Then I lost it, on her voice mail. I relayed quickly what had happened, so I didn't leave her hanging thinking up a hundred different horrific scenarios. When she called me back with several options for appointment times, I was so relieved. Just making the appointment made me feel better. I was partnering with someone to get through this, officially.

Therapy had been a part of my life for years before my losses, and I'm grateful for that. It was easy for me to ask for help because I had experience doing so. It would have been much harder if I'd never been to therapy and I was tasked with finding someone, figuring out cost and insurance, and everything else.

I have a few friends who have had miscarriages who said, "I probably needed a therapist, but I never got around to it." I understand this. Grieving is a full-time job. There are all kinds of barriers to therapy. *How do I find someone good? Can I afford it? How will it even help? My baby is gone, nothing can fix that. Do I even* need *therapy? I'll probably get over it on my own, right?*

These are overwhelming questions when you're already consumed with grief. I wish every OB-GYN had a handout with therapist contact information (and cost) at the ready for patients dealing with loss. Some do have this, so ask. Just asking for help in that way might feel like a proactive step, and taking that step may give you the boost you need to go online and find a therapist (if your doctor doesn't have referrals and you're left to your own devices).

If asking for help is difficult for you, then calling a therapist for the first time can seem daunting. Seeking professional help is not a sign of weakness or failure. It is a recognition of vulnerability which, by the way, is an asset, not a liability. Asking for help is not an indulgence; it's a necessity you give to yourself.

We know there is no one way to grieve, no exact way to frame a loss. A therapist can help you "hold" these feelings when they are most intense as you learn how to navigate the process and define what you need to do for you.

There are many different types of therapy, but one thing is clear—therapy should support your wellness and healing in *your* time, not anyone else's. This is what the term person-centered therapy means. Trauma-informed therapy takes a person-centered approach to help cope with trauma, meaning it is sensitive not only to the person's experience and perception of trauma, but what it means to them in their life, culture, religion, and faith.

Specialized approaches that can provide short-term relief from anxiety and stress and are used by some trauma-informed therapists include:

Evidence-based therapies
(requiring a mental health professional)

EMDR: Eye Movement Desensitization and Reprocessing (EMDR) is a psychotherapy treatment originally designed to alleviate the distress associated with traumatic memories. Among many other things, it can be used to help with anxiety, stress, fears, and resolving the distress due to past events.

CBT: Cognitive Behavioral Therapy (CBT) aims to help individuals better understand the thoughts and feelings that influence their behaviors. This involves looking closely at your thoughts and reframing them. CBT has been used to help with phobias, anxiety, depression, and addictions.

CPT: Cognitive Processing Therapy (CPT) uses elements of CBT to help people suffering from posttraumatic stress disorder (PTSD). The goal of CPT is to free clients of their "stuck points," which are conflicting beliefs or strong beliefs that create unpleasant emotions and problematic or unhealthy behavior after a traumatic event.

EFT: Emotional Freedom Technique (EFT) is a five-step technique that may be incorporated into your session to calm anxiety as your work through your pain. EFT is easy to learn and, with the guidance of a therapist, you can identify ways to use it when difficult emotions hit. It's been used to treat people with anxiety and PTSD. Some say it works in a similar fashion to acupuncture or acupressure, focusing on certain trigger points to relieve and release difficult feelings related to a past experience.

ACT: Acceptance Commitment Therapy (ACT) uses elements of CBT and mindfulness with the goals of 1) learning to stop avoiding, denying, and struggling with inner emotions and 2) accepting that these deeper feelings are appropriate responses to certain situations that should not prevent you from moving forward in your life.

MBSR: Mindfulness-Based Stress Reduction (MBSR) is an eight-week program that offers mindfulness training to assist with stress, anxiety, depression, and pain. It uses a combination of mindfulness meditation, body awareness, yoga, and exploring patterns of behaviors, thinking, feelings, and action.

MSC: Mindful Self-Compassion (MSC) is an offshoot of MBSR that combines the skills of mindfulness and self-compassion to produce a powerful tool for emotional resilience and healing. Research has shown that self-compassion greatly enhances emotional well-being and reduces anxiety and depression.

PE: Prolonged Exposure (PE) is a form of behavior therapy and CBT designed to treat PTSD. It is characterized by two main treatment procedures—imaginal and in-vivo exposures. Imaginal exposure is repeated, "on-purpose" retelling of the trauma memory, and in-vivo exposure is repeatedly confronting the situations and objects that cause distress but are not inherently dangerous.

Somatic therapy: This is a form of body-centered therapy that looks at the connection of mind and body and uses both traditional talk therapy and physical therapies (such as deep breathing and mindfulness) for holistic healing. The goal is to release the pent-up tension that is negatively affecting your physical and emotional well-being since the belief is that trauma has been lodged into the body.

TF-CBT: Trauma Focused-CBT (TF-CBT) is primarily targeted at children and adolescents, but it has been used with adults following a traumatic event. The treatment has core components of CBT with an overarching trauma framework including writing, processing, and developing a new trauma narrative.

Alternative and holistic therapies (requiring a trained mental health practitioner or certified specialist):

Reiki: The word Reiki is made of two Japanese words: *Rei*, which means "God's Wisdom or the Higher Power," and *Ki,* which is "life force energy." So Reiki is actually "spiritually guided life force energy." It involves using the hands either on the body or above it to help move the energy in the body. It has been used to treat PTSD, anxiety, and other issues.

Art therapy: Active art-making bypasses the need for words, especially at the beginning, and can be a powerful way to access deep feelings. An art therapist is specifically trained to use the creative process, applied psychological theory, and human experience within the session to help a person identify, understand, and process.

Therapeutic journaling: Journaling, something many of us do regularly, is actually used as a therapeutic modality for healing. Whether done via stream of consciousness, timed writing about a specific stressor, free writing with a prompt, or list-making, writing helps us develop resilience. Writing—the raw, unfiltered act of it—strengthens a connection to deeper dimensions of ourselves. In addition, research has found that the imaginative process set forth on the page has restorative effects akin to our body's innate ability to heal wounds.

Note: This is not a comprehensive list of all therapies available. Remember, proceed with caution with any practitioner who claims to be able to "cure" you with X number of sessions.

Huong

It can be overwhelming to find a therapist. The process can be daunting, including the fear of making the "wrong" choice. Even as a therapist, when it was time to find a new therapist for myself, I felt frustrated and lost.

One question to start with is, will you be going through insurance or paying out of pocket? If you go through insurance, you may be able to search their network online, or they can also provide you with a list of providers in your area.

I would encourage you to look at a therapist's Psychology Today profile or website and read about their training, credentialing, and treatment approach. The next step would be to call or email them to schedule a phone consultation (most offer a complimentary ten- to fifteen-minute phone consult) to see if it would be a good fit. Please don't be discouraged if you do not get a phone call or email back immediately. A lot of providers have solo practices and only return calls in between clients or on off days.

When you do get someone on the phone, ask them about their experience with pregnancy loss and also their approach to pregnancy loss. Listen carefully. Some of the simple questions you can ask yourself are, "Can I trust this person?" and "Do I believe this person can help me?"

As a mental health provider, I recognize that we have various levels of training and offer different types of interventions and styles. However, at the end of the day, research shows that the MOST important factor in the process of change in therapy is the therapeutic relationship between the therapist and the client. So look for someone you trust to guide you through this journey. And if it's not a good fit after the first session or two, please be direct with the provider and let them know how you are feeling. That way they can discuss any miscommunication issues or offer a referral to another therapist. There is a good fit for you out there.

Where to start

- If you plan on using insurance, visit your insurance provider's website to find help in your area.
- You can also visit PsychologyToday.com/us/therapists to find a therapist, psychiatrist, treatment center, or support group near you.
- Community counseling centers, which are typically nonprofit and funded with donations and grants, often offer sliding-scale fees.

Returning to "normal" life
(whatever that means)

Feeling disoriented

Wait, which way is up?

After my losses, I felt like I was walking around in a world turned upside down. For me, returning to "normal" life meant going back to work, resuming my gym routine, running errands, starting to socialize again. All of these things felt really unnatural, uncomfortable, and unsettling.

At work, I'd listen to drama surrounding particular projects (e.g., "the deadline got moved up! We need weekend work!"), or hear coworkers chitchatting about TV shows or sports scores, and it all seemed so . . . stupid. I could not relate (See "Going back to work"). I was walking around obsessed with things like, oh, MORTALITY, while others were debating where to go to lunch. Sometimes I wanted to scream: "How the hell are you people talking about the Kardashians when there are babies dying?" I knew I couldn't really judge them; I used to be them. But now my perspective had changed—abruptly, dramatically, permanently.

It was strange for me to see how the world just carried on, unaffected, unchanged. The same people came to the gym, wearing the same lame shirts that said things like "Namaste in bed." They smiled and said, "Haven't seen you in a while," then walked off. The cashiers at Trader Joe's were their usual pleasant selves, raving about the new chocolate-covered whatevers in the snack section. Friends laughed as heartily as ever. For me, with each loss, the world had stopped; going out in the world made me aware that for everyone else, it kept spinning. In the grand scheme, my losses did not seem to matter, and that was depressing.

I felt very lonely back in the "real world," grieving privately but in public. I felt kind of like a satellite, revolving around this other planet that I used to inhabit. I had a hard time feeling present, a hard time concentrating. It took me a while to feel like I had my bearings. And even now, I don't interact with the world in the same way I did before my losses. I don't get as caught up in drama as I used to; I don't sweat the small stuff. And if someone comes to the gym who I haven't seen in a while, I ask them if everything is OK.

Meredith

You have never been here before. The landscape is the same, and yet the eyes with which you see it, the lens you're looking through, is entirely different.

When I think of disorientation I think of reentry—finding yourself back in the same spot but with knowledge and experience that renders you different than before. It may feel like you don't belong or don't want to belong here. Many of the old rules no longer apply. The safety net and parameters you relied on are gone. Something new is taking their place, only none of that is certain yet. All this uncertainty is disorienting. And completely natural.

A source of comfort may be realizing that you have been here before, having acclimated to new emotional territory, but at different times in your life and under different circumstances. The uncertainty of those times probably feels now like a distant or forgotten past. That is because you learned something valuable from those experiences. And what you learned got absorbed. You need not think about it any longer because it's become part of you. This is what is called integration.

And it will happen again with this. It is happening now—as you read this, as you reflect, and as you wonder when you'll feel grounded in your old-yet-new life. This is part of the work. You are on your way.

"It took me several weeks to really plug back into normal life and work, as I still felt in a daze some of the time. All conversation felt forced (on my part) and like I was required to do meaningless 'small talk' with people, but that none of it really mattered." —Jessica, on her second-trimester loss

247

Triggers at every turn

It was like the universe was torturing me.

After my losses, I felt like I was walking around without skin. Everything hit a nerve. *Everything.* Here are just a few examples of things that triggered me.

My husband is a soccer coach. I'd go to his games and cry behind my sunglasses as I watched the kids play. My heart couldn't handle watching the kids who ran the wrong way on the field, the ones who kicked and missed completely. They made me think of Miles. Chris had said he would want his son to at least try soccer, and I'd joked that Miles would probably inherit my lack of coordination.

At the grocery store, I watched pregnant women sorting through apples, assessing for bruises, and I couldn't help but gaze longingly at mothers letting their toddlers steer their own mini carts. They seemed so impatient and irritated with their toddlers, and it just broke me. What I would do to have a toddler to wrangle. When I got to the checkout line, the clerk tried to make small talk. In a way, his friendliness was a trigger. I couldn't respond. I pretended to look at something on my phone. He probably thought I was rude. He didn't know that I couldn't chat because if I started speaking at all, I'd cry.

In an attempt at self-care, I booked a massage right after Miles died. When I called, I asked for an appointment with Amanda, who I hadn't seen since before I got pregnant because she was not certified in prenatal massage. I told them I didn't need prenatal massage any longer, hoping they'd get the hint. They booked the appointment and I hoped that was the end of it. Nope. The day of my appointment, they called and said they needed to reschedule because they'd accidentally put me with someone who did not do prenatal massage. I lost it. "I'm not prenatal anymore. I already told you that. My baby died. Thank you for making me say it." When I came in for my massage, they were apologetic. They gave me the Pity Face and I wanted to run out of there like my hair was on fire (I didn't; I really needed that massage).

(A story that's sort of funny now that time has passed: Six months after losing Miles, I went to get a massage at my usual clinic, but with a new therapist. She was young, wearing Converse sneakers. She flipped through my chart as we walked into the treatment room and read aloud, "No longer prenatal. Do not ask her." I peeked over her shoulder and saw that someone had written this on my form in thick, black marker. There were lots of exclamation marks. She laughed. "Your neck is probably sore from looking down at your baby all the time, huh?" I didn't correct her, didn't have the heart. When I was her age, I didn't know a thing about pregnancy loss either. I assumed prenatal was just a hop, skip, and a jump away from a baby. Oh, to be innocent.)

Here's the thing: Babies and mothers are everywhere. Kids are everywhere. Families are everywhere. It's pretty hard to avoid pain completely. But I had to really limit my interactions with the world for a while (See "I just want to hide from the world"). I'm a sensitive person by nature, and I just felt too vulnerable and raw to deal with people in the aftermath of my losses.

Meredith

Your altered reality continues parallel to other women, and the experience can be very lonely. There is no one way to feel about your loss. And how you feel will change. You will eventually come to know what this loss means for you, but that will take time. What is important in the early stages is to understand that you are entering a period of grief even as you must return to your daily life. The smallest, most mundane activities—preparing a bowl of cereal, for example—can trigger sadness for what you associate with them. For example, perhaps you ate that same cereal the day you went to your last OB appointment, and everything was fine. Then, that night, you went home and something wasn't right. Now, here you are. Expect the unexpected jolt of sadness in this period after loss; it's natural and normal to feel fragile. And it won't last forever.

Huong

Trigger warning: We are going to be talking about pregnancy loss triggers.

According to Merriam-Webster, a trigger warning is a statement cautioning that content (as in a text, video, or class) may be disturbing or upsetting. You may have also seen content warnings at the beginning of TV shows or movies to warn people of content that might elicit a strong or potentially harmful emotional response. Overall, there is increased awareness of the usefulness of trigger and content warnings on the internet and in media these days. I am appreciative because it sets the tone of "enter at your own risk."

However, not everything in life will come with a trigger or content warning, especially not after a pregnancy loss. There are the "known" triggers such as dates, anniversaries, holidays, and the like. But what about those triggers that you did not even know you had?

One potential trigger may be related to smells. Some women report a heightened or weakened sense of smell during pregnancy. Therefore, following a pregnancy loss, smelling a familiar smell may trigger old memories and pain. Our sense of smell is one of our most primal memory circuits. Several studies have demonstrated that smells trigger more vivid emotional memories and are better at inducing that feeling of "being brought back in time" than images. So don't be surprised if you find yourself crying after smelling banana bread if that was your comfort food during pregnancy.

Acting like you're fine
(not recommended)

It's exhausting.

Since I was a kid, my mom has said, "Your radar is always up," meaning I'm always very attuned (*overly* attuned) to what other people are feeling. When I was grieving, I could sense their discomfort. And I felt pressure to act like I was fine to ease that discomfort.

Sometimes I did just that—I acted. I put on a smile. I tried to be the "strong" and "brave" person that everyone seemed to want me to be. I said all the right things: "I'm feeling better every day," and "I'm doing OK," and "I'm focusing on all the good things in my life—I'm really so fortunate!"

This just left me feeling like a fraud. I felt inauthentic and . . . icky. The fact that people seemed to like this fraudulent version of me just made me feel even worse.

Now, when I'm going through something, I try to be honest about it (or at least semi-honest, because sometimes I need privacy). I still find myself downplaying—like, instead of saying, "I'm having a really hard time," I'll say, "I'm not having the easiest of times," with a little laugh for good measure. I feel that pressure to be positive, and I let it get to me still. But I figure I can chip away at my own false exterior over time by practicing authenticity more and more.

Meredith

Carl Jung wrote that "persona . . . is the individual's system of adaptation to, or the manner he assumes in dealing with, the world."

Persona is the aspect of someone's character that is presented to, or perceived by, others. This word, interestingly enough, is derived from Latin; it means theatrical mask. Personas are not bad or good, but they are necessary to some extent when you live in a society with others. They can become necessary when you are navigating grief and learning to honor your true self but need to create a protective barrier (for now) from the chatter of people who don't know what to say.

Society encourages us to package things—including ourselves—with a tidy bow. The problem arises when you believe you are your persona, or the persona you are wearing at the moment. To act happy to get through a situation, from point A to point B, can be a lot of work. Sometimes it is necessary. When it is, tell yourself this: I need to leave this situation shortly, and I will smile and say, "See you later."

It's always better not to have to pretend you're happy when you're not. You must meet yourself where you are and remain attuned to what you're up to doing, what feels like too much, and realistically, what amount of social graces you're up for. At the same time, might being with others—but being "with" yourself (translation: being true to yourself)—coexist? Why not?

Being sad is not the problem. The problem is when you judge your sadness. When you do, it has the effect of creating pressure—inside you and out there in the world. People begin tiptoeing around or purposefully trying to ignore your reaction. Their reaction to your reaction becomes an event no one wants and no one wants to talk about.

So, be honest with yourself and them. You're the one with agency here, whether you realize it or not. Tend to your needs, but don't deprive others of your love either. You matter. So set parameters: I'll come for dessert, or I'll stay until brunch starts, and then I'm taking off. Find ways to practice this type of self-care every day, not just on holidays or special occasions. Acquaint yourself with how it feels to say this. Awkward at first? Keep practicing. It'll get better.

Going back to work

You probably won't sleep the night before. I didn't.

After my first ectopic pregnancy, I took two weeks off work to recover from my surgery and cry in the comfort of my own home. I called my company's HR department to inquire about "bereavement leave" (because I really didn't want to use my vacation time). The HR person (a woman, mind you) said, "Well, bereavement leave is only for, like, real people." Way to go, HR!

With my second loss, I went to work and tried to concentrate while waiting for my body to let go of the pregnancy. I bled and bled while trying to pay attention in meetings.

"The thought of going back, facing everyone—especially in a sales job where I had to face different people and re-tell the whole sorry story each day— quite frankly made me feel physically sick."
—Elle Wright, *Ask Me His Name: Learning to Live and Laugh Again After the Loss of My Baby*

When I lost Miles, I took two weeks off again. This amount of time off is considered significant in the world of advertising.

With my fourth loss, I did not take any time off. For weeks, I woke up earlier than usual so I could get blood testing done every other day before work. The testing was necessary to confirm that my ectopic pregnancy was gradually "resolving" (a nicer way of saying the misplaced embryo was slowly dying). Again, I bled and bled while nobody suspected a thing.

Nobody told me I was entitled to medical leave, and I was too distraught to look into it myself. So, I used vacation time. By the time I was done losing babies, I had no time left for an actual vacation, which is probably what I really needed.

People at work knew about my first loss and my third loss, the ones that required me to take time off. I don't know which was worse—suffering through losses that nobody knew about, or suffering through losses that people *did* know about. When people did know, they weren't particularly supportive. Most people didn't say anything to me at all. Nothing. Nada.

I had dreaded going back to work because I was afraid of all the questions, but there were no questions. Maybe some people didn't care, and maybe others felt awkward around my grief (See "When people say nothing at all").

Can you take time off?

Check with your employer about taking leave following a loss. In an effort to support employees who have lost pregnancies, some companies offer lenient leave policies (with pay!). Others, not so much.

   If your employer does not provide leave, you will need to find ways to care for yourself while back at work. This might mean therapy appointments during your lunch break, a short walk during the day to collect your thoughts, journaling behind a closed office door, or texting a supportive friend from the bathroom stall. Create moments of solace for yourself so you can nurture your needs even while you take care of business.

I did a lot of "faking it" at work (See "Acting like you're fine"). I tried to be "professional" and "on." This was EXHAUSTING, like fall-asleep-at-seven-PM exhausting. To get through the days, I took lunch breaks in my car and closed the door to my office as much as I could (I may have also taken a nap under my desk once . . . or twice). I needed a reprieve. If you don't have a door or can't hide away in your car, I feel for you. It did help me to text certain friends (or my husband) on particularly hard days. And I did have a few coworkers I could confide in (godsends!). I had to create a safe bubble for myself, a place where I could let my real feelings just be what they were.

It took a while to feel back in the swing of things. I've always been a high-achiever at work, but I just could not fire on all cylinders when I was grieving. I made a lot of mistakes. I felt like I was in a fog. Whenever we had meetings to talk about projects, I couldn't bring myself to focus. I mean, why were these projects even important? What was the point of them? And I couldn't stand hearing all the workplace chatter, the sounds of people going about life as usual, laughing and joking and planning happy hours. Like I said, it was extremely lonely.

"Then there's the workplace, its own special hell for women who've miscarried. It's awkward enough trying to hide a pregnancy, and all its side effects, in those tumultuous early weeks. How are you then supposed to explain why you need time off to heal or to grieve? And what if you don't get sick days at all, or your job requires manual labor? Maybe you're worried about being 'mommy-tracked'—or worse—if your boss finds out you're trying to have a baby. Even being in the same room as your colleagues as they chatter obliviously about their children's lives can be excruciating." —Lauren Kelley and Alexandra March in their *New York Times* Opinion piece, "You Know Someone Who's Had a Miscarriage"

My losses have changed who I am at work, even now. I don't sweat the small stuff anymore. I don't get caught up in stressful deadlines. I'm firm on my boundaries and prioritize my family life over everything else. I guess I've realized how fragile life is, and I'm not willing to spend my time fretting over work projects when I should be enjoying time with my daughter. That perspective is just one of the many things I've gained from my losses, one of the many things I'm grateful for.

Meredith

Your heart likely cannot keep pace with the demands of your job description, even if you love your job, and it's much harder if you don't.

The emails, the workflow, the meetings, even going to lunch are fraught. And all those coworkers? And the pressure to interact? Difficult. And a lot. (Sometimes even under the best circumstances.)

It's hard to land back in an office or customer-facing job after a loss like this. Returning to work requires insight, planning, and self-care. It means knowing that your pre-loss level of productivity and concentration might be more than a bit off and, at times, impossible. You've been out of the office, but your coworkers haven't, and, sure, they're glad you're feeling better, but they're likely also glad to no longer be covering your workload.

If you're self-employed, you might have a bit more flexibility as far as your schedule. But though you're the boss, you still need to return to work to keep your business going, and that's a different kind of pressure altogether.

"U.S. workplaces have not caught up with the growing recognition that miscarriage is a loss that takes time to mourn. Women and men are burning sick days, taking unpaid leave and relying on the kindness of their supervisors to cope." —Rebecca Dube, "Miscarriage at Work," Today.com

---

Return to work can trigger a lot of emotion. After a week or more of solitude at home (or at least some privacy), it's like being kicked out of the nest and left to fend for yourself—the work, the comments, the questions, the deadlines, the physical and emotional labor are all intense. Plus, a part of you might find you'd like a bit more time to simply think about your pregnancy, to reflect on the baby you lost, to imagine what might have been. No longer having the time (because: work is crazy) can bring its own kind of sadness too.

To make the return to work a little easier for you:

- Pause frequently and take a deep breath.
- When you first go back, find five minutes to be alone at least a few times a day: head to the restroom and lock yourself in a stall; take a walk; sit in your car.
- Keep a journal, and write things down if your feelings start to overwhelm you—putting them on paper is equivalent in the short-term to talking them through. Later, when you have time, you can reread your notes, cry as appropriate, and assess what to do next.
- Set limits to honor the space you still need to grieve. Working overtime won't make you more productive in the long run, but tending to your sadness just might.

Meanwhile, in Korea...

In Korea, there are laws in place granting maternity leave in the case of miscarriage or stillbirth, with leave time based on the number of weeks of pregnancy. The leave is paid, and an employer is not allowed to dismiss an employee during leave.

When grief sneaks
up on you

Because it will.

Grief is a weird thing. I could be going through a day feeling generally OK and then—boom—I'd be reduced to tears by something that wouldn't have affected me so much before. In an attempt to keep a sense of humor, I kept a list in my phone of all the odd things that brought me to tears while I was grieving. Here are just a few:

- Hearing "Halo" by Beyoncé, which I did not even know was in my music library. Damn shuffle!
- A *Dateline* episode about the tsunami in Thailand
- A work meeting scheduled over my usual lunch break (I *really* needed those lunch breaks to get through the day)
- A yoga teacher touching me to make an adjustment
- Bumper-to-bumper freeway traffic
- Some asshole at the pharmacy snapping at me for not seeing where the line started
- A haircut that turned out a bit too short so that I couldn't get all the strands to stay in a ponytail

I can kind of laugh about many of these things now. I was obviously just so sensitive, a 5'11" raw nerve (yes, I know, I'm tall. So is Meredith!). I'm generally a calm, cool, collected person, so my heightened emotionality caught me off guard. But that's what grief does—it catches you off guard. It does not wait for convenient times to show itself. It just shows itself whenever and wherever it wants to. It was humbling for the control freak in me; I couldn't control grief, I had to just let it do its thing. There's really no other choice in the matter.

Meredith

After a time, it seems like the grief work you needed to do is finally easing up. You go for stretches feeling somewhat like yourself again. It feels like you've come to the end of the hardest stuff. Maybe you're excited about what's next—a new class, a trip. Maybe you have decided to try to become pregnant again. You're excited, and it feels kind of . . . *good*.

But then something happens, and you're crying uncontrollably. Does that mean you're not as far along in healing as you think?

Not necessarily. Grief is dynamic, meaning it can change from day to day and hour to hour, and it's nonlinear—there is no step-by-step approach to it. This means that with every move forward you also encounter what I think of as a complementary reaction to your own growth. The excitement about something new might trigger a kind of unconscious reminder of the loss, like *Oh, I'm so excited about this because I've been sad for so long*. You think about your happiness in relation to your sorrow. In a tender way, it's almost as though the grieving part of ourselves wants to be remembered, too, even as we identify less and less with the pain we endured.

"Ugly cry: Heaving sobs, accompanied by a swollen face, active mucous membranes, and running mascara. Known to attack without warning and right before job interviews and first dates." —Rebecca Soffer and Gabrielle Birkner, *Modern Loss: Candid Conversations about Grief. Beginners Welcome.*

So what you can you do? Take a moment to thank the you who lived through the pain, who navigated the grief, who endured the suffering. Thank HER, and let her know you'll never forget her. In truth, your ability to recognize this part of yourself and honor her helps you integrate the strength she holds into your life. You're becoming even stronger. Yes, you are.

Coping with holidays and celebrations

They might sting.

Holidays and celebrations are hard for many people, for many reasons. Even before my losses, these types of gatherings brought up complicated feelings—being around family and resurrecting old dynamics tends to do that. While I was grieving, holidays and celebrations were even more complicated.

The thing with these events is that they come with lots of expectations (and pressure). They're supposed to be happy and fun and joyful. When I was grieving, I felt a big disconnect between myself and the world around me. It was lonely. Christmas was especially hard—there is just so much freaking jolliness, and I was anything but jolly. Plus, one of my babies was due on December 25—something that still casts a shadow over Christmas for me.

But it's not just the big holidays that can be triggering. For me, Halloween was hard—all the kids in their cute costumes just broke my heart, especially the babies dressed as pumpkins or pineapples. Easter was hard because I was surrounded by nieces and nephews at family meals; it felt like everyone's family was growing but mine. Even the fourth of July was hard—listening to people whooping and hollering during fireworks, flaunting their happiness, when I was sad and just wanted to sleep.

Weddings, birthdays—these were hard too. I just couldn't relate to everyone's celebratory mood. I didn't want to be in the middle of a dance floor. I didn't want to play drinking games. I couldn't imagine being that happy again.

Once upon a time, everyone's holidays and celebrations were experienced only by them; now, with social media, we all get to witness the fun everyone is having. In this way, social media really has a way of amplifying feelings of loneliness—all those photos of people living their best lives, showing off their families and good fortunes, overusing #blessed (See "Navigating social media"). It seemed like everyone except me was happy "soaking up family time" or "relishing moments," according to their captions. Of course, I can't predict when a pregnancy announcement is coming, but holidays are predictable, and I had to learn to stay off social media during those.

"I found weddings, baptisms, birthdays—anything celebrating life's milestones—painful. If I smiled my way through the ceremony, I sobbed on the way home." —Mattie J. Bekink, "The Promise," featured in *Modern Loss: Candid Conversations about Grief. Beginners Welcome.* (Rebecca Soffer and Gabrielle Birkner, editors)

My survival strategies for holidays and celebrations:

1. Limit social engagements that require too much "faking it" (aka "Say no" whenever necessary).
2. Focus on creating traditions that really mean something to me.
3. Step away from social media.
4. Be gentle with myself.

That last one is hard. I still beat myself up when I can't feel what I think I *should* be feeling. I find myself asking, *What is wrong with you?* I know, logically, that nothing is wrong with me. It's just that big "happy" gatherings tend to pick at the wounds left by loss.

Meredith

Like Kim says, holidays and celebrations can be difficult under normal circumstances. The pressure to gather and be happy is often too much even when you haven't encountered a significant loss, recent or not. The pressure to gather is deeply rooted—and what if you don't show? Everyone will be disappointed. Or worried. Or concerned. Or maybe they'll think you're selfish. There's pressure not only to attend but to act happy too.

Find a middle ground for yourself. What might it be like to take your understandable sadness to a gathering with people you love and who love you? What might it feel like to cry a bit and then enjoy the company (and cake)? It might feel good, like you're not performing or pretending.

The landmine of Mother's Day

I lost my first pregnancy in April 2015, and I lost Miles in April 2016. When Mother's Day came around a month later, it felt like a hard slap in the face.

Even though I knew better, I made the masochistic mistake of going on social media. I say masochistic because I can't think of another explanation—it was like I was seeking out more pain. Maybe it's the same as when we pinch ourselves to ensure what we're feeling is real.

I realize women are proud of being mothers, but it felt like they were flaunting it. I had never felt so "left out" (not even in junior high, and that's saying something). "Motherhood is the greatest joy," they wrote. "I don't know who I would be if I wasn't a mother," they wrote. *Yes, I know, I wanted to write, all of us who aren't mothers are just purposeless fools. We may as well just jump off a bridge, right?*

Chris and I hosted a Mother's Day family gathering at our house after Miles died. I was in too much of a fog to realize this wasn't a great idea. All I knew is that I wanted to be at home. I didn't want to go anywhere else. At home, I could escape to my bedroom if I needed to.

After dinner, my sister asked if I wanted to hold her two-month-old, and I said OK. It was my first time holding him, aside from the time I held him in the hospital, hours after he was born and hours before I knew that my baby boy was dying (seriously, my doctor's appointment was the same day). The moment I felt the weight of him in my arms, I started crying, and then she started crying. Chris, perplexed, always perplexed by my grief, said, "Why are you crying?" My sister and I managed a blubbering laugh, because that's how my family copes—we look for comic relief, tension-breakers.

This is what I tell my friends who have miscarried, so I'm sharing it with you, too: You're probably going to cry on Mother's Day. I don't know a way around it. If you can't handle the family gatherings, don't go. And take a day (or month or year) off from social media if you can.

Or maybe you've chatted with your circle of friends and family, and they totally understand your reluctance to partake of the communal gathering right now (good). They support you not attending family events just yet (excellent). They get it, and they get you (nice). But then, comfy on your couch, phone in hand, you make the decision to check your social media accounts—or maybe you just open your email. There, the photos and the memes and the missives by women about their gratitude for motherhood are the jolt you didn't need just yet.

We (naturally) don't want to be shown the source of our pain. But might there be another aspect? Maybe it's less about avoiding the source and more about getting acquainted with what it feels like to move through these spontaneous reminders of grief without trying to act like it's not supposed to hurt.

Triggering dates

*Due dates, loss dates, any date
that makes your heart ache.*

April is a hard time for me. April was when I had my first pregnancy loss—an ectopic pregnancy that required emergency surgery. And April was when I lost Miles at seventeen weeks. Every April since these losses, my limbs feel heavy, and I'm generally in a funk. I start to worry that I'm having a depressive episode. Then it dawns on me—*oh, yes, that.*

For me, the loss dates are the hardest. I remember due dates too, but I'm not as melancholy on those. I'm more wistful, pondering what could have been, wondering if the lost babies are having birthdays in another dimension, growing and changing beyond my view. The loss dates, though, those get me. I feel those in my body. I really believe the body remembers trauma. It's stored there in our cells, even if we have mentally "moved on." My body remembers the trauma of my emergency surgery with my first pregnancy. It remembers the trauma of Miles being removed from me. And that makes April difficult.

I don't mind if April is always difficult. It's comforting, in a way, to know that my body remembers, even when the rest of the world does not. My body knows what we went through, together. I've come to welcome the sadness. It reminds me of my own resilience, and it fills me with gratitude for what I have now.

Meredith

Expect to be caught off guard. Expect to be surprised. You count the days—first trying to conceive, then trying to make sense of your loss. Tracking days helps. *It's been this long since* provides reference. *I have this many more days to go* grounds you on a journey that sometimes seems to have no real beginning, middle, or end.

It's not until a particular date suddenly and unexpectedly grabs your attention and gives you a little (or a big) shake that you notice. Maybe this was your due date. There might be many or few of these dates, but each time, you're caught off guard. It doesn't hurt less but, in time, you recover from the reminder more quickly.

Even after you're done with the hardest part of mourning, grief will pull you back just a bit and give you yet another chance to work through more of your loss. (It's very thorough.) This is another way to look at trigger dates—as openings, as facets of love that lay in wait, seeking an outlet.

With or without tears, and in time, a feeling of lightness will follow these reminders. This is how you heal. This is how you grow.

"I still get sad on the day the heartbeat stopped, and I'll probably cry a little on that day, each year." —Jessica, on her second-trimester loss

"That year, that should have been filled with milestone cards, gurgles and weaning, was instead filled with the dread each time a 'first' was on the horizon. First Christmas, first Mothers' Day, my first birthday without my son."
—Elle Wright, *Ask Me His Name: Learning to Live and Laugh Again After the Loss of My Baby*

Dealing with other people having babies

Why does pregnancy seem
to be everywhere?

*At work, at the grocery store, on TV, all
over social media—everywhere*

I lost hair in the first few months after losing Miles. I don't know if it was stress or hormones, but I couldn't brush it without clumps coming out. The white tile of our bathroom floor was covered in a carpet of my loss. The hair that remained was broken and frizzy. Just what I needed when I was already feeling my lowest.

I decided to get it cut. I didn't want to go back to my usual hair stylist because I'd told her I was pregnant when I crossed the first trimester mark, and I couldn't deal with her putting her hand to her chest and saying, "I'm so sorry." When I called to ask what days she worked (so I could schedule another day), they said, "Oh, she's on leave actually." She was pregnant with twins.

It felt like everyone around me was pregnant. There was a baby boom at my workplace. Everyone was making jokes about there being "something in the water." It seemed like every time I turned a corner at the office, I ran into a baby bump.

Even Chris noticed that 90 percent of ads on TV were somehow related to pregnancy or parenthood. After my first loss, there was this stupid Burger King commercial featuring a chicken announcing, "French fries and I are pregnant and we're having chicken fries!" Normally, I wouldn't even notice a commercial like this. If I did notice it, I would think, "Lame," and wonder aloud how much the ad agency got paid for creating it. But as I lay in bed recovering from my surgery, I saw this commercial at least twenty times and every time it infuriated me.

You know how someone mentions an obscure word, and then you suddenly start seeing or hearing that word everywhere? There's actually a name for it—Baader-Meinhof phenomenon. After each of my losses, that phenomenon seemed to apply to anything pregnancy-related. Everywhere I looked, pregnancy was involved.

Obviously, my brain was just more attuned to pregnancy at that time—a cruel and seemingly masochistic phenomenon. I was wired to notice it while my brain was attempting to process my losses. I still notice it, probably more than other people. I still see pregnancy as this mysterious, terrifying, amazing thing that deserves careful attention. But it does not dominate my thoughts like it once did.

Meredith

There are two things going on here. One is catered marketing online—like when you've visited Google or Amazon, for example, shopping for baby supplies or reading about pregnancy. Google or Facebook and other sites then sort you into a "people who are interested in babies and pregnancy" or perhaps "expecting parent" category. So you're getting actual targeted ads about this. This feels personal, because it is—you're literally being targeted. There are ways to minimize your exposure to targeted ads. In most browsers, you can turn off pop-up ads. If you see an ad while you're online, there is often the option to "stop seeing this ad" or "control ads like this." You can also turn off Ad Personalization in browsers like Google Chrome.

Something else is also happening. The Baader-Meinhof phenomenon, or Baader-Meinhof effect, is real. Your awareness of something increases, and when this happens, it isn't that it wasn't there before, but that you simply had not noticed it in the same way. Now you notice all the pregnant women and the babies; they seem to be following you around and showing up on every corner. They're all over your social media feed. Baby clothes come up in ads. Suddenly every other home in the neighborhood is expecting a baby.

This leads you to believe it's actually happening more, even if that's not the case. Your brain is reinforcing newly acquired information. Other names for this are:

- frequency illusion
- recency illusion
- selective attention bias

This can happen at every phase of pregnancy, pregnancy planning, and loss. You are attuned to babies, pregnancy, children, parenthood, mothers, holidays, showers, the list goes on.

At times of joy, this can be comforting and can bring joy. At times of sorrow it's at best bittersweet. But knowing what it is, and that it's normal, can help explain why it happens and help you make sense of it when it does.

Huong

In some ways, pregnancy feels like it's everywhere because it *is* everywhere (or at least it's more of a focus than it was in previous generations). Elaborate birth announcements, over-the-top baby showers, and gender reveal parties are all relatively new to our culture. In general, the focus of marriage has shifted from the couple to their future child(ren). The moment a couple ties the knot, they start hearing, "When are you going to start a family?" For those who are childfree by choice, they wonder, "Why can't two people be considered a family?" For those who have suffered pregnancy loss(es), they begin to feel "left out" of The Best Club Ever.

I was a Peace Corps volunteer in the rural highlands of Peru in my early twenties, and I remember a stark difference between pregnant women there as compared to pregnant women in Southern California, where I was born and raised. Often, I did not even know some of the women in my town were pregnant because of the large and multiple skirts (*polleras*) that they wore. Sometimes I didn't know until the baby arrived! There were no parties, no fanfare or celebration, and I wonder if that made it a little bit easier for some who experienced pregnancy losses.

"Every time going to a grocery store, I was met with tabloid magazine covers of pregnant celebrities, every commercial was Pampers. You start to avoid the areas of stores with baby clothes. Heck, I even got mad at seeing a cat on TV having kittens. Like, how dare this cat get knocked up, and I can't even keep a baby?" —Michaela, after her first-trimester loss

"Wherever I went, women appeared around corners, led by their pregnant bellies. Women stood up from loading groceries into cars and were hugely pregnant or dripping with children, the reminder of something I was meant to be doing, something I had failed to do." —Susanna Sonnenberg, "Twins," featured in *About What Was Lost: 20 Writers on Miscarriage, Healing, and Hope* (Jessica Berger Gross, editor)

Another note: In addition to the Baader-Meinhof phenomenon, there is also the reticular activating system (RAS). In his book *Getting Things Done*, David Allen talks about how the RAS may work: "When you focus on something—the vacation you're going to take, the meeting you're about to go into, the project you want to launch—that focus instantly creates ideas and thought patterns you wouldn't have had otherwise. Even your physiology will respond to an image in your head as if it were reality."

So if you feel like *everyone* around you is pregnant, it may be because your brain is searching and sifting through the environment around you and only showing you those who are pregnant or images and websites related to pregnancy. Our brains seem to be programmed by not only what we focus on but also by how we identify ourselves. It is our brain's way of proving us "right," even if it causes us distress. As a former professor of mine used to say, "You can thank your brain for that!"

All the triggered feelings—
anger, sadness, envy, shame, guilt

All I have to say is . . . ugh.

A few weeks after my first loss, my husband's good friend called to say he "knocked up" his Tinder-acquired girlfriend. Upon hearing the news of this incredibly obnoxious "oops," I cried spontaneous tears, the kind you cry when you pluck a nose hair. The woman went on to have a totally normal pregnancy and delivered a healthy baby (of course).

Around the same time, my sister-in-law announced her second pregnancy. And then my sister announced her third—I believe her words were, "It's kind of a shock. With the two boys running around, I think we only had sex once." Awesome. I was especially irritated with people having multiple kids. So greedy. I just wanted my one, *thankyouverymuch*. Even now, I have "my one," and I still feel painful pangs when others seem to reproduce easily.

At work, it seemed like every Friday there were pink or blue balloons in one of the conference rooms. Our designers were taking time out of their workdays to create Pinterest-worthy signs and decorations for the mama-to-be. Gifts were piled on tables, along with finger sandwiches and cupcakes with pink or blue frosting (or white for those who said, giddily, "We want to be surprised!").

It was impossible for me to avoid other women's pregnancies. I tried, I did. But, frankly, I was running into baby bumps everywhere I went. This meant that I felt pressure to "fake it" a lot. I didn't want people to think I was a bitter bitch. So I forced myself to ask all the usual questions—"When are you due? Boy or girl?" I put a pleasant smile on my face. Then, exhausted and feeling inauthentic and empty, I found a private place and cried or screamed (and if that wasn't possible, I texted a good friend to vent).

I had mixed feelings around babies. Sometimes, I wanted nothing to do with them. I waited a full year to meet my niece (which I still feel bad about). Other times, I was mesmerized by babies. I saw them as these magical miracles, and I wanted to hold them for hours and stare at their eyelashes. Often, I thought I would be fine and then fell apart once the baby was in my arms.

What was so hard about this was that I *wanted* to be happy for these pregnant women and their babies, especially if they were close friends or family. When I couldn't summon that happiness, I felt awful. It's not that I wished anyone harm; it's just that I couldn't look at pregnant women or babies without thinking *Why not me? Why?* It was just so painful. And layered on that pain was guilt for being "such a bitch."

I don't know any woman who has gone through a pregnancy loss and *not* felt emotional around pregnant women and babies. The most evolved, enlightened, Zen women I know say they struggled with it. So, I guess my words of wisdom would be—don't beat yourself up for whatever feelings arise, and find a private place to cry or scream as needed (my car was mine).

> "I remember sitting, two days after my D & C, on Christmas morning, still wearing the giant bulky pad they make you wear for bleeding, watching my sister-in-law opening gifts of baby clothes. That sucked."
>
> —Michaela, after her first-trimester loss

Meredith

Trying to avoid emotional triggers soon after a loss is reasonable—in theory. But even planning ahead to avoid a person or place doesn't guarantee something else won't come from out of nowhere and hurt just as much (or more).

This is actually good news. It's good because it challenges the belief that feelings somehow shouldn't be felt. That losses shouldn't be grieved. That you're not still sad or bitter or envious—because maybe deep down you are. That sounds reasonable. And expected. They are authentic feelings. They arose spontaneously. Let them move through you, and then let them go.

Though it sounds obvious, it's worth repeating because everyone seems to forget: emotions are normal—they come up, you feel them (OK, some are more tolerable than others), and eventually they subside.

It can help to reframe what triggers do and how they can be of service to growth. Again, you need not go seeking out ways to upset yourself—that's the last thing you need after a miscarriage or loss. But, should you find yourself overcome with emotion, or weeping when you see a newborn in her mother's arms, view it as an opportunity to work through more of your pain. Your pain is unique and meaningful.

This need not be viewed as a setback but a springboard forward, further into healing.

> "Just last week I went to visit a friend who had given birth to her third child and, even if I say so myself, my performance was flawless. 'Look at his tiny hands!' 'Oh, her eyes/nose/mouth is just like yours!' 'Of course I'd love a hold!' And, breathe. And, chat. And, smile. Don't think about it, don't think about it, don't think about it. There should be Oscars for that sort of thing." —Liane Moriarty, *What Alice Forgot* (in this novel, the character Elisabeth struggles for years to have a child)

My kind-of-bitchy open letter
to expecting mothers

Must they always be stroking their bellies?
WE SEE IT. You're growing a human.
Congrats.

With each of my losses, I felt so much resentment toward women who seemed to effortlessly reproduce. And there were *a lot* of them in my life during my losses. It was very coarse salt in a gaping wound. Of course I rationally understood that people were not getting pregnant to spite me (duh), but my inner toddler (you may have your own) was not having it (See "The 'It's not fair' tantrum"). I was angry. Like, ANGRY. That's what led me to write this kind-of-bitchy letter.

Dear Expecting Mothers,

I want to be happy for you, but I just can't. There, I said it. In fact, I kind of hate you. It's not as simple as envy—it feels like pure hatred.

I resent how you take your bumps for granted. I resent the ultrasound photos you post on Facebook—some from the first trimester. Some of you post pictures of your pregnancy tests! Don't you know what can go wrong? It must be nice to be so naïve.

Some of you complain about your full bladders, the pain in your lower back, your swollen feet. You don't know what I would give to have these problems.

Some of you are just consumed by things like the décor of your nursery and the games you'll play at your baby shower, as if these things are actually important, as if your baby's health is a given so you have time to contemplate such silliness.

I'm sorry for my anger. It's my favorite stage of grief. I can't help the way I feel. I just wish I was you, I guess. Or I wish you realized how lucky you are.

Sincerely,
The childless woman who can't even look at you without tears coming

Meredith

When you're feeling anger like this, try not to judge it. Try not to compare it to how you think you should be feeling.

In Kim's letter, it seems like part of what is so anger-producing might have less to do with other women being pregnant and more to do with how she perceives these particular moms-to-be as having a kind of blissful unknowing of what might/could go wrong. This ties to the societal belief (and all its pressures) that motherhood—from conceiving to birthing to raising a child—is something that is "meant to be" for women, something that comes naturally, easily. In reality, your experience of pregnancy loss is just as natural and real and deserving of attention. This is the real hurt, that there appears to be no reservoir of attention by society to devote to such grief. It can be lonely.

"I was nearly debilitated by the number-one symptom of life after miscarriage: blinding jealousy of anyone pregnant, recently delivered, or who even appeared to be ovulating. (Don't ask how I thought I could tell who was ovulating. Miscarriage-related insanity is a terrifying thing.)"
—Dahlia Lithwick, "I Went Out Full," featured in *About What Was Lost: 20 Writers on Miscarriage, Healing, and Hope* (Jessica Berger Gross, editor)

Make no apologies for your anger. Take note of the depth of your feelings. Listen to what else that anger might be saying to you. Is it coupled with longing for the baby you still wish you could hold? Or maybe a bit of (natural) jealousy at all that you missed because of your loss? It may be. It may not be. Can you tolerate your anger? Are you OK with it? If you're not, can you get to know it even better? How? Be curious about it.

When angry or hostile or snippy thoughts arise, thoughts you think you wouldn't be thinking if you were more [*fill in the blank—enlightened, healed, able to move on, or something else*], take a moment to listen to them. Really listen. Don't run from them. Is there more to them than you originally thought?

Anger has energy; inside energy is life, strength, and, yes, perspective. Pay a reverent attention to it. I'm not talking about "nursing" a resentment but rather acknowledging that emotion as purely natural. Write to it, sit with it, and don't worry about "making it go away." It will. This mindfulness acts as a kind of grace. In this way you determine what is acceptable for you. There is power in that.

The dreaded baby showers

My RSVP? No, thanks.

Fact: I still hate baby showers. And "sprinkles" (mini showers for second or third or fourth children). And gender reveal parties. And basically any event that treats pregnancy like it's a cute game. I never really enjoyed these events, but they became especially aggravating after my losses.

Even now, I usually decline invitations to these types of events. It just feels too weird to be around everyone laughing and smashing chocolate bars in diapers and guessing belly circumference for fun and prizes. Like, how can these people make light of something so serious? Don't they know what can go wrong?

"Why are we forced to spend gazillions of dollars, attend a cheesy party with not nearly enough booze, 'oooh' and 'aww' at onesies and play stupid games just because you got pregnant?" —Zara Barrie, Elite Daily

Before I realized that I should not attend these events because of the effects on my sanity, I went with my husband to a co-ed, nautical-themed baby shower (Ahoy! It's a boy!). One of the guests said to me, "Why don't you have a baby yet? Don't you want to join the club?" This is another thing I hate about these events—it's like everyone feels entitled to know everyone else's baby business. I felt like ants were crawling on my skin the entire time at that shower. I kept giving Chris eyes that said, "Can we leave?" and he kept missing my queues. I ended up sitting in a corner, texting a friend, until we finally left.

After that, I declined invitations. If I knew the person somewhat well, I explained that it was just too hard for me. If I didn't know the person well, I just made up an excuse, sent a gift, and tried to limit my "feeling guilty" time to five minutes. I had to do what I had to do. End of story. I *still* have to do what I have to do (and oftentimes that means no baby showers).

A personal note: What I have always found so hard about showers—not all, but a fair share—is the performance expectation laid out by the people hosting and, perhaps, from the expectant mother herself. These expectations range but often include guests being required to express their delight in a very specific way.

Also a burden (for me, anyway) is the focus on material gifts, namely on one person's gift being THE MOST SPECIAL, on everyone agreeing that "we all agree" that A's gift is THE BEST and B's gift is THE CUTEST and C's gift is THE MOST DARLING. These are a few more reasons why, even though I am truly happy about your baby, I might not attend your shower but would rather take you to lunch instead.

"I got anger from receiving baby shower invitations and making excuses not to go . . . I really loved these people, and I felt awful. At the time I understood why I didn't go, but I still wonder if I should've." —Michaela, after her first-trimester loss

All this is to say, if you find yourself feeling ambivalent, it does not necessarily mean you are jealous or envious, or, if you are, that those encompass the whole of your feelings. If you really do not feel like attending a shower, check in with yourself. Will you regret not going? Will you be happier if you don't go? Can you process your jealousy or envy and find a way to be happy for your friend too? Then, tell your friend—if you are convinced they will understand—the truth. If not, just apologize. Then offer to find a way to make it up to her—deliver a gift in person, if possible, or take her to lunch, or go on a walk together. Share authentic conversation. Be there for her the best way you can while you are also there for yourself.

How might it feel to be happy for your friend in the face of your grief? It will be hard, yes, but meaningful—not only to her but to you. It takes depth and strength to be there for someone; you've got it. You've got this.

> **Did you know?**
>
> In some cultures (for example, Russian, Jewish, Muslim, Japanese), it is considered taboo to have a shower before a baby is born, as it could be tempting fate and/or the gods.

Huong

On a personal note as well, I have thrown quite a few baby showers for dear friends. I do love "showering" them with love, but I cannot stand being asked, "When are you next?" I imagine this question is even more torturous for a woman going through infertility or pregnancy loss.

A client shared with me a painful moment while attending a baby shower for an Indian-American colleague. She described how all the women placed silver bangles on the expecting mother's arms. The belief was that the jangling of the bracelets warded off the evil spirits. The next portion of the ceremony was choosing another woman to sit next to the expecting mother to "pass on" her good fortune and to receive bracelets as well. My client, who recently struggled with a pregnancy loss, was encouraged to receive bracelets. She stated, "I was so uncomfortable with the ceremony because I felt like I would be letting everyone down (and the culture) if I told them about my doubts of ever having a healthy baby."

Rediscovering (and loving) who you are

Finding faith

In something divine, maybe. Or in yourself.

Before my losses, I believed in a God who dictated events—rewarding good, punishing evil. That belief system left me feeling betrayed and angry. The result: a crisis of faith that surprised me. I was forced to really consider the role of God in my life. If I believe in God, what does that mean?

Since my losses, I've come to accept that my previous belief system was limited and simplistic. I do think there is a higher power, something larger than myself. But I think this higher power is no more in control than I am. When bad things happen, it is not a punishment. It is not a result of something I did. It just happened. God is not a dictator or commander; God is a partner. And my God is just as saddened by bad things happening as I am. We can commiserate, in a way. We can grieve together, in a way.

What the studies tell us

According to a review of research on religion and pregnancy loss:

"Religion has a significant effect on parents' acceptance of such mishaps and it may have a considerable effect on their recovery from such tragic events." *(Journal of Education and Health Promotion, 2015)*

When I was a kid, I used to pray for things to happen—getting an A on a test, winning a softball game. Now, I don't formally pray, but I do have meditative moments when I reflect on surrendering and trusting my own strength in the face of whatever comes. That has been a new cornerstone of my faith—recognizing my own strength. My higher power is there to witness and encourage that strength.

I realize religion and faith are very personal things. I make no judgment of anyone's beliefs. All I know is that losing a baby can rock your world and disrupt those beliefs—whatever they are. Part of grieving can be letting go of old beliefs and welcoming new ones. I've welcomed this new trust I have in myself. I've welcomed the idea that a higher power might not have all the answers and explanations—those are inside me.

Meredith

Grief is not only about mourning. You find, when you're in it, that something else occurs. You need to navigate the darkened corners and unfamiliar passageways that connect the depths of your heart to the new reality of your life.

Faith is like a companion. And you have it already. It is there in your willingness to take the next step even when you're not sure where this journey will take you.

Faith means complete trust or confidence in someone or something. But it's also the connection between you and what you trust—something larger than yourself that helps shoulder the fears and burden, and gives you just enough hope to keep you going as you surrender to the process of growth and change.

Maybe it's nature that you trust. Or our ability as a species to seek survival and growth. Maybe it's something more ethereal.

Julie Mussché, director of St. Joseph Hospital Center for Spiritual Development, says that with the loss of a pregnancy, it is vitally important to pay attention to "the biology of what has happened." It's important to recognize that "God is in the mix," she said, "or whatever a person chooses to call that divine presence, that third party in the room—and outside the room."

This divine presence is different for everyone. Some use prayer to connect to that presence; some use stillness and quiet. Some terms for this divine presence include (but are not limited to): God, higher power, Jesus, Christ, Christ love, Akal Murat, timeless one, Allah, Shiva, Buddha, The Gracious, The Merciful, creator, protector, savior, messiah, father, mother, lord, infinite love, the universe, infinite wisdom, divine guidance, intuitive light, shakti, chi, life force.

Faith is not the same as religion, though religion can provide a lens through which to view faith. Faith is far more complex than religion, because it stems from the inside rather than something external you practice.

Religion can give you a framework—services, observances, prayer. Guidelines and structure. Some people use religion to tell them what to think. But often the problem with religion as the sole method to navigate grief is that religion cannot discern between your needs and its own. Only you can do that. And that is where faith is most important.

A MEDITATION FOR YOU

Intuition.* I have it and am learning to use it.

"The only real valuable thing is intuition." —Albert Einstein

And yet, I wonder: is my intuition—my internal North Star, so to speak—just now starting to emerge, or am I just finally seeing it for the first time? It's an interesting question. The good news is that I have an internal North Star, and today I am learning how to look for and follow it. I trust that my North Star appears to me in myriad ways. It might be an emotion—a pristine calm or a flow of unexpected tears. As I continue to practice focusing on myself, I'll connect more easily and readily to my North Star, and the seamless union of my heart and mind will feel more natural and less like work.

Life will become simpler in the long run if I follow my North Star. At the very least, I will be on the right path—for me.

I accept that the true answers for me are already inside me. Today I'm learning to spot them.

*Use this term, or substitute what you call divine presence.

Religions, gurus, thought leaders, influencers, anyone other than yourself will not be able to make sense of the loss for you. Faith reminds you that, sometimes, not having an answer is the answer.

Try to keep your focus with where you are right now, today. Trust the hours to pass and things inside you to change. Looking too far ahead, although that is where the mind wants to go, isn't where you are going to find your answers. The answers truly are inside you. It's your mind that is trying to protect you from pain *righthererightnow*, but its best intentions won't work. When you feel fragile, when a loss has propelled you into unknown dimensions, there is an impulse to figure it out fast to make the pain stop. The mind is always trying to figure things out, but it tends to complicate things along the way.

Losing a pregnancy is a crisis of faith—whether you believe in God or not. Everyone has some kind of a paradigm, a lens by which they see and experience their life. A loss this huge expands that lens—how could it not?

Huong

To see the potential impact of religious faith after pregnancy loss, we can look at a study comparing and contrasting responses of women in Qatar versus women in the United Kingdom.

According to the research, Qatari women rely on strong faith to positively frame their losses. Women, their families, and medical professionals all talk about lost babies as "birds in heaven" who their mothers will see again and who will help their mothers enter paradise. A belief in a higher power enabled women to see their loss as "God's will," which led to a decreased grief response as compared to the UK respondents.

This shows the power of faith. As Kim and Meredith both discuss, this faith does not have to be in a traditional "higher power"; the faith can be in YOU.

"I told myself I didn't have to understand why it happened, that it is for God to know and understand. It lifted my anxiety and control to place it on Him being 'in charge' of the situation. I know this doesn't apply to everyone, as people have different faith/religious beliefs, but this viewpoint did help me."
—Michaela, after her first-trimester loss

"My faith survived something substantial. I realized how real I could be with God and that love would remain. I wear the battle wounds, but I grew from it."
—Wendy, who experienced two first-trimester miscarriages

Will I ever feel like me again?

A new me.

Here's a conversation I had with my therapist:

Me: "I feel like I'm just going through motions."

Her: "That's fine for now. Some people can't even do that."

Me: "But am I ever going to feel like myself again?"

Her: "You won't always be depressed. But you'll always be different."

At the time, I was a little let down. I wanted her to say, "Yes, you'll feel like your old self again in X weeks." But I'm glad she was honest.

I remember someone saying that when you lose a child (during pregnancy or beyond), you spend the rest of your life impersonating who you were before that loss. To me, impersonating sounds exhausting. Instead, I've worked on accepting that I am not that person. This means mourning the old me, the more carefree me, the innocent and naïve me. Of course, this is another layer to grief.

"Grief is a cocoon from which we emerge new." —Glennon Doyle

I don't see how losing a baby could *not* change me. But change isn't bad. The new me is much more grateful, much more appreciative of all that is good in my life. The new me is more compassionate, more aware that people are suffering with secret things all around me. The new me has a better perspective on life, takes things in stride, sees the proverbial forest for the trees. Maybe all these changes would have come naturally with age, but maybe not. All I know is that I quite like who I am now.

When you wonder if you'll ever feel like the old you again, try to pinpoint what you find most different. Grief has forced you to grow. While you're still in the midst of this process, you won't have perspective—not yet anyway. See if you can name what has changed without labeling or judging it. This new facet of you has always been there, but until now it has remained untapped. Grief changed that. You will emerge anew. You will be you, but you will be deepened.

"This was not a blip in my reproductive history or a fleeting brush with heartache; this was a cosmic shift that would impact every area of my life."

—Adriel Booker, "How to Keep Your Marriage Intact After a Miscarriage," *Relevant Magazine*

"Losing your child is losing yourself. She died, I died."

—Sarah Agaton Howes, "Lessons from Dying," featured in *What God Is Honored Here?* *Writings on Miscarriage and Infant Loss by and for Native Women and Women of Color* (Shannon Gibney and Kao Kalia Yang, editors)

"You will heal and you will rebuild yourself around the loss you have suffered. You will be whole again but you will never be the same. Nor should you be the same, nor should you want to."

—Elisabeth Kübler-Ross and David Kessler, *On Grief and Grieving*

Self-compassion and self-care

I couldn't heal without it.

I have never been a big "self-care" person. My thought has always been: *That sounds time-consuming. I have things to do.*

One good thing that has come out of my losses is that I've learned so much about slowing down and being kind to myself. Mostly, I had no choice. My life as I knew it came to a screeching halt starting with my first loss, and it became painfully obvious to me that to survive grieving, I had to stop and deal with all the feelings that were coming up for me. I felt so much anger (at my body, at my naïveté, at my fantasies and dreams) and therapy helped me see that the only way to resolve that was to forgive my body and my heart. Forgiveness required getting in touch with myself in a new way and developing self-compassion that I'd never really had before. It wasn't doing any good to berate myself for getting my hopes up with each pregnancy, for example. It was so much more healing to have compassion for my hopeful spirit, like, *Oh, you wanted this so much, sweet self.* (I know it sounds corny, but it really did help me).

"I learned that all pain and loss is in fact a gift. Having miscarriages taught me that I had to mother myself before I could be a mother to someone else."
—Beyoncé

While I was grieving, I indulged opportunities to truly care for myself, to do whatever possible to help myself feel better. Some of that self-care has carried over to today. I'm still the first in line to try the latest self-care fad (my last experience was floating in a sensory deprivation tank. It wasn't my favorite. My favorite was a Korean spa day with Huong).

Here are some of the self-care practices that helped me (and still help me) connect with myself in a compassionate way:

- Yoga—at home or in a studio (in my "cocooning" phase, I didn't want to go to a studio)
- Reading
- Writing/journaling (formally, in a dedicated book, or just venting in the Notes app of my phone)
- Hot baths (with Epsom salt and bubbles and all that good stuff)
- Getting a massage (I found someone who would come to my house—bonus!)
- Therapy
- Making a new recipe
- Going for a run by the beach
- Napping
- Saying "no" to social situations that caused me even a smidge of anxiety

Huong

While self-care can include baths and massages, it goes much deeper—to self-compassion.

Kristen Neff, PhD, is the leading researcher on the topic of self-compassion. According to Neff, self-compassion is the "compassion directed inward, relating to ourselves as the object of care and concern when faced with the experience of suffering" and "involves the capacity to comfort and soothe ourselves and to motivate ourselves with encouragement when we suffer, fail or feel inadequate."

You may be surprised to learn that self-compassion and its impact on mental health is a highly researched field. You may think, "Self-compassion? That's not a real thing." Or, "I have enough self-compassion for myself. I don't want to be weak." Or, "Self-compassion? We all need to toughen up more instead of becoming so soft." Or, similarly, "I need to be tougher on myself, or else I won't get X and Y done."

Those above statements are some of the reasons we suffer.

According to Neff, with self-compassion, we give ourselves "the same kindness and care we'd give to a good friend." How many times have you found yourself expressing kindness and grace to a good friend after hearing about a hardship they have struggled with, only to then berate and reprimand yourself for going through a similar hardship?

"Caring for myself is not self-indulgence. It is self-preservation..."
—Audre Lorde, *A Burst of Light and Other Essays*

I often reference Neff's book, *Self-Compassion, The Proven Power of Being Kind To Yourself* (2011), in my sessions with clients to encourage them to view their grief, loss, and pain through another lens, one that allows them to heal instead of continuing to self-flagellate. According to Neff, we have been indoctrinated in a "stiff upper lip" type of society that we rarely "take the time to step back and recognize how hard it is for us in the moment."

The three main components of self-compassion are self-kindness, common humanity, and mindfulness.

1. **Self-kindness** is the ability to be gentle and understanding with ourselves instead of harsh and judgmental. So in the case of a pregnancy loss, what kind of thoughts are you having? Are you thinking, "This is a hard time for me, but I'm not weak for crying. It is normal to cry and grieve," or, "What is wrong with me? Why is it taking me so long to get over this?!"

2. **Common humanity** is the feeling of being connected with others in the human experience instead of feeling cut-off and isolated in our pain and suffering. Consider these two thoughts: "No one understands me, not my partner or my friends. I can't believe they have the audacity to complain about their kids when they know I am dying to have one"; versus "We all know what it feels like to hurt and have pain. While my friend and partner may not know EXACTLY how I am feeling, they are trying to understand my pain."

3. **Mindfulness** is acknowledging our pain rather than ignoring or magnifying it. In this case, are your actions aligned with taking care of yourself and doing healing practices such as acknowledging and sitting with the uncomfortable and difficult feelings from pregnancy loss, or are you already googling other ways to get pregnant, giving away any baby items, or trolling mommy blogs to berate mothers who complain about their children?

Sounds like common sense, right? But oh so very hard to implement. One of the biggest barriers to self-compassion is the fear of laziness and self-indulgence: "If I'm too self-compassionate, won't I just be lazy and selfish?" Take a moment and see if this is a belief you have been taught.

I am raising my hand, both hands. Growing up with refugee parents, I was constantly told that hard work, diligence, and perseverance were the keys to unlocking the so-called American Dream. In addition, when I wanted to rest or play like my similar-aged peers, my parents reprimanded me for being "lazy" and "slothful" and reminded me incessantly that they got on a boat for me (it's the immigrant version of "I used to walk ten miles in the snow to get to school").

On one hand, I am grateful for the insane work ethic that has been finely tuned and solidified over the years. However, I came to realize that one of the main reasons self-criticism and self-flagellation worked was because of FEAR. According to Neff, we "become motivated by the desire to escape our own self-judgment. This approach works to a certain degree, but one of the biggest problems with fear as a motivator is that anxiety itself can undermine performance."

This is often the case for many of my clients. The coping tools that once worked and produced results reach a point where they no longer work and, in addition, are causing pain. It is at that juncture when change can happen. Maybe you are starting to realize that beating yourself up over the pregnancy loss is no longer helping, and you are tired of feeling bad. There is hope. There are many different tools you can find on the self-compassion website (www.self-compassion.org). You can also take the self-compassion quiz to see where you currently land.

One specific tool that I like to use with clients (which Neff also recommends) is writing oneself a self-compassion letter. Imagine yourself as a kind, loving friend sharing supportive words with someone going through this loss. Imagine what you would want to hear from a friend. Or imagine yourself writing a letter from future you, from the wise you twenty years from now. What would you want to hear? Because remember, *most of the time, we know what we most need to hear but somehow we withhold that from ourselves as a form of self-punishment.*

Coming back to my body

It went through this with me.

Pregnancy loss takes a toll, not just on your physical body, but on your relationship with your body. After each of my losses, I felt very angry with my body (See "Feeling betrayed by my body"). At certain points, I detached completely. My body was doing whatever it needed to do and I was just annoyed with the process—the bleeding, the hormone fluctuations, the waiting to be back to "normal."

Meredith: Living in the home where a loved one died can be difficult. At every turn there are reminders, little and big. Everywhere you look, another memory alights. Too much of this too soon is way more than most people can endure.

When your body is that home, there is no way to separate the experience from the space. You don't ever really get a respite. Hot spots throughout the body turn on and off with seemingly no warning; the pain may be physical, but it comes with a message: pay attention to the emotions that might be contributing to, or exacerbating, the pain. Your body is Nature personified; she will return to a kind of homeostasis, though it may be different from what you're used to. Everyone's body responds differently.

I still feel guilty for all the anger I harbored. My body went through so much—five pregnancies in a couple years is a lot. Nothing that happened was my body's fault. I see now how much my body wanted to carry a baby. It was as desperate as I was for a happy outcome. When I felt so out of sorts with each loss, my body did too. I shouldn't have seen my body as an adversary; it was my comrade.

—————————

Meredith: This kind of positive self-regard can spread across the rest of you, too—your resilience of body, mind, and spirit, all connected. Your body carries everything inside it. Even when you aren't feeling like you can handle another day of this, your body is trying to heal and, in that way, is a testament to why all this suffering is meaningful.

—————————

I have so much appreciation for my body now. I look back at how it "bounced back" with each loss, how it never gave up on me. I remember being mystified at how my period resumed within a month or two of each loss, as if my body was saying, "OK, I'm ready. Let's do this." How amazing is that? After each surgery, my body healed—I had no patience for the healing process at the time, but I can see in hindsight that it was so quick. I was able to go for runs again, able to go to yoga classes. It's incredible, really, what the body can endure.

—————————

Meredith: It's miraculous, really. We are resilient as a species, even despite the most unbearable suffering. A quote I love: "Since time immemorial we have rebounded from our relentless wars, countless disasters (both natural and man-made), and the violence in our own lives." (Bessel A. van der Kolk, *The Body Keeps the Score: Brain, Mind, and Body in the Healing of Trauma*)

—————————

Today, I respect my body more than I ever have before. I still have my critical days, but I don't see how I could ever be angry at my body again. I'm so grateful for its resilience and persistence.

A little something that helps me
It might sound cheesy, but I have looked in the mirror on several occasions and apologized for the less-than-kind things I've said to my body in the past. And I try to make a regular habit of saying "I love you" to my body when I come out of the shower, naked. It's a small thing, but it matters to me to acknowledge my body's amazingness as often as I can.

Unfortunately, women have a long history of being at war with our bodies. Whether you believe you are too fat, too skinny, too dark-skinned, too light-skinned, too something, or not enough something else, a pregnancy loss may worsen your relationship with your body, especially if you believe it has failed you.

Also, if you have ever struggled with dieting—56.4 percent of women in the US reported being on a diet within the last year and 75 percent of women reported disordered eating (meaning unhealthy thoughts, feelings, or behaviors related to food and their bodies)—a pregnancy loss can either trigger a history of disordered eating or push you into disordered eating behaviors as a way to control and cope.

"I remember feeling sorry for my body that was so happy to prepare for this baby by swelling up and increasing my breasts several sizes already and all kinds of hormonal changes ... only to be halted. ... It was the saddest thing."
—Jessica, on her second-trimester loss

Some clients have reported trying to punish their bodies by under-eating and losing any the of pregnancy weight that they no longer "deserve" to have or overeating and/or bingeing as a way to emotionally numb and blunt the grief.

This is a complicated issue. For starters, I typically encourage my clients to practice self-compassion and learn about the anti-diet culture as they explore how these issues are affecting them. If these issues arise, professional help is warranted. Remember that your body is listening to you all the time, and this is the only body you will have.

Moments of joy

I felt guilty about them at first, then grateful.

The first time I laughed hard after losing Miles, I covered my mouth, instinctively. The way you would when you burp or curse or do something else socially inappropriate. I felt my cheeks flush, as if I'd been caught doing something sinful, disobeying a rule. I don't know why; I was alone, watching a TV show (*It's Always Sunny in Philadelphia*). In the most basic sense, I think I was startled by my own outburst—*what is this strange sound I have not heard in eons?* On a deeper level, I felt guilty, like I was dishonoring Miles with this brief moment of joy.

"Yuck yuks: The combination of shock, relief, and guilt arising from the first time you find yourself doubled over in laughter after a deep loss."
—Rebecca Soffer and Gabrielle Birkner, *Modern Loss: Candid Conversations about Grief. Beginners Welcome.*

Because I had four losses, I was fresh off a loss for the better (or worse) part of two years. I think when people envision grieving, they picture consistent sadness. I envisioned that myself. So when I did have flashes of joy, it was confusing. Was I supposed to have these flashes? If people caught me in them, would they think the losses hadn't affected me, that I didn't really love my babies?

When I struggled with these questions, I came back to Miles. I decided there was no way he would want me to feel nothing but sorrow. He would want me to engage with the world and find enjoyment. I was alive; I owed him that much.

A few weeks after losing him, I suggested to Chris that we venture out for a brunch outing. I've always loved brunch—my favorite kinds of food, my favorite time of day. From there, we graduated to seeing a movie and going to a comedy club. I felt like an alien visiting another planet for investigational purposes, but in time, I also felt more "like me."

My grief wasn't all tears and sadness; there were moments of joyful reprieve. In the beginning, they were so brief, fleeting. But then they became more common, more substantial. I learned to see the joyful moments as evidence that I would make it. I collected this evidence and held it as tightly as a security blanket.

"Joy is grief inside out."

—George Valliant, psychiatrist, quoted in *All Joy and No Fun* by Jennifer Senior

"Tucked inside the moments of this great sadness—this feeling of being punctured, scrambling and stricken—were also moments of the brightest, most swollen and logic shattering happiness I'd ever experienced. One moment would be a wall of happiness so tall it could not be scaled; the next felt like falling into a pit of sadness that had no bottom. I realized that you could not have one without the other, that this great capacity to love and be happy can be experienced only with this great risk of having happiness taken from you—to tremble, always, on the edge of loss."

—Emily Rapp, *The Still Point of the Turning World*

Now, I experience joy regularly. Like, all the time. Every day. I'm one of those annoying people (but I still would never use #blessed). Before my losses, I was not this type of person. I was prone to negativity. I think the darkness of grief gave me a new appreciation for light. Sometimes, I've learned, life is dependent on contrast. For example, I wouldn't enjoy the freedoms of weekends if the week wasn't such a grind. Now, knowing grief, there is a new depth to joy. I never take it for granted.

Meredith

After shedding so many tears, after being inside so many dark spaces of your heart, feeling happy can feel unfamiliar. But even in the midst of grief, moments of elation and of unexpected joy are natural.

You've been changed by your grief. That change will have an effect on how you experience joy. You have a new perspective on life. This perspective can make happier times feel even more poignant.

Your joy may take you by surprise, at least the way you express it. It may even come through tears. This can be one of the first flashes of gratitude that you feel; you know you've made it through some of the roughest parts, and your capacity to feel something other than pain has remained intact or has even been heightened. Something to be thankful for indeed.

Finding meaning

There's so much there.

In the midst of my losses, someone said to me, "You'll grow from this," and I thought *I don't give a shit about growing. I just want to have a baby.* But I *did* grow, in spite of myself. I just had to recognize it on my own terms, in my own time. Nobody but me could attach meaning to my experience. The meanings I found are mine alone.

Some may say people aren't themselves while grieving, but I think they are exactly themselves, stripped of all the illusions of control and safety they had before their loss. In this way, grieving exposes us; it gets to the heart of the universal fears and hopes that make us human. It is impossible to be unchanged by it.

I've gained so many things from my losses. I'm more confident in my own fortitude and resilience. I realize I can survive more than I ever thought I could. This has made me less fearful, bolder.

I have such a deep appreciation for life, every breath of it. I realize how fragile and fleeting it is, how it can be gone in a second. This scares me sometimes, but mostly it liberates me to just live as fully as I can. I've learned the beauty of surrender.

My perspective has changed, for the better. Grief and loss demand thinking about death. And thinking about death demands reassessing life— what matters, what *should* matter. I don't fret about stupid things as much. I focus on my passions, my relationships. I try to live in the direction of nurturing those things.

I feel more connected to others, more compassionate. I have a new understanding of the suffering out there, much of it silent and private. I know so many people feel alone, and my heart hurts for that. My experiences have encouraged me to share my story, to reach out however I can to alleviate just a little of the collective loneliness.

All of these things, all of this meaning, does not make up for the heart-ache of my losses. I'm not *glad* I lost pregnancies. It was awful. But I figure the best way I can honor my lost babies is to show them how they changed me. They meant something. They had lasting impact. They mattered.

"Mourning and surviving a baby's death demands change. Some of your old ways of being and doing are simply inadequate. It's as if you've been broken and forced to become wiser." —Deborah L. Davis, *Empty Cradle, Broken Heart: Surviving the Death of Your Baby*

"...because I had already lived through the absolute worst thing I could imagine, I was suddenly afraid of nothing and in a bit of a mad rush to live the life I wanted to live...Seizing the day is not just bumper-sticker territory for me. I am aware at every moment just how brief our time here is, and I seize the crap out of it." —Haley Tanner, "F is for Forgiveness," featured in *Modern Loss: Candid Conversations about Grief. Beginners Welcome.* (Rebecca Soffer and Gabrielle Birkner, editors)

"If I could survive this, I could survive anything. I was going to survive. That was my moment of enlightenment." —Kim Cooper Findling, Mamamia.com

"Although we would never do the work of raising them, we had to raise ourselves, do the hard work of living in the absence of who they and we could have been together." —Shannon Gibney and Kao Kalia Yang, "Reclaiming Life," in *What God Is Honored Here? Writings on Miscarriage and Infant Loss by and for Native Women and Women of Color*

Meredith

It's so much more than surviving "surviving."

Rather than "finding meaning," I prefer the term "deepening," at least in the beginning, when it can be hard to assign meaning to the loss. Deepening suggests rooting. Plants receive nutrients through their roots as well. The deeper the root, the greater the foundation.

Meaning will come to you organically as a result of this rigorous, internal process. So much in today's world and in contemporary society is outwardly directed, a product of a results-driven world. With grief, the results you are seeking will always be internal, and the deeper you go, the greater chance you have of emerging with more of yourself. Deeper is relative, of course. Deep, like grief itself, is different for everyone.

One study of women who experienced miscarriage or stillbirth used the term "posttraumatic growth" to describe one effect of the grief and posttraumatic stress that accompanies this type of loss. This growth means getting to know the unknowns of yourself. It's a big leap, often in the dark, without much warning to prepare.

Depth suggests something that exists underground where the atmosphere can feel alien and frightening, as the interior depths often do.

This is where primal loss lives.

"I feel like I'm more grateful and appreciative each day for my family and loved ones. I also see children as little miracles and think it's just amazing how any of us get here, against many odds, and are able to live and breathe and be healthy and functioning. As cheesy as it sounds, I really do see life as a gift now. Mine and everyone else's."—Jessica, after her second-trimester loss

"I've always been quite a calm guy (or so I've been told) but this experience has mellowed me out completely. Very few things stress me since we lost Teddy ... I'm just grateful to have all those that I love around me and in good health, and I feel like a richer person for having had Teddy in our lives to bring me that perspective." —Nico (husband of Elle Wright, author of *Ask Me His Name: Learning to Live and Laugh Again After the Loss of My Baby*)

A tree or flower won't bloom unless it has rooted in the way its particular genus requires. Succulents are different than roses, eucalyptus are different than oaks, and you are different from the next woman, and the next and the next and the next. When the flower blooms—or when you discover the meaning behind all this loss that had at once seemed unattainable—stand in awe of what you endured to get here.

Bite-sized activities will help you move through your day, sure, but this is not a performance. No one should be judging you, and if they are, well, that speaks to their level of discomfort with loss.

On harder days, occupy your mind with something productive. Give yourself small, manageable tasks. Set your timer. Five minutes here, ten minutes there. These tiny increments of structure provide a nice reset. They are manageable, doable, tolerable. Short bursts of respite like this can refuel your mind, body, and spirit as you continue to find meaning in your loss both now and in the months to come. Because you've spent time with it before, it is no longer a stranger.

Huong

In 2019, David Kessler, a world-renowned grief expert (he co-wrote *On Grief and Grieving* with Elisabeth Kübler-Ross) identified "finding meaning" as the sixth stage of grief (joining the original five—denial, anger, bargaining, depression, and acceptance). He said, "Loss can wound and paralyze. It can hang over us for years. But finding meaning in loss empowers us to find a path forward."

Kessler states that many people look for a sense of "closure" after a loss. However, he argues that it is finding meaning after the loss that can transform grief into a more hopeful and peaceful experience.

For some women, this may take months and years. The meaning of the experience may also change and morph into different iterations that one needs to hear and believe at certain times. You have lost control after a pregnancy loss. Do not let others take away your meaning. You get to create that meaning and you get to change your mind about the meaning.

"The world breaks everyone and afterward many are strong at the broken places." —Ernest Hemingway, *A Farewell to Arms*

Trying again . . .
or not

Should we try again?

You might not know the answer right now. That's OK.

After my first loss, I swore up and down that I was done, not trying again, over it, moving on. Then time passed, and we tried again.

After my second loss, I said, "Nope. OK. Fool me once, shame on you. Fool me twice . . . "

Then time passed, and we tried again.

After my third loss, I said, "OK. Three strikes, and you're out. Done deal."

Then time passed and we tried again.

After my fourth loss, I didn't even bother saying anything. I knew, in my heart, that I would want to try again.

And we did.

And, somehow, my daughter came into the world with a look on her face that said *Oh, hey, it's you.* As if she'd been there the whole time, waiting in the wings while I grieved and grieved.

When women lose babies and say they don't want to try again, I totally understand.

When they lose and say they need to try again, I totally understand.

After each loss, I wavered for weeks (sometimes months) on whether or not to try again. I wasn't sure if I could mentally endure another loss. I wasn't sure if I wanted to put my body and my marriage through that. It's not an easy decision, though everyone around you will imply it is: "Just try again," they say. They think they're being supportive. They don't realize how "try again" completely dismisses the gravity of the loss of the baby you were just carrying. So, screw them. Take your time.

One thing: Consider a new doctor if the thought of your old one makes your stomach churn. To this day, thinking about the doctor who confirmed Miles died makes me feel like I'm going to throw up. I could not handle seeing him again. The doctor I began seeing after him was incredible, the quintessential breath of fresh air.

Another thing: I don't think you need to "resolve your grief" to try again. Sometimes, that's just not realistic. I don't even know if my grief is fully resolved today, and my daughter is two.

A good friend said to me once, "Maybe humans are wired for happiness." Her point was that no matter what decisions we make, we will learn to frame them in a positive way because we *want* to think they were for the best. We don't want to be regretful and miserable. This helped me when I was pondering whether to try again. I knew that no matter what, I would go on to have a fulfilling life. There was no "right" or "wrong"; there was only my choice and the life lived in the wake of that choice.

Here we go again…

The unhelpful thing someone said	My imagined response	Let's unpack this
"You guys should just try again!"	"Would you go skydiving again if your parachute didn't open correctly the first time?" (Fun fact: I've been skydiving twice. The second time, the parachute did not open. The guy strapped to me said, "Fuck," and then pulled the emergency chute just in time. I will not go again).	There is no "just" in trying again. When people told me to "just try again," I felt like they were 1) glossing over the existence of the baby I'd lost, and 2) dismissing the physical and emotional pain I'd endured during that loss. I know they meant well. To them, "trying again" seemed like the quickest, easiest way for me to get what I wanted (a baby) so I wouldn't be sad anymore. In their minds, I got pregnant once, so it could/would happen again, and "what are the chances of something going wrong then?" (someone actually said this to me and then probably felt like a jerk when I proceeded to lose three more babies). I think the pressure people put on me had more to do with their own discomfort with my pain than anything. People have a hard time being patient with grief. See "Grieving in a society that sucks at grief." I felt a disconnect between the enthusiasm of others and my internal fears and apprehensions. It was lonely. Each time my husband and I decided to "try again" (that phrase still raises my blood pressure), I told fewer and fewer people. I didn't want to admit to my own longing. I wanted to protect my desire, hold it close. You may want to do the same. Or you may want to tell your loved ones so they can comfort you through the anxiety of trying again. See "To tell people, or not to tell people." It's really up to you—like everything in this process.

Meredith

Trust that you are capable of loving again.

Trust that the grief may never be completely gone.

Trust that all the work you've done to process your pain counts.

Trust that you are more resilient, more in touch with your desire, and even more in touch with your needs this time around.

Trust that your ability to decide if you want to try again will lead you to the right decision.

Trust that the circular and overlapping nature of grieving a loss will always lead you back to the thing that broke your heart.

Trust that your loss forced you to open more fully, that it will be forever intertwined with your life going forward.

Trust that even if you think your brain forgot, your soul will remember your baby.

Trust the joy you feel to try again if that is what you want. Follow your joy and your desire.

Trust yourself.

"After my stillbirth and miscarriages, there was a part of me that kept saying, 'enough now, stop, it's not fair, you can't keep putting yourself and your body through this.' But there was the other part nudging me, saying, 'let us do this one more time, just to be sure, just to say we tried absolutely everything' . . . Looking back now I'm not sure how I did it, and if I could mentally go through it again, but you do what you need to because inside all of us there's a huge reserve of strength and hope tucked tightly away to help us climb any mountain." —Georgie, who had a stillborn daughter (Ella) and two first-trimester miscarriages. She now lives in Uganda with her husband and two children.

"I became maniacal in my desire for another baby, any baby. Those crazed women who kidnap children began to make perfect sense to me. I told my husband to 'give me another baby.' I didn't care about anything else." —Sarah Agaton Howes, "Lessons from Dying," featured in *What God Is Honored Here? Writings on Miscarriage and Infant Loss by and for Native Women and Women of Color* (Shannon Gibney and Kao Kalia Yang, editors)

I want to try again, but I'm terrified

How could I not be terrified?

When I lost my pregnancies, I also lost my innocence. I became more aware than I ever wanted to be of what could go dreadfully wrong. So, of course, when I approached getting pregnant again, I was scared.

In addition to the discomfort of just feeling scared in and of itself, I also felt resentful of my fear. After all, so many other people seem to approach getting pregnant with joy and enthusiasm. They make jokes about enjoying "practicing." They start brainstorming baby names, just for the hell of it. They seem to have no anxiety at all. Why would they? They haven't lost a baby.

For me, deciding to try again meant coming to terms with the fact that pregnancy would not ever be this light, fun experience for me. Even now, I still envy women who pee on a stick and throw a nine-month-long celebration party, women whose greatest worry is weight gain and what color to paint the nursery, women who obsess over their gender reveal shindigs and baby showers, women who post their ultrasound photos on Facebook with reckless abandon. I will never be one of them.

"I missed the child we lost and I wanted another and these seemed like two absolutely separate aches." —Elizabeth McCracken, in her memoir *An Exact Replica of a Figment of My Imagination*

I've come to see my fear and anxiety as representative of the love I felt for the babies I lost. I knew how painful it was to lose. My mind and body remembered that pain, and I felt programmed to try to avoid it again. So, yes, the idea of trying for another baby was very unsettling. It's like how humans instinctually step back if they come upon a snake in their path; it's ingrained. Trying again felt like continuing to walk forward, staring the snake in the eye. I took the most careful steps I could and hoped for the best.

Meredith

Until now, grief may have been your main focus. The baby you lost, the pain you endured as you recovered. Now something new is happening despite your fear. You're looking ahead. You're thinking about the future.

As you go about trying to decide whether or not to try again, you have far more information, more data—both textbook and experiential, derived from your own experience—to drawn upon. And you have more knowledge about yourself.

The loss has changed your reality, changed you, changed your relationships. All that knowledge, used to define and understand one set of circumstances, has begun to shed some light on which path you'll ultimately decide to take in the future. At some point—in fact, it might be happening now—the urgency of those details will subside, though their importance will not. They still matter, still inform. Let them be *part* of the mortar that paves that path. Let them help you make decisions about what is right for you, using the wisdom they bring and the lessons they taught you *beyond* the sadness (that you're strong, resourceful, and resilient, for example).

Perhaps you will try again. Or maybe you'll make the decision to keep thinking about it for now, to hold the possibility in your hands, to let yourself, allow yourself once again, a tiny bit of space to dream.

Huong

Some of the fear that comes with trying again may be related to what we call anticipatory grief. In "The Long Road: An Article on Anticipatory Grief," Jennifer Allen shares that anticipatory grief is "the challenge of holding both hope and grief, staying close and letting go—all at the same time." I believe this concept rings true for women and couples who are contemplating the idea of "trying again." Although the word "try" is a verb, meaning to make an effort to do something, it often first starts with the emotional and psychological burden of starting to entertain the notion of life and death.

In my practice, for some women who are considering "trying again," this may bring up a mixture of feelings including hope and joy for the possibility of pregnancy but also grief and dread at possibly having to experience a pregnancy loss. They tell me, "I want to try again so badly, but the idea of another loss seems insurmountable. I don't know if I can deal with yet another loss." Some have to make the painful decision to weigh the literal costs and benefits of trying again versus other actions.

"No amount of anxiety can change the future. No amount of regret can change the past." —Karen Salmansohn

When you and your partner
aren't on the same page

You want to try again; he doesn't. Or vice versa.

After our fourth loss, my husband said, "Would it be so bad if we didn't have a child?" and I wanted to slap him. He was ready to throw in the towel. Our losses had taken such a toll on us—emotionally, physically, financially (See "When your loss causes financial stress"). He hated seeing me suffer. And I'm sure he hated suffering himself, though he was very stubborn in insisting that he was "fine."

We had several talks about whether or not we should keep going in our attempts to have a child. When he sensed my apprehension, he'd start rattling off all the pros of *not* having kids: "We'll have so much more freedom! We'll have more money! We can retire early! We can get another dog!" He seemed to have no problem flipping the switch back to a life without kids. I found it impossible to flip that switch.

**"He, I know, really really wants a second kid, and I don't know.
That's where little fractures start to happen."**
—Whitney Port, on her hesitancy to try again after her miscarriage, to the Today Show

---

Ultimately, he let me decide. "It's your body," he said. It sounded cold and harsh, but it was the truth. It *was* my body. I was the one who was forming a biologically based attachment to the baby the moment I peed on a stick (and, as a woman, I had to bear the brunt of all the societal messages about the mother-baby attachment). I was the one who had to undergo various medical procedures if something went wrong (and even if everything went right).

"The only thing that seems eternal and natural in motherhood is ambivalence."* —Jane Lazarre

---

At times, he resented my resolve. My resolve was putting us through the ringer. He would have preferred to move on and try to find happiness as a childless couple. But I had to keep going. It was something I just knew, at a gut level, that I had to do. Thankfully, he didn't fight me too much. I'm sure he thought I was crazy at times (I probably *was* crazy at times), but he let me make the final decision each time we contemplated trying again. All I needed from him was a confirmation that he still wanted to be a father. He always gave me a very businesslike response to that question: "If it were up to me, I would be a father." That was all I needed to hear.

Meredith

Some couples will never share the same vision for parenthood. This complicates things when it comes to getting pregnant and trying to have a baby.

Maybe that was you—or is you. Trauma can, of course, unify couples. But the deepening that grief forces you and your partner to do can also bring about completely different visions for the future regarding a baby.

Degrees of ambivalence can persist even for the person who would like to have a baby. They often become more pronounced, it seems, if there was hesitation from the start.

If you want a baby, but your partner does not, and this longing or desire is not met, it can be acutely painful and at times very lonely. Our tendency might be to try to fight the "awareness" of this; to try to work harder to get the other person to see our side, to get on board, to move together, side by side, in the same direction. It can feel like a betrayal—in a way—if your partner's path is headed east, but yours is headed north. It can almost be more difficult if you are aligned on many other things too. It brings this single disparity—a big one already—into extremely sharp relief.

As you work through differences, as you navigate this space together and separately, how do you tolerate a new level of not knowing what comes next, this time with your partner?

Some ideas to hold loosely and use as needed:

- This step in your journey together is about vulnerability.
- While you will want to share your feelings and desires, be equally interested and curious in your partner's perspective. Ask questions, listen, and refrain from trying to sell or convince.
- Ask: Am I hearing what the other person is really saying? Dare to ask: "Can you tell me more? I want to know."
- Say: "I'm affected by this deeply. And I know you are too. Let's keep talking about it for now, even if we disagree."

Deciding not to try again

There's nothing wrong with that choice.

"Trying again" after a loss is never simple, and sometimes it's especially complicated. Maybe you had a pregnancy complication or a genetic issue that you fear repeating again. If you have fertility concerns, maybe you don't want to go through the stress of trying again or going through extensive medical procedures. Maybe you can't tolerate the emotional rollercoaster that would come with another pregnancy. There are so many valid reasons.

After I gave birth to my daughter, people started to ask if we had plans for another baby. I found this super annoying. I felt so grateful to have our daughter and had no interest in pressing our luck. In fact, just two months after our daughter was born, my husband got a vasectomy. It wasn't something he would have done on his own, but I felt strongly about it. I didn't want to be pregnant ever again. Pregnancy, for me, had been so tied to pain. I considered it a miracle that our fifth pregnancy had been successful. I plan to spend the rest of my life counting my lucky stars.

"I was not able to attempt getting pregnant again;
I didn't have the fortitude to risk that horrific pain a second time."
—Cindy Harkin, featured in the *New York Times* Opinion piece,
"You Know Someone Who's Had a Miscarriage" (Lauren Kelley and Alexandra March)

When I tell people about the vasectomy, they look at me a little funny. They don't really understand how painful our losses were and what a toll they took on our marriage (and our life, in general). I'm relieved that the pregnancy stage of my life is over. Yes, there are times I wish my daughter had a sibling, but I knew I would feel that way when making our decision to end our fertility as a couple. For us, the relief that came with the vasectomy outweighed any lingering desires to grow our family. It's a very personal choice. We all have to do what works for us and our relationships.

Meredith

You may be struggling to decide whether or not to try to become pregnant again. Or maybe the decision to not try came easily. Either way, letting go of something that you cherish—in this case, the idea of having another baby or having a first—can be hard. You may find yourself walking through the stages of loss as you say goodbye not to a baby, but to a significant phase in your life that is now drawing to a close.

You may feel ambivalent about all this. A part of you may still long for parenthood. At the same time you may find yourself exploring other valuable experiences, big and little. These won't be the same as having a baby, and they won't change the gravity or meaning of your loss, because nothing could do that. You may have never wanted this to be your decision, but here you are. The path your life is taking holds promise and value; it will be different than having a baby, but it will be equally meaningful in ways you have yet to discover.

"Trust yourself. You've survived a lot, and you'll survive whatever is coming."
—Robert Tew

Getting pregnant after a loss

When it feels like you're holding your breath for nine months

The anxiety is real.

For me, pregnancy will always be a fraught experience with so many complicated emotions. Don't get me wrong—I was excited each time I got pregnant. I was hopeful and eager and grateful. But I was also terrified. The fear made me feel lonely, because other pregnant women seemed to be joyous and carefree (my perception, of course. I didn't know their personal stories).

After my first loss, pregnancy became completely anxiety-ridden. With each subsequent loss, it got worse. Crippling. When I got pregnant for the fifth time, I didn't even bother taking a picture of the positive pregnancy test. When we heard a heartbeat at our first ultrasound (eight weeks), I got so light-headed and dizzy that I nearly fell off the table. The stress of the appointment gave me a two-day migraine.

During my fifth pregnancy, I would only allow myself to mark the baby's age—eight weeks, nine weeks, ten weeks—once that week had passed. I refused to get ahead of myself. In a way, I thought if I marked ahead, the baby would die, a punishment for my overconfidence.

As my bump started to grow, I hated that I had to announce that I was pregnant. Actually, I didn't announce it. Someone at work blurted out, "When you stand that way, it looks like you have a baby bump." The proverbial cat was out of the damn bag. Shortly after that, the receptionist at work touched my belly and proclaimed, "Look at you!" I felt assaulted, exposed. For months, my desire to be a mother had been this sacred secret, something I kept protected. Now, everyone knew. If I had another loss, everyone would know that too.

On social media, I'd see people announcing, "We're having a girl!" and I'd shudder at their arrogance. Even when we found out my fifth pregnancy was a girl, we simply said, "It's a girl." We didn't know if we'd be lucky enough to *have* her.

As my bump continued to grow, I resisted buying maternity clothes. It got to the point that my husband had to buy them. I was angry with him, convinced he'd jinxed the whole thing. The only time I bought anything for our daughter was when I went to return something my husband had purchased and they mandated I do an exchange. I chose newborn pajamas because they were the right price. When I got home, I pulled them from the bag and said to my husband, "I did a bad thing."

What the studies tell us

"Women with a history of prenatal loss are consistently reported to exhibit significantly elevated rates of anxiety and depressive symptoms during a subsequent pregnancy."

(The British Journal of Psychiatry, 2011)

"I had been given a pregnancy journal and didn't start writing in it until after twelve weeks. I tried not to 'look ahead' of what was to come past the week I was in until probably around thirty-six weeks... There is a difference between women who have gone through pregnancy loss than those who don't... Your ultrasound appointments are different. Each milestone is different. Even the physical ailments don't seem as bad, because you know that that still means you're pregnant." —Michaela, on her pregnancy after a first-trimester loss

"I was scared. Every. Single. Second. I obsessed over hormone counts. Breast tenderness. Nausea. I took everything as a sign that things were either thriving or they weren't. Dissected everything. Prayer helped. But I knew the reality of loss, having just endured it twice. There was an element of surrender that occurred at some point. It probably taught me more than I can even conceptualize to this day." —Wendy, on pregnancy after her two first-trimester miscarriages

I told everyone I didn't want a baby shower. They thought I was just being coy, but I was serious. Just the thought of accumulating all those things before she was born—the clothes, the toys, the gadgets—made my heart race. Many people insisted I have a shower, and I kept adamantly refusing. In the end, I got my way, but loved ones seemed strangely irritated with me and my refusal to follow the usual happy-pregnant-lady narrative.

I think people assumed that I'd "loosen up" as the pregnancy went on. I made the mistake of assuming this as well. I told myself, "I'll relax when I hear the heartbeat," then "When I get past the first trimester," then "When the genetic screening tests come back," then "When the anatomy scan is normal," then "When she's bigger than a bell pepper," then "When I feel her move." I've come to accept that I'll never be at ease. I've come to accept that this is motherhood.

Meredith

Anxiety. Unease and worry while you wait once again. It's completely understandable. But don't let that frightened inner voice go too far. If you find yourself worrying more, even just a bit more each day, or if fear is interfering with your ability to separate your past loss from your current pregnancy, it might be more than anxiety. Please, understand that your worry is natural, but recognize that you might be dealing with some posttraumatic stress (See "Posttraumatic stress: It's a thing"). There is help available for you (See "Getting professional help").

"Traumatic experiences get imprinted on us. There is an evolutionary benefit to us remembering. So when a woman gets pregnant again after having a miscarriage, her body and mind remember and she can have significant anxiety and can re-experience aspects of the trauma."

—Tessa Sugarbaker, a gynecologist who now works as a therapist treating clients who have experienced pregnancy loss, to *Washington Post*

Coping with the anxiety

Do what you need to do.

When I got pregnant for the fifth time and passed the seventeen-week mark (when I'd lost Miles), the anxiety decreased a little, but then I just began worrying about all the horrific ways I could still lose my baby. I hadn't had a preterm delivery yet, or a stillbirth—were those in store?

My doctor knew I was anxious, so he arranged for me to see a specialist who would more closely monitor the baby's development, the placenta, my cervix, et cetera. I had *a lot* of ultrasounds. I was hooked up to monitors to measure contractions starting at twenty weeks. Toward the end of my pregnancy, I was in the specialist's office multiple times a week.

The close monitoring did help reassure me, but it also raised my anxiety at times. In earlier weeks, they saw my placenta was lying very low, so that gave me something to worry about. Eventually, it moved. During the anatomy exam, they noted small deposits of calcium on my baby's heart—which they said could mean nothing but was also a marker for Down's Syndrome. It turned out to be nothing. They encouraged me to do kick charts (counting the baby's kicks at certain times of day), which can make the sanest woman completely neurotic. I would lie awake at night, waiting for my daughter to kick the prescribed number of times before I would allow myself to sleep. Throughout my pregnancy, they said my daughter was measuring large. This, in combination with the fact that I was borderline for gestational diabetes, caused me to fret about what I was eating. It was a lot of stress for nothing— they thought she would be over nine pounds, and she was six and a half.

Ultimately, I think the close monitoring was good for me. It helped me feel more "in control." But, of course, the control was an illusion. It's not like the specialist could have prevented every terrible thing from happening.

Something could have still gone wrong; it just didn't. Still, sometimes we need illusions, something to cling to.

I also hired a doula so I would have someone available to talk to me about my fears. I warned her early on that I was going to be anxious, and she was the calmest person ever, so that helped.

"It was very difficult to attend each doctor's appointment in my second pregnancy. I wanted to be positive but also not presumptive; I didn't want to believe the worst, but I also feared that at any moment, I would be given another round of bad news. To combat the anxiety, I had to rely on a spiritual part of myself that allows me to 'let go' and recognize that I am not in full control of everything in my life and/or in this world. For a control freak, not at all easy, but a very important practice that was/is necessary during and post pregnancy with my daughter."

—Jessica, on managing anxiety when pregnant again after her second-trimester loss

I continued going to therapy and talking aloud about my worries and my ongoing grief for my previous losses. Because I'm an overachiever, I also consulted with a psychiatrist, and she agreed it was best for me to stay on medication throughout my pregnancy to handle the inevitable anxiety.

I started doing restorative yoga and used the classes to really think about my baby and connect with her. I still love restorative yoga.

Something I didn't do but wish I'd done is take medical leave from work. My advertising job was very demanding and stressful, and I don't think it was good for me to be there during my pregnancy. I often had up to ten meetings a day, coupled with crazy deadlines. I began insisting on lunch breaks, which meant missing meetings. I had to fight for those damn lunch breaks. A pregnant woman should not have to fight for lunch breaks. On my review that year, my boss wrote: "Schedule rigidity results in the absence of leadership." So, yeah, I should have excused myself from that type of environment. I'm just grateful my daughter arrived safely, despite the stress.

Meredith

Trauma has a way of pulling opposite forces together inside us. Meditation, in addition to any other therapy or self-care, can help you hold both without being overwhelmed.

Meditation Is Not What You *Think*

Your mind is always looking for new possibilities—answers to your problems (thank you, mind!). Unfortunately, the mind sometimes complicates things, kind of like a neighbor who meddles. Being mindful means understanding this and accepting it. You don't need to wrestle the mind into submission or be hard on yourself for thinking too much.

See page 125 for exercises to help you practice mindfulness and ease your anxiety.

I'm having trouble connecting
with my baby

Because connection means love,
and love makes loss painful.

When I got pregnant after my first loss, I told myself not to get too attached. When that pregnancy resulted in a loss, and then another, and then another, I had become so hardened that I found it very hard to connect with my daughter during my fifth pregnancy, even as the weeks ticked by and everything seemed to be going well.

There were times I'd ask my husband, "Are you sure I'm really pregnant?" I genuinely wondered if I was so grief-stricken about my previous losses that I'd become delusional. I'd have dreams all the time of losing the baby, of waking up in a pool of blood. Nearly every morning, it would take me a moment to orient myself, to confirm reality. I'd step on the scale daily, not because I cared how many pounds I was gaining, but because the weight assured me that a baby was really inside, growing.

Actress Kristen Bell said about her pregnancy with her daughter, "It could've been a water bottle in my belly, that's about how connected I felt to her during my pregnancy." I understood this. And then I felt ashamed for understanding this. After all my losses, I felt like I should have been even more deeply connected to my baby, awash in gratitude and joy. I just wasn't. It was too hard for me to get attached. I felt like keeping my distance would lessen the pain of a loss. Ultimately, I think I just wanted to feel like I had some control over my pain.

Eventually, I started writing letters to our daughter, in an attempt to connect with her, after so many weeks of attempting *not* to connect with her.

I didn't tell anyone about these letters. If we lost her, only she would know how I got attached to her when I should have known better. In the letters, I told her how scared I was. It helped to get it out, to share my reality with her. I still write her letters, even though she's here. I still tell her how the amount of love I feel for her scares me at times.

"When I got pregnant again last summer, I tried for a few days to pretend that this time, I wouldn't fall in love with the baby until I knew we were in it for the long haul. Ha ... I decided that being pregnant meant keeping two colliding realities in my heart and mind from week 1 to week 40: My baby needs me to take care of him and to anticipate his birth. My baby may not be born."
—Emily Bazelon, "I Went Out Full," featured in *About What Was Lost: 20 Writers on Miscarriage, Healing, and Hope* (Jessica Berger Gross, editor)

"This time I did not let myself map out my pregnancy the way I had the first time, writing into my calendar what my due date would be, or imagining how I would look in maternity clothes, or planning what I would say to my boss when it was time to apply for leave. I kept my hopes small, and limited my excitement to cautious postings on the Internet bulletin boards, where I graduated from the 'Dealing with Loss' board to the one titled 'Pregnant After Loss.'" —Andrea J. Buchanan, "Misconceptions," featured in *About What Was Lost: 20 Writers on Miscarriage, Healing, and Hope* (Jessica Berger Gross, editor)

"Pregnancy after loss is a whole other thing."
—Domino Kirke, singer

Meredith

It almost seems counterintuitive that after having endured a pregnancy loss (or losses) it could be difficult to bond with your baby while he or she is still in utero. And not just mildly difficult. But hard.

Women who become pregnant after having prior pregnancy losses commonly experience feelings of depression, anxiety, and even trauma-like symptoms—and problems bonding with the baby. After such loss, a new layer of grief surfaces when you become pregnant. You now have the challenge of grieving the loss of one baby while bonding to another.

That's a lot.

But there is hope—lots of it. It might surprise you to learn that giving meaning to your parenting role for the unborn child who has died can aid in your ability to bond and attach to the baby in this pregnancy. This reminds us (again) that prior loss, like new life, is to be revered and cherished. Your current pregnancy doesn't make up for the pregnancy you lost—it's not an either/or equation. Understanding your own mental experience of your loss and your related feelings can help you mourn the loss of one baby while attaching to another, and this in turn can lower the chance of having potential attachment problems after birth. (See a few mentalization exercises in Huong's entry).

All the love we need to talk about? There it is—the baby you lost and the baby you will meet one day. Love is deep enough and wide enough to hold them both—and you—forever.

Huong

In the appropriately titled article "'Ghosts' in the Womb," psychologist Rayna Markin discusses how pregnancies following loss(es) are often characterized by feelings of depression, anxiety, trauma-like symptoms, and potential difficulty with bonding to the baby while in utero due to fears of another pregnancy loss. This difficulty with bonding during pregnancy may lead to impaired mother-infant attachment relationships following birth.

Some studies suggest that babies born after a pregnancy loss are at the highest risk for insecure attachment with their mother. One such treatment intervention that has proven effective for increasing mother and child bonding during pregnancy is mentalization-based therapy.

The goal in mentalization therapy following a pregnancy loss is to allow the mother to mourn the loss of one baby while also attaching herself to another. Though it may seem counterintuitive, part of attaching yourself to your new baby is remembering the baby you lost.

Here is how remembering the baby you lost can help you, according to PALS (Pregnancy After Loss Support):

1. Remembering your baby who died helps you to understand the trauma of losing a child. It also helps with how that loss is affecting you.
2. Remembering the baby who died is a way of recognizing that these are two different babies.

3. By both remembering and celebrating, you are realizing that you are capable of holding multiple, conflicting emotions in your mind. Yes, you can be both happy and sad at the same time. Yes, you can switch from one emotion to the other.
4. By honoring the child who died, you are thinking about how you can change your future. This isn't a guarantee that bad things won't happen again, but a recognition that we can healthily respond to our emotions.

A few mentalization exercises include:

1. Imagine the two babies talking to each other, which will help create separate and distinct identities for them.
2. Write a letter to each of your children and introduce them to each other. Talk about how they can support each other going forth in the world and how they will always be connected.
3. Practice holding in your body both the emotions of happiness about your current pregnancy and the sadness about your previous loss. Locate where you feel the happiness (e.g., your heart can feel like like it is bursting), and locate where you feel the sadness (e.g., your stomach is in knots). The more you can tolerate and practice holding conflicting emotions, the more you will make space for both children.

To tell people, or not to tell people

That is the question.

A story: When my sister was in college, she had a male roommate who became more than just a roommate. But she didn't tell anyone about the relationship. She continued insisting they were just friends. For years. When they eventually broke up, my sister felt like she had nobody to turn to because the entire relationship had been a secret. A friend of hers, upon hearing the whole story, said, "Well, closed mouths don't get fed." And that's what I think about sharing pregnancy (and loss): Closed mouths don't get fed.

After my first loss, I decided I would open up to a select group of friends and family if I got pregnant again. So that select group of people knew about each of my subsequent pregnancies (and losses). I did not tell the general public about my pregnancies though—it just didn't feel right for me. I was more than halfway through my pregnancy with my daughter when a coworker noticed my baby bump. The "telling" was essentially done for me, whether I liked it or not.

Ultimately, it's up to each woman to decide what she wants to do. Lately, I've seen more women on social media announcing their pregnancies early— not with blissful ignorance, but with clear knowing and intention. They state that they don't want to be quiet, they want people to know what's going on so that if something goes wrong, they have support. I am a private person, so a public declaration like this would make me break out in hives, but I am in full support of whatever each woman needs to do to feel supported during her pregnancy.

If you do not want to announce your pregnancy on social media, that is OK. If you want to, that is fine too. You know intimately, now, about loss and the way it can affect you. There is nothing about that you need to hide. What is key here is the honesty with yourself, with, as Kim says, the knowing and intention. That strips away the veneer and is one less thing you have to work at keeping up.

"I wanted to keep it a secret. After posting my last pregnancy on social media and then losing the baby, I didn't want the same thing to happen again."
—Amy Whatley, who hid her pregnancy for nine months after suffering multiple losses, DailyMail.com

"Here's the problem with keeping pregnancy a secret: If friends and relatives and coworkers and neighbors don't know about your pregnancy, how will they provide support if the worst DOES happen?"
—Jessica Berger Gross, *About What Was Lost: 20 Writers on Miscarriage, Healing, and Hope*

"If you were to lose your pregnancy, who would you want to know about it? Who would you want to be there to support you? Maybe entrusting the people on that list with one's news—however long or short the list may be—would help women feel less isolated."
—Lauren Kelley and Alexandra March in their *New York Times* Opinion piece, "You Know Someone Who's Had a Miscarriage"

More unhelpful things
people will say

Oh yes, there are more.

When I got pregnant again after my first loss, I was understandably very anxious. After all, my only experience with pregnancy had been very traumatic. But when I expressed my anxieties to friends and family, I was surprised when they didn't seem to understand. Instead of saying, "Of course you're worried," they waved off my fears and assured me that everything would be fine this time. Lightning doesn't strike twice, as they say.

Except it did, for me. And when it did, I directed some of my anger at all the people who made false promises and lobbed vague optimism at me when I'd expressed concerns.

"Vulnerability is not winning or losing; it's having the courage to show up and be seen when we have no control over the outcome."
—Brené Brown

It really irked me to have my anxieties invalidated and dismissed. In addition to feeling scared, I also felt self-critical of my fears, like *Why couldn't I get over it? Why couldn't I trust things would be OK?* I wish someone had just acknowledged the truth of the matter: "You're scared because this awful thing happened to you before. All we can do is hope that it doesn't happen again."

Here are just a few of the things you might hear if you get pregnant again.

The unhelpful thing someone said	My imagined response	Let's unpack this
"Don't worry, you've paid your dues."	"Actually, I don't think it works like that."	My sister said this to me after my first loss. It was clear that she, like me, had been going through life believing in tidy equations—if X, then Y. In her mind, I had already had this terrible ectopic pregnancy. She could assume that was meant to "teach me something." With the lesson learned, I was in the clear. My conclusion: When people say things like this, it's a reflection of their own belief systems, the ones they cling to because of their own fears about life's randomness.
"I'm sure everything will be fine this time!"	"OH MY GOD, are you psychic?" Alternative: "LIAR!"	During my third pregnancy, when the fifteen-week ultrasound showed that my amniotic fluid levels were dangerously low, a family member said, "Oh, I'm sure the baby's fine" with a dismissive flick of her wrist that told me I was silly for fretting. When I think of this moment and the look on her face and that wrist flick, I still get angry. I guess, statistically speaking, things with any pregnancy will probably be fine. Pregnancy loss is more common than many people realize, but, still, most pregnancies are fine. But if you've had a loss, the "most" is not comforting. If you've been on the wrong side of the statistics, you realize there are no guarantees. Once again, I think when people say this it's more about *them*. They feel good about themselves when they offer optimism. They like the idea of infusing positivity. Even though the intention is good, trite phrases felt very insensitive to me. I wish my family member would have said, "I can imagine you're really worried. I hope everything is OK."

The unhelpful thing someone said	My imagined response	Let's unpack this
"You must be so excited!"	"If by excited you mean scared shitless, yes."	When my bump grew during my fifth pregnancy, people would say they were "so excited" for us, and I felt weird about it. I just couldn't match their enthusiasm. I would force a smile and struggle to refrain from lecturing them on all the things that could still go wrong: placental abruption, umbilical cord issues, listeria, toxoplasmosis, cervical incompetence, premature labor, unexplained stillbirth. Didn't they know about these things? How could they speak with such confidence about the baby's arrival? How could they think I would be planning a baby shower or constructing a nursery?

It was so lonely for me to feel that disconnect during interactions with others, when my internal feelings just didn't match what the world was telling me to feel. I also felt like their enthusiasm meant they didn't understand (or want to understand) the pain of my losses. Had they already forgotten what I'd been through?

I know people probably were genuinely excited for me, and they were probably excited to be able to celebrate something good (instead of awkwardly supporting me through grief). Still, I would have appreciated someone saying, "I'm sure this pregnancy has been hard for you because of your previous losses. I'll be thinking of you as you get to your due date." That's it. |

"Unbridled positivity in an experience of failure or distress makes people feel worse, not better." —Dr. Kelsey Crowe and Emily McDowell, *There Is No Good Card for This: What to Say and Do When Life Is Scary, Awful, and Unfair to People You Love*

"Since I have no investment in the outcome of this situation, it costs me nothing to be optimistic." —Gabrielle Zevin, *The Storied Life of AJ Fikry*

The unhelpful thing someone said	My imagined response	Let's unpack this
"Is this your first?"	[Awkward pause]	I never knew how to answer this question. I didn't want to burden people with information about my sad history (and it did feel like I was burdening them). Sometimes, I would say something like, "My first that's made it this far," and that just elicited confusion. When they "got it," they stuck out their bottom lip and furrowed their brows (See "The Pity Face"). Sometimes, it was just easier to say "Yes, this is my first." My heart always hurt after this lie though. I felt like I was denying the existence of the previous lives I'd carried (however briefly).

Meredith

Just like you may have been bothered by what people said to you after your loss, you may feel bothered by what they say when you are pregnant again. This time around, you may feel that upbeat responses to your pregnancy fail to authentically address—even remotely—your unique experience. Granted, some responses are innocent in nature, maybe the person doesn't know you or your history, and they are probably not intentionally trying to sidestep or overlook your pain. But that doesn't mean you don't feel a twinge or aren't momentarily at a loss for words.

We all make assumptions. Some we keep to ourselves, and others get blurted out. Some aren't intended to be insensitive but are; other times we say just the right things.

More important than what people say or trying to figure out their intention is speaking the truth of your situation.

If you find that you keep returning to the things people say that upset you, ask yourself how *you* can give voice to what's inside that needs to be heard. It may be awkward to talk about pregnancy loss, but if you are honest and direct, you not only validate your own experience, you help someone else understand what you and so many other women have gone through.

Why do I still resent pregnant women?

When you're one of them again, you expect the resentment to go away, but it might not.

Even now, having had a healthy baby, I resent pregnant women. That sounds crazy, I know. You would think I'd be "over it," but I'm really not. I'm still grieving the loss of a "fun" pregnancy experience. I feel gypped, cheated of that.

When I see pregnant women who seem to be going about their day without a care in the world, it bothers me. *Still.* I guess it's that I assume they are taking for granted what they have. Don't even get me started when I see a pregnant woman drinking wine or going to a hot yoga class. It takes a lot of restraint not to scream, "Why would you risk anything?!"

I overheard a pregnant relative say, "Sometimes I forget I'm pregnant" and I wanted to slap her. At work, I was in a meeting with two pregnant women complaining about their swollen ankles, and I felt that desire to slap again. I've had the same anger arise when I hear pregnant women obsessing over their "babymoons" or baby showers or "sprinkles." It's just weird for me to see people treating pregnancy like a fun, cute event to document on Pinterest. Don't they know the dark side?

But that's the thing—they don't. Or, they do, but they have no reason to think it will happen to them. As Deborah L. Davis writes in her book *Empty Cradle, Broken Heart: Surviving the Death of Your Baby*, pregnant women are "reminiscent of promises broken and a blissful ignorance never to be recaptured."

Whenever I overhear pregnant women talking about two-thousand-dollar cribs and state-of-the-art strollers and all-natural pacifiers, I think, *If you have a healthy baby, who cares about that shit?* But, see, these women *get* to care about that shit because they don't have any other serious worries associated with their pregnancies. They still have the illusion of control. They still have innocence. That's what I envy. I know my anger toward them is really just a reflection of the sadness I feel for what I didn't have, but it's still there. When it comes up, I try to connect with that sad part of myself. I know, long-term, that's where the healing is.

Meredith

There are a couple of things that might be going on if you find yourself resentful of pregnant woman.

Like Kim, you see them out there, all these pregnant bellies having what appear to be textbook pregnancies, swollen ankles and a few odd cravings they write about on their blogs. You may be sad that you didn't get to experience the joy of pregnancy, to know what carrying a baby feels like without having complications, emergency tests, multiple miscarriages, loss. The burden you carry is that you know from experience what could go wrong. You've lived it. Grieved it. Feeling resentful might just be part of the process you move through.

"When I returned for every successive appointment, the pregnant women in the waiting room made me sad: there they sat in the present, dreaming of the future. I couldn't bear watching. I wanted a separate waiting room for people like me, with different magazines. No *Parenting* or *Wondertime* or *Pregnancy*, no ads with pink or tawny or pearly smiling infants. I wanted *Hold Your Horses Magazine. Don't Count Your Chickens for Women. Pregnant for the Time Being Monthly*. Here I was, only in this second, and then the next, and nothing else. No due dates, no conversations about 'the baby' or what life would be like months from now. No 'This time will be different' or 'Listen, it will all be worth it when you hold your child in your arms.' What I wanted, scrawled across my chart in shaky physician's cursive: *NOTE: do not blow sunshine up patient's ass.*"
—Elizabeth McCracken, in her memoir *An Exact Replica of a Figment of My Imagination*

Another less personal reason could be that pregnancy and childbirth have become, in a way, status symbols. Status implies hierarchy, popularity, and, to some extent, belonging—though status is more about exclusivity than inclusivity. In this case, it's the perceived and cultivated reality of a perfectly manifested What-to-Expect-When-You're-Expecting (only the good things!) pregnancy "experience" worthy of documentation on social media that "matters."

There might be one more reason, and it is far more poignant than you realize. That is your resentment might be masking the anger you might be carrying toward yourself for your own naïveté about pregnancy. For not being prepared *enough*—but for something that was impossible to prepare for. Did you feel ill-prepared? Can anyone ever really be fully prepared? The answer, of course, is no.

Knowing this, understanding it, and taking it in might enable the resentment and anger to give way. Look inside. See that you did all you could, that you tried your very best.

Allowing for hope and gratitude

And all the daydreams and fantasies.

At some point in my pregnancy with my daughter, I chose to let go. I accepted that things could still go wrong—she could be born premature, she could be born still. But I made the active choice to try to enjoy my pregnancy. I knew it would be my last one. I wanted to feel gratitude, not fear.

I started to take "bump photos" about halfway through my pregnancy. I didn't share them with anyone, but I did include them in letters I wrote to my daughter, telling her how we were growing together. Toward the very end of my pregnancy, my sister took maternity photos. I shared a couple on social media.

I'd told myself not to entertain too many fantasies. I thought less fantasizing would mean less pain if I lost the baby. But, you know, fantasies are . . . fantastic. At a certain point, I was doing myself a grave disservice by not allowing them. I started small—thinking about baking cookies with my daughter, taking her to the beach for the first time, reading books at the library. To this day, I keep lists of things I want to do with her. I've realized that I can be excited for an expected future while also acknowledging that I might be thrown several curveballs.

I cried often toward the end of my pregnancy, marveling at my daughter's visible movements in my belly. It was just all so incredible. I don't know if I would have had that same sense of awe and wonder if I hadn't gone through so much loss. I know my pregnancy with my daughter was very much colored by the losses that came before her, but that wasn't a bad thing. Yes, I had a hard time connecting with her for the first half of my pregnancy because I was so afraid, but in the second half, I let go more and was able to truly enjoy the miracle.

"This pregnancy is not like the first. My elation has been colored—not diminished, but informed—by my experience of loss. I am a little wiser this time, a little more cautious in my joy. I am hopeful, and I am excited. I am aware of the fragility of this miracle I'm carrying, and I am so grateful to have another chance." —Jessica Jernigan, "Unplanned," featured in *About What Was Lost: 20 Writers on Miscarriage, Healing, and Hope* (Jessica Berger Gross, editor)

"I saw it as, this was supposed to happen in order for my daughter to be born. That if I didn't miscarry the first pregnancy, I wouldn't have had her. I didn't want to lessen the meaning or feelings I had for the first pregnancy. I still cherish the couple months I had. It was a different baby and a different journey. I don't think of that pregnancy as any less meaningful than the one I had with my current child. I want to thank that pregnancy for helping me to be able to appreciate the one I had with my daughter."

—Michaela, on how her first-trimester miscarriage affected her pregnancy with her daughter

Meredith

You might like to think of gratitude as groundedness in what is, right now—in your life, in what is in existence, in that which you are a part of and relate to. Think of gratitude as being here, being present and mindful, and being able to struggle through something difficult, experience your own growth and transformation, and emerge anew.

A common view of gratitude is that it is something to be felt when something is bestowed upon you, or when the worst doesn't happen, or when you're lucky. But we can use the term for something far bigger and whole, which encompasses not only the feelings we want to feel or getting the experiences we want to have, but rather those which awaken us to the unthinkable. Those awakenings come far more frequently than the obvious "gifts" we hope to receive. And gratitude itself might come years after that awakening you were forced into. You might be grateful for your ability to extend a hand to help someone in pain—the same pain you are in now.

Then you can feel gratitude for this, maybe.

Having a baby
after a loss

Giving birth

It's an emotional thing.

My contractions started at seven o'clock on a Tuesday night. My husband and I were watching a Twins versus Yankees playoff game on TV. When the contractions started coming regularly, I pulled out a notebook to record the intervals. I was excited but also nervous. I knew labor was a major medical event, and I didn't want anything to go wrong.

I had contractions throughout the night, and they became gradually more painful. The next morning, around nine o' clock, my husband and I finally drove to the hospital. It was the same hospital where I'd had emergency surgery after my first ectopic pregnancy. The full-circle-ness of it all wasn't lost on me, even in the midst of labor. *I'm on a different floor this time*, I told myself. *This time, I'm having a baby.*

They took me to triage and said I was only one centimeter dilated. ONE. After fourteen hours of contractions. I was a wreck. My thoughts went to the worst place—my daughter was stuck, there would be an emergency c-section, something would go horribly awry. Thankfully, my doula was there to calm me down.

At ten that night, after twenty-seven hours of labor, my daughter emerged. My first thought was, "She's so tiny." The specialist I'd seen had predicted she'd be over nine pounds; she was only six and a half. My second thought was, "She's purple. Why is she purple?" My third thought was, "Why isn't she crying?"

Her eyes were open. She was alive. But she was silent. A bunch of blue-gloved hands passed in front of my face, handling the baby. They let me hold her, then took her from me. "What's her name?" they asked, some urgency in their voice. "Mya," I said. One of them turned to Mya said, "We need you to cry, Mya." I shrieked: "Is there something wrong? What's wrong?" I was convinced she was dead.

"I know everybody's situation is different, but I also think you never truly get over that kind of loss and you never trust your body again until you see a healthy child come." —Lela Rochon, actress

---

Then she cried—just once, like the test beep of a smoke alarm. Then I cried. They were tears of happiness, but mostly relief—relief that my daughter had survived all those months inside of me, unlike the others before her. Relief that she was now here, alive. When my husband cut the umbilical cord, I felt sadness in the form of a walnut-size lump in my throat. She was on her own now, in a world that may be more dangerous than my womb.

After they warmed her and checked her over, they lay her on my chest, and I felt like I exhaled for the first time in years. Her Apgar scores were high. I still don't know why everyone seemed so frantic when she was first born. Maybe it was just frantic in my memory; maybe I was just terrified.

I know all mothers feel grateful to have a healthy baby, but when you've lost, that gratitude is of the heart-exploding variety. It still is. I haven't taken a single day of Mya's life for granted. I don't see how I ever could.

Meredith

Women who have given birth to a preterm baby who didn't survive or who had a stillborn baby may have posttraumatic stress flare up from the whole birth experience. The last time they went through labor, their baby was dying (or had already died).

Why wouldn't anxiety be understandable in a new scenario that bears so many of the same elements—pregnancy, hospital, doctor, delivery room?

Being in this "space," both physically and emotionally, presents a kind of power struggle between your body and your mind. Your mind cannot differentiate between then and now; it all seems like one and the same. Meanwhile, your body is ready to have this baby. But in the midst of contractions, belly and lower back pain, and the memory of what happened before, it may seem impossible to separate the past from the present.

This is natural. It is difficult, but yes, it happens. All the more reason to find ways to keep your anxiety in check. By definition, anxiety is an overwhelming sense of apprehension and fear often marked by physical signs (such as tension, sweating, and increased pulse rate), by doubt concerning the reality and nature of the threat, and by self-doubt about one's capacity to cope with it.

Anxiety dials up your worst fears, then keeps them at a level where you suffer equally if you try to ignore them or face them. You can't win! You become afraid of what might occur and fear your inability to get through it.

Calming anxiety with breathing

Dr. Andrew Weil teaches an easy breathing technique that is highly effective for calming anxiety. The 4-7-8 Breath (also known as the Relaxing Breath) truly combats stress in the moment. Dr. Weil calls it "the perfect, portable stress antidote" and for good reason. You can do the exercise in any position. He suggests doing this exercise twice a day for the first month, then increasing gradually if desired.

Preparation:

Place the tip of your tongue against the ridge of tissue just behind your upper front teeth, and keep it there through the entire exercise. (You will be exhaling through your mouth around your tongue.) Purse your lips if that feels more natural or comfortable.

1. Exhale completely through your mouth, making a whoosh sound.
2. Close your mouth and inhale quietly through your nose to a mental count of four.
3. Hold your breath for a count of seven.
4. Exhale completely through your mouth, making a whoosh sound to a count of eight. This is one breath.
5. Now inhale again and repeat the cycle three more times for a total of four breaths.

—Dr. Andrew Weil, DrWeil.com

Anxiety doesn't so much "blow your fears out of proportion," but, because it diminishes your ability to stay connected with yourself, everything feels unmanageable.

This can happen for anyone and especially women who have had earlier-term miscarriages, or if you've been through single or multiple rounds of IUIs or IVF and have lost a baby before. If you've conceived through expensive and rigorous fertilization procedures, your fears may also include cost to both your health and the bottom line.

Acknowledge the complexities of your situation on every level. Remember the details. Try to breathe through the anxiety (See Dr. Andrew Weil's exercise above). Just as you prepare with birthing techniques, equip yourself with a range of remedies to deal with anxiety during the birth.

You will get through this. You will do the best that you can—which is often likely more than you give yourself credit for.

A word about "rainbow babies"

The sentiment is sweet, but . . .

"Rainbow baby" has become a common term to describe a baby who arrives after a loss. I might be in the minority on this one, but I don't love this term. For me, it's too simplistic and cutesy. I don't like that it makes my first four pregnancies "storms." They weren't storms; they were lives, however brief. I don't like thinking of my daughter as a "rainbow" after these "storms." It seems like it's putting pressure on her to be this amazing bringer-of-color after all the dark days. She is amazing, and she does bring color to my life, but that's independent of whatever happened before her.

"Those who are lucky enough not to be a part of the loss community feel that somehow having a rainbow baby fixes everything. I have heard over and over again: *'after every storm comes a rainbow.'* I don't believe that to be true because infant loss is not a temporary storm but something we must weather every day for the rest of our lives."
—Allison, "To the Mom Who Isn't Sure She Wants a Rainbow Baby," StillStandingMag.com

There is this implication that a "rainbow baby" heals everything after a loss, and that's just not the case. I am so grateful to have my daughter, but that does not mean I'm "over" the losses that preceded her. It's just not that simple. Grief is complex. Emotion is complex. Even with my daughter here, I still have "cloudy" days.

I do appreciate that people acknowledge the need for a term like "rainbow baby." That means they are thinking about how hard it is to lose a baby and long for another. But that term does not do justice to all the emotion involved. At least not for me.

Meredith

Researchers have studied if the birth of a healthy baby makes the sadness of a previous loss go away or if the symptoms persist. They found no evidence that emotions associated with prior pregnancy loss went away with the birth of a healthy child. They did find that previous prenatal loss showed that depression and anxiety symptoms still persisted after what would conventionally be defined as the postnatal period.

This means two things: One, you must still deal with your prior loss and cope with sadness about that, and, two, the subsequent birth of a healthy baby is no replacement for the grieving you still need to do. Does this mean you should not be overjoyed with your new baby? Absolutely not! But it is a gentle reminder to see that little one as her own unique self.

Though I found myself nodding in agreement as I read Kim's entry, another question, related to the research, kept popping into my mind—a concern, really. What happens if a parent becomes fixated on the rainbow? Is this rainbow business for the sake of social media? By posting and focusing on the rainbow, are they actually trying to avoid something? Their grief and pain? If not, that's good. But what about the pressure to be happy when a baby is born? What about postpartum depression? A person can divulge feelings with details about what the sadness looks like, but that does not mean they have addressed those feelings.

This rainbow baby, we hope, grows into a toddler into a teenager and, eventually, an adult. This is what is important, right? The fact that a human has made it safely onto the planet. The fact that parents are joyful about that is what matters.

Pregnancy and parenthood talk is riddled with language that is either good or bad, normal or not normal. Rainbow or storm? How about simply my baby, my child?

I'm still afraid something
bad is going to happen

Yes, still.

Confession: My daughter is two years old, and I am *still* afraid of losing her.

My pregnancy losses forced me to realize life is tenuous. I know nothing is forever. This has made me extraordinarily grateful for every moment I have with my daughter, but it's also made me anxious. Some examples:

- When my daughter was just a few days old, I made my husband move all the medications and cleaning supplies to upper cabinets, even though it would be months before she would be able to crawl.
- I became obsessed with the possibility that my daughter could drown in the dog's water bowl. Again, this was when she was just a few days old.
- My sister-in-law gave me a mug that says, "Goals for today: Keep the tiny human alive," and, while I thought it was funny, it also made me nervous—what if I failed?
- When our neighbor, the quintessential "nice older lady," commented on how adorable my daughter was, I felt a rush of adrenalin, thinking *You can't have her.* Then I asked my husband to stick a piece of wood in the track of the window in my daughter's room, so it couldn't be easily slid open by intruders. I didn't tell my husband that it was the "nice older lady" I feared.
- On car rides, if my daughter was quiet, I had to pull over to make sure she hadn't somehow suffocated herself on the blanket I'd used to cover her legs; I was relieved when she was old enough for us to turn the car seat facing forward—now a quick glance in the rearview is enough to reassure.

- Any time I left my daughter at home with my husband so I could run an errand, I'd return gripping the steering wheel tightly while turning onto our street, expecting to see ambulances outside, lights flashing, neighbors standing around, wondering how they would tell me the unthinkable had happened.
- Even now, if my daughter sleeps in past her usual wake-up time, I brace myself when I open the door, wondering what I'll do if she isn't breathing.

She's been in our lives two years now; we are so tightly and intricately interwoven. She is our heart, our center, the beat of our days. Sometimes I think about how this would make the loss of her impossible to survive. How can someone extract the heart without killing the human? Not possible.

"Every day your first thought is not 'I love him' but 'how is he?' The world, overnight, rearranges itself into an obstacle course of terrors." —Hanya Yanagihara

I look at the tick marks we've started keeping on the wall, measuring my daughter's height, and I think about how those would gut me if we lost her. On the wall across from those tick marks are her dirty handprints, marking where she touches the wall for balance while going up and down the steps to the garage. Those handprints would gut me too.

As Jennifer Senior says in *All Joy and No Fun*, "all parents are hostages to fate." All parents fear loss. The sense of vulnerability can be agonizing, but as Senior writes, this agony is "the price mothers and fathers pay for elation, and for fathomless connection." In other words, fear is a side effect of immense love.

"The sound of her breathing reminded me, as it so often did, of how vulnerable she was. And how vulnerable we were because of how much we loved her." —Dennis Lehane

For me, the fear is heightened because I *have* lost. I cannot be in denial of the possibility. I cannot think, *Oh, it won't happen to me.* It might. It could.

But instead of focusing on the fear, I try to focus on gratitude. I know life can be gone in an instant, so I'm deeply thankful for all the instants that I get with my daughter, especially the ones that are ordinary and unremarkable.

Meredith

What Kim shares are natural feelings about losing someone you love. The echoes of loss do stay with us. But so does the love. Love and loss are forever intertwined. We can and do know this, but, thankfully, love takes over and lets us connect with the people we care for and who care for us. Love carries risk, but that love is so worth the cost of risk.

However, when worry about loss turns to obsession, it's important to ask if what you think you're worried about is, in fact, what you are most afraid of happening. This does not negate your fears or your worries regarding miscarriage and pregnancy. Those are real, and you are well aware of them.

But if you are obsessing about that, and it's not getting better but worse, there is likely something else just beyond your awareness that is causing you more fear. Something percolating right beneath the surface. Something that is too emotionally scary to look at straight on.

"I watched him to make sure his chest rose and fell for eighteen months. I held him while he was asleep and awake ... I never let this child out of my sight. Once on a plane the flight attendant offered to watch him so I could use the bathroom, and I said, 'I don't know you!' She leaned in and said, 'Ma'm, we're on a plane, where will I go?' But she didn't know that I was a soldier, and I dreamed magical thoughts, and I was terrified every day that my child was going to die."
—Sarah Agaton Howes, "Lessons from Dying," featured in *What God Is Honored Here? Writings on Miscarriage and Infant Loss by and for Native Women and Women of Color* (Shannon Gibney and Kao Kalia Yang, editors)

Fear of death is natural when you've been so close to loss. It's on your mind and in your heart. It's defined much of your days as you've slowly but surely worked your way through the grief process, the mourning, and all the emotions that go with that. When you've faced loss like this, "endings" kind of become your theme song, and appropriately so.

Obsessing is something entirely different.

Obsessing is progressive. It may be triggered by something that happens, but its purpose is to keep you from thinking about something else. You may be obsessing about someone you love dying, or you may be obsessing about eating only raw food or exercising in a regimented fashion or sticking to a particular schedule. The list of possibilities is infinite.

If you cannot stop thinking about something, if those thoughts preoccupy you and cause you their own mental anguish, recognize them as obsessions. If the underlying cause of your worry is not addressed, your obsessions tend to increase. The underlying cause often turns out to be less frightening, but identifying it can lead to ways to address it. Addressing it means you get to heal and integrate that part that has been unseen and neglected inside you.

"Through the blur, I wondered if I was alone or if other parents felt the same way I did—that everything involving our children was painful in some way. The emotions, whether they were joy, sorrow, love or pride, were so deep and sharp that in the end they left you raw, exposed and yes, in pain. The human heart was not designed to beat outside the human body and yet, each child represented just that—a parent's heart bared, beating forever outside its chest." —Debra Ginsberg

---

If you don't address what is underlying, you are subject to the whims of the mind and what might become a new obsession. This is your mind's way of avoiding what it perceives as most frightening to you—only you are not fully consciously aware of what that deeper fear is. Obsessions keep it that way.

Obsessions can take on a life of their own, contributing to the feeling of being out of control. If you find yourself unable to stop thinking about death, or any topic for that matter, if you've tried to stop but can't, it's time to talk to someone who can help, preferably a licensed therapist who can help you identify the root of your fear and provide tools as necessary to help you address obsessions when you notice them flaring up again.

Huong

It is a natural reaction to catastrophize when you have experienced loss. Catastrophizing is a part of something called automatic negative thoughts (ANTs), which involve creating the worst-case scenario as a tool to help you cope. Some of us think that if we allow ourselves to constantly go to the worst-case scenario, then we will be fully prepared in every situation and that it may take away some of the "sting" of the potential loss.

The thing is that life doesn't work like this. Mentally preparing for a catastrophe does not take away pain if that event actually happens. In fact, some people feel angry that they essentially experienced the catastrophe twice—once in their imagination, and once in reality. There's a quote I share with my clients: "Worrying doesn't take away tomorrow's troubles. It takes away today's peace."

The interesting thing about ANTs is that they can find their way into our lives in some pretty sneaky ways. They might be negative thoughts as well as distortions and rigidity that seem to become a pattern. Other ANTs include:

- Black or white thinking/All or nothing thinking
- Focusing on the negative
- Fortune telling
- Mind reading
- Thinking with your feelings
- Being ruled by "shoulds"
- Labeling
- Taking things personally
- Blame

If you find yourself stuck in automatic negative thoughts, cognitive behavioral therapy (CBT) can help (See page 89 and "Getting professional help" for more information on CBT).

Is it normal to *still* be sad?

Probably. Yes. It's been my normal.

Having my daughter brought so much happiness to my life, but I still have moments of sadness. Even when I feel peace about losing the four pregnancies that came before my daughter, I still deal with a more general sadness about life's unfairness. I haven't gotten over that fully. I'm not sure I ever will.

"Sometimes my grief sneaks up on me, and I'll start crying if a TV show mentions the word miscarriage. I couldn't even say that word for years after the losses. I've done a lot of healing, but it still conjures feelings of deep and inexplicable sadness. The hardest memories for me are the ones linked to seeing the ultrasounds. It breaks my heart to think about those moments in my life." —Wendy, on her two first-trimester miscarriages

It is bittersweet to see my daughter grow. As her appearance changes and her personality develops, I can't help but wonder who the other babies could have been. I realize how individual each child is; the others would not have been like my daughter. They would have been their own unique selves. I wish I could have known them. At the same time, I know that if I'd gotten to know them, my daughter wouldn't be here. That's another kind of sadness.

In *Empty Cradle, Broken Heart: Surviving the Death of Your Baby*, Deborah Davis talks about "shadow grief," a sadness that remains in the background and occasionally reappears. This is how I would describe my grief—a shadow. I don't mind it. It reminds me of what I've been through, and that helps keep me grateful for what I have now.

You may not be sad all the time now, but when your sadness hits, all the pain comes rushing back. It might not be as strong or intense as it was when you first lost your baby, but the melancholy might take you by surprise. Even in the face of happiness, of wellness surrounding you, of life feeling "really good," you can feel the longing for the baby who is gone.

These feelings, which seem to be so opposite, can coexist. In fact, they may surface just when you are at your happiest, at a joyful event or a seemingly unrelated one, like a promotion at work. This kind of sadness catches you off guard. Somehow the joy and happiness bring the loss into sharper relief, calling out facets that you didn't see before but you notice now. Feeling blue amid the joy is real.

It is also natural. It usually means you've found ways back into your life, and they are meaningful. It means you are able to hold both the sadness and the happiness up to the light and honor their value both within yourself and out there in the world.

What the studies tell us

- Symptoms of anxiety and depression can persist for up to three years following a miscarriage. (*The Primary Care Companion of CNS Disorders*, 2015; *British Journal of Psychiatry*, 2011)
- Mood symptoms following a prenatal loss do not always resolve with the birth of a subsequent healthy child. (*The Primary Care Companion for CNS Disorders*, 2015; *The British Journal of Psychiatry*, 2011)

Am I allowed to think the newborn days are hard?

*They were so hard, even though
I was so grateful.*

I've come to believe there are no "easy" babies; there are hard babies and hard*er* babies. Given my losses, I expected to be so overcome with gratitude that I'd welcome the difficulties of the newborn days. In some ways, that did happen. I was able to keep things in perspective better than I probably would have if I hadn't been through my losses. But, BUT, the newborn days were still hard. I didn't sleep more than a half hour the first week, and in the weeks that followed, sleeping three hours a night was considered "good." My daughter cut my left nipple the first time she latched (the lactation consultant actually gasped and said, "That is a *wound*"). My daughter was having reactions to something in my breastmilk, so I had to go on an elimination diet to figure out the culprit (it was tomatoes, so I could not consume tomatoes for the months I nursed her. No salsa, no pizza sauce, no pasta with marinara). I had all the usual emotional swings that come with hormone fluctuations, fatigue, and the general overwhelm of the task of caring for a tiny human. There were many days when I made to-do lists to feel "accomplished," and I felt elation when checking off "take a shower."

I think many women feel uncomfortable talking about the difficulties of the newborn days. They don't want to seem ungrateful. They see all the "#blessed" posts on social media when others have babies and feel guilty. Let the shame spiral begin! Because I lost four babies, I felt *really* disallowed to discuss any difficulties. I still do. After all, in the midst of my losses, when I heard new moms complain about how tired they were, I resented them.

I didn't understand how they could be anything but grateful. *The nerve*, I thought. Then I had a baby, and I understood.

What I've decided is this: My gratitude can live in parallel to my feelings of exhaustion, helplessness, and despair (let's be real—trying to get a baby to stop crying at one AM is cause for despair). I allow myself to cry tears of joy; I also allow myself to cry tears of frustration. Motherhood, and the path to it, require grace over judgment.

Meredith

Bear with me as I lay out the issues that affect some—many—women after the birth of a child. Stay with me as we explore how they collide, and what you can do if it happens to you.

Postpartum depression

The hormone levels your body achieved to support your pregnancy, and the increase predelivery to support the actual birth, take a sudden drop after the baby is born. The levels of estrogen and progesterone plummet. This leads to chemical changes in your brain that may trigger mood swings. In addition, many mothers are unable to get the rest they need to fully recover from giving birth. Constant sleep deprivation can lead to physical discomfort and exhaustion, which can contribute to the symptoms of postpartum depression.

The feelings of sadness and anxiety that we associate with postpartum depression can happen to women who have experienced pregnancy losses and those who have not.

Medical Experts from the National Institute of Mental Health tell us that "postpartum depression does not have a single cause, but likely results from a combination of physical and emotional factors. Postpartum depression does not occur because of something a mother does or does not do."

Posttraumatic stress following childbirth—Childbirth Induced Posttraumatic Stress Syndrome

In "The Mothers Who Can't Escape the Trauma of Childbirth" (*The Atlantic*, 2015), Ilana E. Strauss writes, "For some women, the psychological toll of childbirth leads to a form of PTSD—distinct from postpartum depression— that follows them into new motherhood." This type of PTSD is known as Childbirth Induced Posttraumatic Stress Syndrome.

Posttraumatic stress related to a prior pregnancy loss or losses

Research shows that it is not unusual for women who miscarry or have an ectopic pregnancy to experience some degree of PTSD (See "Posttraumatic stress: It's a thing"). This might be anxiety that could be moderate or severe, and depression—though depression is less likely. These symptoms can last at least three months following pregnancy loss.

"To take care of a baby, you have to become accustomed
to the constant sound of unhappiness; to spit-up and yellow poop;
to long hours of doing nothing that requires your mental acuity,
your wit, your carefully cultivated self. You will be so very tired."

—Polly Rosenwaike, *Look How Happy I'm Making You*

Looking at these three issues, we can see how hormones can affect mental health. Likewise, we can also see that trauma related to a lost pregnancy could trigger anxiety following a healthy birth and certainly following a birth with complications.

So, what can you do to prepare yourself just in case it happens to you?

Please note, I'm not trying to scare or worry you, but I want you to have context that this does happen, it's not unusual, and while science can say certain individuals are "more" likely to be affected, science is not able to say who they will be.

- First, become desensitized to the term PTSD. Learn to say the words. Many of us are frightened to ever utter the syllables yet are walking around experiencing its very symptoms. The same goes for postpartum depression.
- Talk to your partner, friends, and family about depression, anxiety, and PTSD. Explain to them that you are trying to prepare yourself in the event it happens to you—or one of them.
- Talk to your doctor. If you see a specialist for high-risk pregnancy (as Kim did), ask them for guidance.
- If you deliver in the hospital and feel the slightest twinge of anxiety—or even if you don't—ask to speak to the clinical social worker. They have at their disposal a wealth of resources, and some have lived through exactly what you may be experiencing. Talk to them.

- See a therapist. See a trauma-informed therapist. Don't go this alone if you don't have to.
- Medication may be warranted. Consider talking to your physician, therapist, or psychiatrist. Don't use alcohol or other mood enhancers, or food or no food to auto-manage the stress. The goal is to productively mitigate the pain as you actively deal with it, not to mindlessly subvert it so it lies in wait for you at every turn.
- If you can't afford private therapy, seek care from a community clinic or attend a support group offered by the hospital.
- Trust your ability to build resiliency by finding tiny ways each day to confront your fear and turn these challenges into opportunities to grow.

What if I forget the baby I lost?

Moving forward is not forgetting.

Since having Mya, I don't think about Miles that often. Interesting fact: I did not consciously realize the similarity in their names until Mya was at least six months old. Mya, Miles, Mya, Miles. I find this very strange.

When Mya was an infant, I asked my husband, "Do you still think about Miles?" and he said, curtly, "Nope." For him, we had moved on. We had succeeded in our struggle to have a child. For him, there was no reason to think about Miles.

I think about Miles, but not nearly as often as I used to. I feel guilty about this sometimes. I picture him "on the other side," and I wonder if he's lonely, if he feels forgotten because Mya is here now, occupying all our attention (See "Where is my baby now?").

What I choose to believe is that Miles knew Mya "on the other side." He helped her make her way to us. He's happy she's here. He's by her side, a brotherly angel. I do not think he is lonely; I think it's impossible to be lonely where he is. I think he's relieved to see that we (his family on Earth) are together and healthy. I think he knows it's natural that we don't think of him all the time anymore. I think he takes comfort in the fact that he'll see us all again.

Each totem you hold or ritual you create helps you process your loss. In the earliest stages of grief, as your heart adapts, you may seek something tangible to carry with you to maintain a connection with your baby. Tiny objects in your pocket, placed around the house, or worn next to your skin can be a great source of comfort. As you move through your grief you may find that how you remember your baby changes. For example, you may think about them less frequently, or smile instead of weep when you say their name. The depth of your mourning has yielded just enough that the pain of their absence has become more integrated. And as this continues over days, weeks, months, even years, the ways you choose to remember your baby will evolve, too.

Ways you may like to remember your baby

- An engraved charm on a necklace you wear 24/7
- An anklet with the baby's initial
- A tattoo with a particular symbol you associate with your baby
- Tiny notes you tape to your computer with their name
- A container garden or garden in the ground
- Planting a tree in their honor
- Naming a star in their honor
- Creating a dish in their honor and serving it on special occasions
- Saying a prayer in their name
- Creating a tiny shrine that you greet in the morning and before you go to sleep

How loss taught me about mothering

There are so many lessons.

I can say this for certain: My losses have made me a better mother.

There are times I wonder how things would have been different if I'd never had a loss, if my very first pregnancy had been successful. I don't think I would have come into motherhood with nearly as much gratitude and joy. I would have taken it for granted. I think I would have struggled more in the postpartum period.

With each pregnancy, the plans I made and the daydreams I had prepared me for motherhood. Motherhood requires so much opening, so much cultivation of love, so much self-sacrifice. Each pregnancy, each loss, prepared me for that.

There are moments with my daughter now when I see, clear as day, how my losses have made me into the amazing mother I am (and I am really amazing, if I do say so myself). Here are just a few things I've noticed:

I'm able to be in the moment with my daughter

My losses showed me how tragedy can strike at any time, so I really do cherish the ordinary moments with my daughter. It's not that I don't feel bored when she wants to diaper her doll one hundred times (I am human), but I'm able to *be* with her and appreciate that being-ness.

I do not sweat the small stuff.

With parenting, there is lots of small stuff, all day, every day. I've learned to roll with it. Nothing is that big of a deal. My losses taught me that I can handle a lot.

I am more compassionate and loving with my daughter

And in general. My losses made me painfully aware of so many other losses. At any given moment, many of us are grieving. This realization made my heart grow bigger, and a bigger heart comes in handy with a child.

I know the value of letting go

My losses helped me realize that I'm not in control of everything—and that's OK. Motherhood may have been a big shock to my system if I hadn't already started to come to terms with my lack of control. As a mother, I've had to let go even more. I'm becoming a pro at it. I know surrender is important as I stand beside my daughter and watch her grow into her own person. I'm sure I'll shed more illusions of control in the teenage years.

"My misconception, my miscarriage the first time around was an abrupt introduction to the pure essence of parenting: the sheer chance of it all. The intensity, the joy, the grief, the fear of loss. The incontrovertible fact that the secret life you have created is simply out of your hands, beyond your control, beyond the scope of any other experience. It readied me, in ways I could not know until I was finally there, for motherhood, for the powerful rush of love and other overwhelming emotions, the depth and breadth of which I mistakenly thought I already knew." —Andrea J Buchanan, "Misconceptions," featured in *About What Was Lost: 20 Writers on Miscarriage, Healing, and Hope* (Jessica Berger Gross, editor)

Meredith

Loss forces you to be even more vulnerable. Being more vulnerable deepens you, connects you to more of yourself. It is difficult and uncomfortable, and you may have, at times, thought the process would never end. This tolerance of discomfort is a sign of resilience. It is a sign of deepened maturity, of inhabiting one's deepest self.

As you walk each step on your journey, you deepen. And in that deepening, you grow empathy. You fill in blanks that didn't need filling until that loss happened. It is no surprise that with such depth, awareness, and experience with pain, you can be there more fully for your child on a profoundly emotional level.

Whether you are a parent or not, will be or won't, for now, become aware of your increasing ability to tolerate uncomfortable feelings. You are learning to be comfortable with being uncomfortable, knowing the discomfort will not last.

"Trauma changed me forever. But now my heart so gouged, my heart so billowed, my heart so open can explode with love. My heart has depth I am certain grief gifted me." —Sarah Agaton Howes, "Lessons from Dying," featured in *What God Is Honored Here? Writings on Miscarriage and Infant Loss by and for Native Women and Women of Color* (Shannon Gibney and Kao Kalia Yang, editors)

"The best thing that experience gave me was a broadened appreciation for having a healthy baby . . . I didn't take any of that for granted (her healthy lungs and ears and eyes etc). Even yesterday, she woke up several times throughout the night to some neighborhood noises, and I was quick to be grateful for the fact that she has great hearing and that she is healthy and alert (rather than feeling sorry for myself and the lack of sleep that night). . . . I hope that experience continues to make me a more grateful and loving mother to my daughter." —Jessica, on mothering after her second-trimester loss

When grief gets (more) complicated

When you have multiple losses

Because one wasn't torturous enough.

After my first loss, people said the usual things—"Just try again!" and "It'll happen!" When I went on to have two losses, then three, then four, those optimistic encouragements and promises turned to silence. I felt like people really didn't know what to say. I felt like they were questioning my sanity, wondering why we kept pursuing this thing that was "obviously not meant to be."

"I could not have prepared for what would happen. For the first, the second, the third, the fourth, the fifth, and the sixth child that I lost, or as the Americans call it: miscarried. In Hmong we call in *nchuav menyuam*, to spill children. It does not matter what language we are expressing in, it is the language of loss, the language of almost but never, the language of forever and ever." —Chue Moua, with Kao Kalia Yang, "Either Side," featured in *What God Is Honored Here? Writings on Miscarriage and Infant Loss by and for Native Women and Women of Color* (Shannon Gibney and Kao Kalia Yang, editors)

Chris and I were wondering this too, in the midst of grieving the losses themselves. I was obsessed with the "why." After all, only 1 percent to 2 percent of women will experience more than three consecutive pregnancy losses. It's not exactly common. I assumed people were thinking *There must be something wrong with her*. I was convinced this was true. I became weighed down by questions about underlying medical issues affecting our fertility. That led to so many doctor's appointments, begging professionals to reveal a magic answer (See "Looking for answers"). There was no magic answer, though, nothing to give me back a sense of control. It was maddening.

In addition to being exhausted searching for answers, I was increasingly frustrated at my body. I felt guilty for failing my babies. I felt ashamed for not being able to do this thing (reproduce) that so many others were able to do so easily since the beginning of time. I felt stupid for continuing to try and fail. I felt angry at Chris for his gentle suggestion that we give up.

So, is grief more complicated with multiple losses? Yes. YES. The emotional turmoil is in a league of its own.

Meredith

Multiple pregnancy losses intensify grief's darkness in exponential ways. Each loss you've been through can amplify longing—for a baby, for an explanation, for a promise of hope. Maybe there's a new doctor, a new test, a new modality to try. Grief follows at every turn. With each pregnancy you lose, you'll instinctually mourn each pregnancy you already lost. Each time, you'll grieve for your body, too, and all it's been through. You'll grieve for the fantasies you harbored for each baby, and for the vision of yourself as a mother.

Amid this, you may not realize how incredibly resilient you are. Of course, that what's enabled you to keep moving forward as you digest the not-great news and process the disappointment. It's not desperation that holds you up; it's fortitude. Resiliency works silently in the background, simultaneously embracing your grief and your hope with every step.

When your external world is increasingly unpredictable, the only antidote is to turn inward and lift all that you have inside of you up to the light. It could mean trying to organize your days to prioritize checking in with yourself. Do it before you call the doctor or go to an appointment, before you consult your ovulation calendar or take another pregnancy test.

The stillness inside you always makes the outer world manageable; it's never the other way around.

"I'd seen enough of pregnancy to understand that the road from pink line on a plastic stick to a healthy baby is long, and far from simple."
—Rebecca Johnson, "Risky Business," featured in *About What Was Lost: 20 Writers on Miscarriage, Healing, and Hope* (Jessica Berger Gross, editor)

When there is no "happy ending"

At least not the one you expected.

There is that John Lennon quote: "Everything will be OK in the end. If it's not OK, it's not the end." I have mixed feelings about this quote. It is comforting in that it is basically saying that however things go in our lives, we will frame them to be "OK"; we are a resilient species. But this quote denies the pain of those of us who have to come to terms with the very real end to a particular journey, and the very real not-OK feelings.

I have an acquaintance who had a stillborn son after undergoing years of fertility treatments. Given their age and all they've been through, I don't know if they will try for another pregnancy. I try to imagine what it must be like to carry a baby all those months, only to lose him, and then have to come to terms with a life without a child to hold.

The vast majority of women who miscarry go on to have a healthy baby. What if you are not one of these women? Having been on the wrong side of the statistics, I can imagine how rage-inducing and painful this would be. I'm sure you feel nudges from others to consider adoption, and I'm sure that's complicated too. Even if you're open to adoption, there is grief upon closing the door to the possibility of having your own biological child.

If you were planning on parenthood, if you started adjusting your life to accommodate a child, diverging from that path is not easy. Diverging from the path comes with big questions: What will we do now? What is our purpose?

When my husband suggested we diverge from that path after our fourth loss, I told him it wasn't as simple as flipping a switch. Opening myself up to having a child was like turning on all the lights in a once-dark room. There was no going back to blackness. I knew in my heart that even if we did have to walk down this other path, away from parenthood, it wouldn't be because I'd managed to flip the switch; it would be because I'd learned to walk in the midst of the blinding light, sometimes closing my eyes as the only way of coping.

Meredith

This loss presents an entirely unique and poignant facet of grief. There is a finite aspect to it, like traveling through the woods on a winding path that suddenly, abruptly ends.

But you're used to this path, to wearing these shoes; you don't want to start over somewhere else. Besides, you've tried before to walk away and couldn't.

This time feels different.

Then why does it hurt so much?

Because you've invested so much of yourself. Because you're scared. Because you're saying goodbye to a part of your life. Because you're letting go of motherhood and a baby you loved in your heart long before you can even recall.

"I will never 'get over' not having a family (it's not the flu), but that doesn't mean that I can't build a new life." —Jody Day, *Living the Life Unexpected: 12 Weeks to Your Plan B for a Meaningful and Fulfilling Future Without Children*

Now is the time to trust that something entirely new awaits you. Something different, yes, but something worthy of your love and desire. You are not so much abandoning the old way but transitioning into something new, so that experience, those lessons, the importance of having tried will always live in an important space inside you. Weep and mourn the end of this journey, and trust that the beginning of something new is already in place, patiently waiting for you.

Be patient with yourself, and be kind. You're in the starting gate of a new adventure. Goodbye to one, then hello to another. Travel forward. So much of yourself and life awaits to be discovered, lived, and loved.

When racial, cultural, and socioeconomic issues come into play

For no good reason the burdens are multiplied.

In talking with my clients who identify as Black, Indigenous, People of Color (BIPOC), their range of experiences after a pregnancy loss follows a similar trajectory as those described in this book. Pain *is* pain, as I often reiterate to my clients.

However, as a member of the BIPOC community, specializing in cross-cultural awareness and competencies, I would be remiss not to speak to how the experience of pregnancy loss intersects with the experience of identifying as a BIPOC (this is the concept of "intersectionality" that I introduced on pages 14–15). Being a BIPOC can give a person a certain resilience when facing hardship, but there is also the potential additional layer of stress due to the minority experience and shame due to cultural expectations and values.

Please note that what I have included here are brief and cursory thoughts on this intersection that in no way speak to all the unique experiences and the beautiful tapestry of cultures, races, and identities of people who experience pregnancy loss.

About minority stress theory

Minority stress theory is a social research and public health model designed to help us understand the lived experienced of people of oppressed communities. The model stresses the importance of understanding that certain groups in society experience greater incidences of minority stress due to their "other" category (such as racial/ethnic minority, sexual minority, gender identity minority, a religious minority, or others). The model highlights how members of marginalized communities experience chronically high levels of internal stress (for example, hiding one's identity out of fear of retribution and potential negative feelings about one's minority group) and external stress (for example, prejudice and discrimination).

The stressors could be caused by several factors, including socioeconomic status, poor social support, and oppressive and antiquated structures that perpetuate inequality. Overall, minority stress theory encapsulates numerous scientific studies that explain how stigma, prejudice, and discrimination can create a hostile and stressful social environment that may lead to increased medical and mental health concerns. In Black females, this phenomenon is called the "weathering effect," where Black females experience accelerated aging due to a combination of chronic stressors.

For example, Black females are not only three to four times more likely to die during and after childbirth, but they also experience pregnancy loss at a much higher rate as compared to their White counterparts. For additional in-depth reading about the Black pregnancy loss experience, I suggest *Black Middle-Class Women and Pregnancy Loss: A Qualitative Inquiry* by Lisa Paisley-Cleveland or *Battling Over Birth: Black Women and the Maternal Health Care Crisis* by Julia Oparah, Helen Arega, and Dantia Hudson.

How pregnancy loss gets more complicated

If you are a BIPOC or an "other" living in your country, there may be additional layers to contend with during your pregnancy loss. One example would be socioeconomic differences. Are you getting a different quality of service at a community clinic as compared to a private hospital, or from a government-subsidized health-care plan versus private pay? Do you have savings or work/government subsidies to cover you following a pregnancy loss? These layers add complexity to the pregnancy loss and the physical and emotional pain associated with that loss.

When I worked at a federally qualified community mental health clinic, I was witness to myriad barriers that exacerbated pregnancy loss for some of my Spanish-speaking clients, including language barriers, socioeconomic barriers, transportation barriers, and lack of cross-cultural understanding from medical providers of different cultural norms and reactions to grief. One client shared, "*me hacia el dolor de mi bebe mas dificil porque tuve que manejar mucha cosas a la misma vez*" (translated to say, "it made the pain of my baby more difficult, because I had to juggle so many things at the same time").

In addition, during my time at the clinic, I noticed that some of my Black or Black-American clients also experienced the intersection of racial/ethnic disparity while grieving their pregnancy loss. One Black-American woman stated, "I am so mad at the doctor for how she treated me after my miscarriage. She told me 'everything was going to be OK.' I wanted to scream at her and tell her, 'you don't understand,' but I didn't want to be seen as the angry Black woman. I was also afraid I would be taken away or called crazy."

Your culture may also impact how you react to your pregnancy loss and how you show your grief (if you show it at all). Some of my BIPOC clients talked about the increased stigma of talking about pregnancy loss because that "just wasn't part of the culture."

"African-American women are at higher risk for premature birth, and so we are losing our babies. If you're dealing with that and you don't have anybody to talk to and you're a person of color, that's added sorrow."
—Keisha Wells, counselor, to the *New York Times*

One Pakistani-American client stated, "In my culture, there are so many things that are considered 'taboo' to talk about, such as sex; and so miscarriage and pregnancy losses also fall into that category. I initially felt so alone following my pregnancy loss at twenty weeks. However, when I finally did open up with some friends about it, some of the older aunties began to share their stories as well." My client expressed feeling less socially isolated and more accepted following this experience of sharing but recognized that she had to "break through" the taboo and wall of secrecy.

One of my Chinese-American clients expressed increased mental fatigue and frustration following her pregnancy loss because she had to switch back and forth in language, content, and tone when speaking with her parents. She noted that her parents followed a traditional type of grieving, which included stoicism and avoidance of difficult topics. This client stated, "It's so frustrating because I was raised in a Chinese home but went to an American school and so I lived in between worlds. After my pregnancy loss, it was tiring to try to explain things to my parents and Chinese family members while also processing my grief by talking with more Americanized friends."

Another client stated, "My parents did not understand why I wanted to have a ceremony for my unborn child. In their culture, it is highly discouraged to air our pain, and it can be seen as 'showing off.' I have to fight my grief, cultural expectations, norms, and rules and make sure I'm not offending some God along the way. It is just too much."

How some cultures may exacerbate feelings of shame

The World Health Organization dedicates a section of their website to why we need to talk about losing a baby: "The experience of losing a baby may differ around the world, yet stigma, shame, and guilt emerge as common themes."

Here are some examples of different cultures and their interpretations of pregnancy loss and grief:

In some sub-Saharan African countries, there is a belief that pregnancy loss was caused by voodoo, a curse, witchcraft, or evil spirits. In some African countries, the pregnancy loss is surrounded by stigma because some people believe there is something wrong with a woman who has had recurrent losses. One theory is because she may have been promiscuous, and so the loss is seen as a punishment from God.

In India and for some Indian-American women in the United States, a woman who has miscarried is often perceived as "barren" or "infertile," which further adds to the shame. One Indian-American client stated, "My family told me that if I would have just stayed in India that I would have had plenty of babies. They told me that coming to American 'ruined' me."

According to research, Spanish-speaking women responded similarly to Westernized women following a pregnancy loss. But in some Latino and/or Hispanic cultures, there may be an additional layer of shame. A Mexican-American client informed me that her mother and family made fun of her due to her "lack of fertility" and said she was not a "real Mexican woman."

In El Salvador, there are strict anti-abortion laws (up to eight years in jail for an abortion), even when the abortion is performed to save the life of a mother. Unfortunately, for some women who experienced miscarriages and/or stillbirths, they were accused of a "botched" abortion attempt and imprisoned. In addition, advocates state that due to the strict laws, some women fear seeking medical care for their miscarriages since they could be suspected of intentional neglect.

As a Vietnamese-American, Spanish-speaking psychologist who has lived in, worked in, and traveled to more than forty countries, I understand that culture is nuanced. I do not want to point fingers or add further blame and shame to groups whose cultural practices may further intensify the pain of pregnancy loss.

"Initially people will talk about the five stages of grief, going through the denial and anger and ultimately ending up at acceptance, but it's different for Black women… I can't tell you how many clients that I've had that have experienced a miscarriage and it comes up almost like an afterthought. We're just so used to not acknowledging some of the traumas that we go through."

—Angela Ford Johnson, psychotherapist, to *Essence*

I believe the underlying thread through these cultures is fear. Shaming is a way to instill fear and promote change and obedience on a societal level. Often, in working with clients who come from a shame-based culture, we start to sift through the beliefs they want to hold onto and the beliefs they want to let go. We pay honor and respect to traditional customs and values but also acknowledge that those beliefs may not be the best map for moving forward at this time.

Kim

Before talking with Huong, I hadn't heard of this concept of intersectionality. Learning about it has opened my eyes to how and why each of our losses is so unique. Even if the physical process of losing a baby may be the same between two women, there are so many factors in each of those women's lives that impact how the loss will affect them—factors ranging from their baseline mental health to their socioeconomic status to their cultural values and the messages they've grown up hearing. This is something that health-care providers need to keep in mind. They approach each of our losses as if they are the same—because, for the provider, who is only concerned with the physical process, they are the same. It would make such a difference if providers just considered what the women sitting on their exam tables may be dealing with. They don't have to know or understand all the intersections for each patient; they just have to know that they exist. That seems like a good step toward greater empathy.

Meredith: There are various ways that medical providers can improve how they interact with patients during and after pregnancy loss. For example, having a clinical social worker in the practice (or shared across medical practices in the same building or hospital affiliation) to proactively make contact with patients during the initial stages of the crisis, during a follow-up appointment, or by phone to check in is a great place to start. A professional can help address fears and concerns and can provide referrals for emotional support so the patient does not feel "dropped" as soon as the doctor or nurse leaves the room to care for another patient.

In addition, having access to language interpreters—in the office or through a phone service—who specialize in medical and psychological terminology can help staff with patients in real time during the office visit when fears and worries surface.

When you have a history of loss or trauma

Separating past and present.

A new loss can reactivate grief from a past loss, even one from long ago. Echoes of former, and perhaps unrelated, losses rise into consciousness. They don't necessarily have form or words but to the individual, something familiar and painful is recurring. Be curious. Are you grieving only for the baby? Or is there also something from the past that's calling for your attention?

The psyche works in mysterious ways, but as you notice how you feel and what thoughts arise, also notice trends and patterns. Paying attention is all that's required; that's valuable work in and of itself.

Trauma is part of one's history. Emotion from past losses resurfaces and mingles in the present day. One of the best things about grief work—which, in a way, all therapy is to some extent—is that we can work toward taking what we've thought of as our story (what happened TO me) and converting it into fuel for our lives (what I DO with what happened). Understanding what happened as part of our history and how it shaped us points to move-ment, something we can reflect on that makes us more aware and attuned to ourselves.

Integration, processing the grief, is what neutralizes the stinging pain. Processing implies something occurring in the present. Use the present moment to reflect, to look at your loss from different angles. Are you also hurting from something that happened a long time ago? This is not uncommon and explains why grief is so complex.

Grief is intertwined with life. Trauma from the past affects how we live and how we grieve (or don't grieve). The trauma after loss has been shown to affect us many years afterward, and in profound ways. How you grieve is a chance to honor your true self—and a way to discover it as well.

Kim

My pregnancy losses were the first real traumas of my life. Or, the first traumas I would label "traumas." When I encounter trauma in the future—when losing loved ones, for example—many of the same feelings will likely resurface. Fear, anxiety, anger. And those feelings will tie me back to my pregnancy losses. I'm sure it will surprise me. I'm sure I'll think, *I thought I was over those*. Then I'll have to realize that we're never truly "over" things. They live in us. We are continuously processing. I don't see this as a bad thing. I see it as part of being alive and open.

See the **Life Events Checklist** in the "Questionnaires and screeners" section at the end of this book to help identify traumas you have experienced. This will be helpful when talking with a mental health professional about how your past is impacting your present.

When your loss happens at the same time as another loss

So many feelings, compounded, intertwined.

First you lose the pregnancy. You know that difficult days of grief lay ahead. You accept this and take the time you need to recover. You commit yourself, surrender to it. You know there is no other way.

But what if the next day you receive a phone call—your best friend passed away suddenly, in her sleep. You go into deeper shock, despair. She was your rock; you had plans to see each other that afternoon. Now your grief is multiplied exponentially.

This kind of consecutive loss happens, and when it does it is incredibly stressful. You may have had your hours cut at work; maybe your partner lost their job. Your elderly dad died, and your mother is a wreck. Your child gets sick and misses school. The family cat goes missing. The stock market tanks. Then a natural disaster or pandemic comes from nowhere. Social justice protests are happening in the streets.

The single point they have in common is you: you're affected—deeply— by each and every one. Any crisis can intensify the devastation of your pregnancy suddenly ending.

After the shock of each of these losses begins to dissipate, and that may take awhile, you will still be left with an accumulated amount of grief. This is known as cumulative grief. This amount of grief can be overwhelming, often too much to navigate alone.

If you are facing multiple losses, get emotional support to help you navigate the complex internal landscape in order to negotiate the multiple changes you're facing externally.

A licensed therapist who specializes in grief work and trauma-informed practice is a good place to start. The goal is to process—on an ongoing basis—the inner effects of these losses for you.

Kim

Nora McInerney (creator of my favorite podcast, "Terrible, Thanks for Asking") writes in her memoir, *It's Okay to Laugh (Crying is Cool Too)*, about how she lost her husband, father, and unborn baby within months of each other. Here is one of my favorite quotes from her:

"I'm not stronger than anybody. I mean, physically, I can do three pull-ups, so I'm stronger than some people, but emotionally, I'm the same as anyone else. This strength isn't superhuman. It's the most human thing of all, a muscle we're all born with but need to exercise rarely at best. And lucky for us, it's a tenacious little thing that bounces back from atrophy as soon as you need to flex it."

I can't even imagine having to grieve someone or something in addition to grieving the loss of a baby. I imagine layers of grief like rows of bricks in a wall; I imagine you lying beneath this wall, bearing the increasing weight. But, like Nora McInerney says, we all have this innate strength that we don't know we have. We take on the weight, somehow. We survive, somehow. I'm sure it becomes next to impossible to tease apart the feelings of the different losses. I'm sure the intertwining of the losses feels chaotic and messy and confusing. But we survive, in spite of the chaos and mess and confusion. We survive.

When your loss feels
overshadowed by a major event

And it's hard to get the support you need.

Sometimes I think about major events in history, and it occurs to me that there were women in the process of losing babies during all of them. During the Great Depression. Shortly before or after 9/11. In the midst of the recent COVID-19 crisis. How do you endure, then process, the loss of a baby while also dealing with a major world event? What if it's not a major world event but a major event in your personal life—moving to a new state, starting a job (or losing a job), preparing for a wedding, for example? Suddenly, there's so much to tend to—your thoughts and emotions about the event as well as your grief over the loss of your baby. How do you make room for both?

The thing with major events is that they come with their own kind of grief. In an interview with the *Harvard Business Review* during the COVID-19 pandemic, David Kessler said, "We feel the world has changed, and it has . . . The loss of normalcy; the fear of economic toll; the loss of connection. This is hitting us and we're grieving. Collectively."

But what if, on top of this collective grief, you also have the very personal, agonizing grief of losing a baby? If the major event affects lots of people around you, and they are all distracted or consumed, how do you get support? How do you deal with the very real sense that nobody is thinking about you or your loss?

In an essay for the *Independent*, Katie Ingram wrote about how she was mentally preparing for her first Mother's Day after her daughter was born still—a hard enough task as is, made harder by the social distancing protocols during the COVID-19 pandemic. Many of us, even diehard introverts, felt some loneliness during the isolation of lockdown. I can only imagine how difficult it must have been for those grieving.

Grief is hard in the best of times. During my losses, my life was pretty quiet otherwise. I could make room for the din of grief (I didn't *want* to, but I could). I had the luxury of time to contemplate; I had support from loved ones. If I'd been preoccupied with a major event, it would have delayed my grief, or at least made it even more confusing—after all, how do you tease apart all the feelings with so much churning in your head at once? I have to assume (or hope) that the teasing-apart is possible, in time, as calm resumes and there is space for grief to be what it is.

Meredith

At the time Kim, Huong, and I were writing this book, the novel coronavirus had each of us self-isolating in different parts of southern California. At the time we began the editing process, the Black Lives Matter protests for social justice had captivated our collective attention and awakened us to the need for allyship with Black women who lose their children—during pregnancy or years after giving birth.

Now, in terms of pregnancy loss, this got me thinking about when there is a death and you are grieving, how jarring it is to overhear someone in the next room talking (or worse, laughing) about something completely unrelated to your loss. It's happened to me, and it served as a reminder that the world—and people I love—continue on with their day-to-day lives even as I navigated my own grief-dominated universe a few feet away. Of course, I, too, have been the person on the other side of the door. We all have, in varying degrees.

"I had seven miscarriages in two years (during which time 9/11 happened and my mother died). Suffice to say I was a basket case."
—Anonymous, the *Atlantic*

It's very different when a natural disaster strikes or a pandemic rises up out of nowhere. Unlike the laughter from the hallway that distracts, the coronavirus pandemic disrupted and shattered the sense that sadness from, say, your pregnancy loss can have your complete attention.

As someone who was already grieving a loss, your attention is now split between two enormous life events, neither of which is easy or pleasant or wanted. Plus, everyone around you who would normally be by your side is trying to cope with the unknowns themselves. It's not that you grieve less for the loss of your pregnancy—your emotional pain may well be amplified as you're confronted with a broader, far more sweeping loss of innocence, as you witness that in the faces of loved ones around you.

This is all to say that you will still need to carve out time to turn inward, to pay attention to the emotions that rise up about the pregnancy you've lost. In the next breath, and without much room for respite, you'll be forced to think more globally and about how to protect yourself.

There are moments and events in time that are beyond comprehension, that jar us out of our private worlds. It won't always be like this. But this will change you. It will change all of us.

When your loss causes financial stress

Because that's what you need right now—money worries.

By my estimation, my losses cost Chris and me well over $10,000. Here are some of the expenses:

- OB-GYN and lab appointments—So. Many. Appointments. (See "Dealing with all the doctor's appointments")
- Special procedures: Two hysterosalpingography (HSG) exams, salpingectomy (surgery to remove my fallopian tube), D&E (dilation and evacuation surgery with general anesthesia), methotrexate injection
- Fertility specialist appointments (which came with their own exams and procedures)
- Prenatal vitamins (and many other supplements that I took in desperate hope they would help my pregnancies)
- Architecture plans to add on to our house (this cost $5,000 alone, and we never used them; we never gained the courage to start a renovation, thinking it would jinx us. Then we moved.)
- Maternity clothes
- Baby clothes and supplies

Medical cost site Healthcare Bluebook estimates that, before insurance, a D&C (dilation and curettage, which surgically clears the uterine lining after a first trimester miscarriage) can range anywhere from $2,400 to upwards of $7,500. $7,500?! Who has $7,500 lying around? Even if you do, you don't want to spend it on something that is already so painful.

Fortunately, Chris and I had insurance, and that did cover costs associated with our losses—kind of. We had high deductibles and large co-pays.

Most distressing is that the bills trickled in for what felt like a year. Just for my salpingectomy, we got a bill from the hospital, a bill from the anesthesiologist, a bill for my follow-ups. It felt never-ending. Talk about adding insult to injury.

"For sale: baby shoes. Never worn."

—Ernest Hemingway (according to legend)

I was lucky in that we had savings to help with all the costs. But they were still a big blow when we were already feeling terrible. What if you don't have the money you need? What if you're even more strapped because your loss required you to take time off work and forego income? It's just all . . . messed up. How can someone properly grieve when they are worried about paying rent or mortgage?

I could go off on a tangent about health care in the United States, but I won't. This book isn't about that. It's about supporting you through this time, helping you through the grief while the bills come in the mail. Still, I'll say that I wish health care was better—easier to access, with transparent cost and less hassle.

Meredith

Pregnancy loss creates many different kinds of stressors. Financial stress is an added layer of worry for many people who have lost a pregnancy. Many have spent a lot of money on medical care, others have invested in infertility treatments, and for some, the stress from both might have made it difficult to work. You or someone you know may have even gone into financial debt in the midst of loss or fertility treatments.

Coupled with and apart from these expenses are the expenses of daily life: food, clothing, car payments, gas or public transportation, school, daycare, insurance, alimony and child support payments, phone bills, and debt from past purchases. These strains alone, without the loss of a pregnancy, can be difficult. Life—and bills—continue. And you will eventually have to face them.

If you are in a financial situation that is causing you stress, even if you have money in the bank, you may want to explore how to get on track so your stress goes down and you have a solid grasp of what you can afford, what is most important to you, and how to proceed.

Here are a few books that may help you gain control of your finances:

- *Financial Recovery: Developing a Healthy Relationship with Money* (Karen McCall)
- *The Total Money Makeover: A Proven Plan for Financial Fitness* (Dave Ramsey)
- *Your Money or Your Life: 9 Steps to Transforming Your Relationship with Money and Achieving Financial Independence* (Vicki Robin, Joe Dominguez, Mr. Money Mustache)

When things get political, religious, or otherwise emotionally charged

Emotions can run high—yours and others'.

You may have turned to a collective belief in the past because it spoke to the real you—or the you at a certain time in your life.

But something about this loss, the baby you were so close to that slipped away, means that the same rules that guided your healing in the past don't seem to work.

You're grieving. Suddenly, it no longer matters to you on which side of the political aisle you sit, how you vote, whether you live in a red, blue, or purple state, worship or don't, identify with a religion or not. What had given you solace, places and collectives you thought you wanted to belong to, now anger, repel, and confuse you.

And, yet, the sheer numbers of those groups/collectives/movements (and counter movements) can, inadvertently, overwhelm the grieving you so that, once again, you're standing all by yourself. *They* think you need to examine how you're viewing things and assume the way *they* do it is right, and if you do it that way you'll eventually be fine. You wish it were that simple, that everything happened for a reason, that a power greater than yourself guided this loss. That might help address some of the pain, but certainly not all of it. These can help support your process:

- Recognize that your priority is you—body, mind, spirit.
- Tend to your body as it recovers from the loss.
- Try not to internalize another's perceived anger or disappointment at you. Instead, use the feelings that come up to connect more deeply to

yourself. Are you judging yourself? Are you disgusted or angry with yourself? These are deeply held feelings that develop over time and might have been triggered by the loss. Pay attention so you can begin to address them so their unseen (but definitely felt) impact lessens and neutralizes.

- Limit outside stress (you have enough internal stress to deal with).
- Steer clear of the pontificators who seem to know how YOU should feel. They don't. You will determine how you "should" (translation: do) feel in real time.

Keep in mind that even when you surround yourself with understanding, like-minded people, there will always be someone whose deeply held views oppose yours in some way, and vice versa.

People have opinions on many things. Some of those things are *none of their business*.

If they have a specific way *they* think you should view the loss, remember that you are discovering the way that is right for you. And it's a process. You do not have to agree, disagree, or make a choice.

They may believe that thoughts create feelings. They may imply that you must be thinking the wrong thoughts and, therefore, why you've had this loss. That's neither helpful nor supportive—furthermore, it's not true. Sitting across from someone who has a one-track reply to your grief or experience is difficult and disconcerting. It may be even harder to see (or very eye opening) if you once held that similar belief.

When you are in a vulnerable frame of mind, too many opinions, even ones you agree with, can feel like an attack in the form of a tidal wave. Remember that no one person or entity knows how you should deal with your loss. Remain open to conversations with those who will listen, reflect, be curious about, and consider your process apart from their own. They will help you hold your pain as you sort things out at your own pace.

Kim

In my mind, there is a "bigger level" to pregnancy loss, something that transcends the individual and speaks to society as a whole. And when I started thinking about these things in the aftermath of my losses, I became even more upset.

I couldn't help but feel extremely bonded to other women after my losses, in awe of how we were all suffering through this terrible thing that nobody was really talking about in society at large. If it was so common, why was there so much silence? Why were women fumbling around on message boards together, swapping information about bleeding, for example? Why wasn't there more infrastructure set up to support people through pregnancy loss? (See "The care you're probably *not* getting").

In the *New York Times* Opinion piece "You Know Someone Who's Had a Miscarriage" (Lauren Kelley and Alexandra March), a woman identified as Carol D. says, "If it were men who went through this horrible emotional trauma, would insurance not cover them going to the hospital—perhaps to a special ward?—where their hands would be held, their discomfort alleviated, their grief recognized and listened to?" This is so true, not just about pregnancy loss, but about so many things related to women's health (if you have not seen the "If Men Breastfed" video, you need to google that right now).

As I thought about this, it exacerbated my grief. I wasn't only sad about losing my babies (and my fantasies for my future as a mother); I was sad about larger social issues that were clearly at play.

At the end of 2019, a bill was introduced in Ohio's legislature that would make physicians who end pregnancies guilty of "abortion murder." The suggestion was that doctors should try to save ectopic pregnancies (by re-implanting them). This is something that is *not even possible*. With this bill, doctors could be jailed for failing to perform a procedure that does not exist.

As someone who experienced two ectopic pregnancies, this infuriated me. I would have given anything to save my embryos with those pregnancies, but my life was in danger. In both cases, measures had to be taken to save my life—and doing so meant the embryos died. It is cruel to suggest—to women, to doctors, to society at large—that there is any choice in the matter for women with ectopic pregnancies. There isn't.

Many women are presented with terrible circumstances and need a pregnancy to be terminated (See "When you had to make the difficult decision to end a pregnancy"). As Dr. Jen Gunter writes in "What you learn from doing abortions after 20 weeks," these procedures are "mostly very sad because no one is there because they are happy." In the majority of cases, a wanted pregnancy is causing physical harm to the woman, or a wanted pregnancy has severe malformations that were not discovered until after twenty weeks.

In some states, there is a ban on "elective" pregnancy terminations after twenty weeks (I've put elective in quotes because the baby's heart is still beating, so the woman does have to "choose" to terminate. I just don't see how it's a real "choice" when the pregnancy is irreparably doomed). Sometimes insurance will not cover the procedure, even if the procedure needs to be done for the patient's own safety. Some women end up going out of state, paying thousands of dollars. Women shouldn't have to do this. This isn't about being pro-choice or pro-life; this is about being pro-women.

Dr. Gunter goes on: "Let's be clear, if you are truly 'pro-life' you'd agree with these procedures because they save women. Not in an abstract way, but sometimes it is in a this-infection-is-killing-you-and-we-need-to-help-you-right-now kind of way. The one thing I've learned from my experience is that efforts to stop abortion after 20 weeks are nothing about life or compassion or good medicine, it is simply wielding the misery of women (and those who love them) as a political tool."

When I lost Miles at seventeen weeks, I was given the option of giving birth to him or having a D&E (dilation and evacuation). I chose to have a D&E. My hospital (a religious hospital) did not perform the procedure, for reasons I can guess but were never explained to me. I had to go to a different hospital, nearly an hour away. It made me feel like I had done something "bad" or "wrong." The whole thing felt strangely clandestine, hushed.

All of these underlying larger issues were salt in my wounds, making my grief more complicated. Even today, when my wounds are mostly healed, I'm still triggered by things I see in the news. Recently, for example, I read that African-American women have more pregnancy losses than White women, and this bothered me. It left me thinking again about the overall infrastructure around pregnancy loss—where the system is failing, how we all have blind spots. Wrapped into pregnancy loss are issues of sexism, racism, classism—so many isms. If you're like me, your awareness of this will stay with you long after the initial stages of grief.

Moving forward from here

We hope that you've found yourself in these pages, and that what you've read has brought some comfort and humor, as well as deeper ways to reflect and define what your loss means *for you*. We hope reading this has brought you some solace and, perhaps, a bit of newfound hopefulness as you consider what comes next *for you*.

For ongoing support and information, visit our website (alltheloveafterloss .com), or follow us on Instagram and Twitter @allthelovetalk.

Your loss matters; your perspective matters. Let's keep the conversation going and continue to spread all the love.

From our hearts to yours,

Kim, Meredith, and Huong

Acknowledgments

Kim

First and foremost, thank you to Turner Publishing for being so supportive of my novels and of this book. It's been such a passion project, and having a partner help bring it to life is a writer's dream. Thank you to my co-authors, Meredith and Huong, for your friendship and insights. Thank you to all of those who shared their personal experiences with me—I am so sorry that we have this pain in common, but so heartened by our abilities to comfort and validate each other. Thank you to the therapists and researchers committed to helping those through pregnancy loss. Last, thank you to my husband, Chris, and my daughter, Mya. Our experience, the three of us, has been my greatest inspiration.

Meredith

All my love to: Kim and Huong for this experience; Barbie, Jillian, Mary, Laura, Mary, Lynne, and Sharon for support, belief, understanding; Olya and Anya, for family; Jonathan, for everything.

Huong

My sincerest gratitude and appreciation to my fellow co-authors, Kim and Meredith. Thank you for sharing your knowledge, wisdom, and insight. Thank you to my clients who inspire me every day with their vulnerability and bravery. A heartfelt thank you to Tatiana, Mina, Jeanie, Emilia, Elia, and Tara, for your lifelong support and love. And thank YOU, dear reader. I am humbled by the collective voices and narratives worldwide who share in this journey of loss, pain, and healing.

Bibliography

Berger Gross, Jessica, ed. *About What Was Lost: Twenty Writers on Miscarriage, Healing, and Hope*. New York: Plume, 2006.

Bigwarfe, Alexa, ed. *Sunshine After the Storm: A Survival Guide for the Grieving Mother*. Kat Biggie Press, 2013.

Boggs, Belle. *The Art of Waiting: On Fertility, Medicine, and Motherhood*. Minneapolis: Graywolf Press, 2016.

Bueno, Julia. *The Brink of Being: Talking About Miscarriage*. New York: Penguin Books, 2019.

Cohen, Jon. *Coming to Term: Uncovering the Truth About Miscarriage*. New Brunswick: Rutgers University Press, 2007.

Crowe, Kelsey, and Emily McDowell. *There Is No Good Card for This: What to Say and Do When Life is Scary, Awful, and Unfair to People You Love*. New York: HarperOne, 2017.

Davis, Deborah L. *Empty Cradle, Broken Heart: Surviving the Death of Your Baby*. Golden: Fulcrum Publishing, 2016.

Freidenfelds, Lara. *The Myth of the Perfect Pregnancy: A History of Miscarriage in America*. Oxford: Oxford University Press, 2020.

Gibney, Shannon, and Kao Kalia Yang, eds. *What God Is Honored Here?: Writings on Miscarriage and Infant Loss by and for Native Women and Women of Color*. Minneapolis: University of Minnesota Press, 2019.

Kelley, Lauren, and Alexandra March, "You Know Someone Who's Had a Miscarriage," *New York Times*, October 10, 2019, nytimes.com/interactive/2019/10/10/opinion/miscarriage-pregnancy.html.

Kessler, David. *Finding Meaning: The Sixth Stage of Grief*. New York: Scribner, 2019.

Kübler-Ross, Elizabeth, and David Kessler. *On Grief and Grieving: Finding the Meaning of Grief Through the Five Stages of Loss*. New York: Scribner, 2005.

Layne, Linda L. *Motherhood Lost: A Feminist Account of Pregnancy Loss in America*. Oxfordshire: Routledge, 2002.

Levy, Ariel. *The Rules Do Not Apply: A Memoir*. New York: Random House, 2017.

Lewis, C. S. *A Grief Observed.* New York: HarperOne, 2009.

McCracken, Elizabeth. *An Exact Replica of a Figment of My Imagination: A Memoir.* New York: Little, Brown and Company, 2008.

Ptacin, Mira. *Poor Your Soul: A Memoir.* New York: Soho Press, 2016.

Soffer, Rebecca, and Gabrielle Birkner. *Modern Loss: Candid Conversations About Grief. Beginners Welcome.* New York: Harper Wave, 2018.

Thorburn, Matthew. *Dear Almost: A Poem.* Baton Rouge: LSU Press, 2016.

Van der Kolk, Bessel. *The Body Keeps the Score: Brain, Mind, and Body in the Healing of Trauma.* New York: Penguin Books, 2015.

Wright, Elle. *Ask Me His Name: Learning to Live and Laugh Again After the Loss of My Baby.* London: Lagom, 2018.

References

A loss like no other

Betz, Gabrielle, and Jill M. Thorngren. 2006. "Ambiguous Loss and the Family Grieving Process." *The Family Journal* 14 (4): 359–65. https://doi.org/10.1177/1066480706290052.

Boss, Pauline. 1999. *Ambiguous Loss: Learning to Live with Unresolved Grief.* Cambridge, Mass.: Harvard University Press.

Farren, Jessica, Maria Jalmbrant, Nora Falconieri, Nicola Mitchell-Jones, Shabnam Bobdiwala, Maya Al-Memar, Sophie Tapp, et al. 2019. "Posttraumatic Stress, Anxiety and Depression Following Miscarriage and Ectopic Pregnancy: A Multi-center, Prospective, Cohort Study." *American Journal of Obstetrics and Gynecology* 222 (4). https://doi.org/10.1016/j.ajog.2019.10.102.

Lang, Ariella, Andrea R. Fleiszer, Fabie Duhamel, Wendy Sword, Kathleen R. Gilbert, and Serena Corsini-Munt. 2011. "Perinatal Loss and Parental Grief: The Challenge of Ambiguity and Disenfranchised Grief." *OMEGA - Journal of Death and Dying* 63 (2): 183–96. https://doi.org/10.2190/om.63.2.e.

Mcgee, Katie, Morgan E. PettyJohn, and Kami L. Gallus. 2018. "Ambiguous Loss: A Phenomenological Exploration of Women Seeking Support Following Miscarriage." *Journal of Loss and Trauma* 23 (6): 516–30. https://doi.org/10.1080/15325024.2018.1484625.

Rubin, Simon Shimshon, and Ruth Malkinson. 2001. "Parental Response to Child Loss across the Life Cycle: Clinical and Research Perspectives." *Handbook of Bereavement Research: Consequences, Coping, and Care.*, 219–40. https://doi.org/10.1037/10436-009.

Different kinds of loss

Almasi, Alireza, Fariba Almassinokiani, and Peyman Akbari. 2014. "Frequency of Molar Pregnancies in Health Care Centers of Tehran, Iran." *Journal of Reproduction & Infertility* 15 (3): 157–160. https://www.jri.ir/article/591.

Cacciatore, Joanne. 2013. "Psychological Effects of Stillbirth." *Seminars in Fetal and Neonatal Medicine* 18 (2): 76–82. https://doi.org/10.1016/j.siny.2012.09.001.

Centers for Disease Control and Prevention/National Center for Health Statistics. 1997. "State Definitions and Reporting Requirements for Live Births, Fetal Deaths, and Induced Terminations of Pregnancy." https://www.cdc.gov/nchs/data/misc/itop97.pdf.

Crenshaw, Kimberlé . 1991. "Mapping the Margins: Intersectionality, Identity Politics, and Violence against Women of Color." *Stanford Law Review* 43 (6): 1241–99. https://doi.org/10.2307/1229039.

Hitzeman, Nathan, and Kelly Albin. 2014. "Misoprostol for Incomplete First Trimester Miscarriage." *American Family Physician* 89 (7): 523–524. https://www.aafp.org/afp/2014/0401/p523.html.

Hoyert, Donna L., and Elizabeth C. W. Gregory. 2016. "Cause of Fetal Death: Data From the Fetal Death Report, 2014." *National Vital Statistics Reports: From the Centers for Disease Control and Prevention, National Center for Health Statistics, National Vital Statistics System* 65 (7): 1–25. https://pubmed.ncbi.nlm.nih.gov/27805550/.

"Information about Miscarriage & Pregnancy Loss." n.d. The Miscarriage Association. https://www.miscarriageassociation.org.uk/information/.

Mattingly, Patricia J, and Saju Joy. 2019. "Evaluation of Fetal Death: Definition of Fetal Death, Frequency of Fetal Death, Diagnosis of Fetal Death." Edited by Carl V Smith. Medscape.com. November 9, 2019. https://emedicine.medscape.com/article/259165-overview.

Michels, Thomas C., and Alvin Y. Tiu. 2007. "Second Trimester Pregnancy Loss." *American Family Physician* 76 (9): 1341–1346. https://pubmed.ncbi.nlm.nih.gov/18019878/.

Speer, Linda. 2019. "Misoprostol Alone Is Associated with High Rate of Successful First-Trimester Abortion." *American Family Physician* 100 (2): 119–119. https://www.aafp.org/afp/2019/0715/p119.html.

Tenore, Josie L. 2000. "Ectopic Pregnancy." *American Family Physician* 61 (4): 1080–1088. https://pubmed.ncbi.nlm.nih.gov/10706160/.

Tong, Stephen, Anupinder Kaur, Susan P. Walker, Valerie Bryant, Joseph L. Onwude, and Michael Permezel. 2008. "Miscarriage Risk for Asymptomatic Women after a Normal First-Trimester Prenatal Visit." *Obstetrics and Gynecology* 111 (3): 710–14. https://doi.org/10.1097/AOG.0b013e318163747c.

Different circumstances

Bhat, Amritha, and Nancy Byatt. 2016. "Infertility and Perinatal Loss: When the

Bough Breaks." *Current Psychiatry Reports* 18 (3). https://doi.org/10.1007/s11920-016-0663-8.

Burden, Christy, Stephanie Bradley, Claire Storey, Alison Ellis, Alexander E. P. Heazell, Soo Downe, Joanne Cacciatore, and Dimitrios Siassakos. 2016. "From Grief, Guilt Pain and Stigma to Hope and Pride—a Systematic Review and Meta-Analysis of Mixed-Method Research of the Psychosocial Impact of Stillbirth." *BMC Pregnancy and Childbirth* 16 (1). https://doi.org/10.1186/s12884-016-0800-8.

Gameiro, Sofia, and Amy Finnigan. 2017. "Long-Term Adjustment to Unmet Parenthood Goals Following ART: A Systematic Review and Meta-Analysis." *Human Reproduction Update* 23 (3): 322–37. https://doi.org/10.1093/humupd/dmx001.

Kersting, Anette, and Birgit Wagner. 2012. "Complicated Grief after Perinatal Loss." *Dialogues Clin Neurosci* 14 (2): 187–94. https://doi.org/10.31887/dcns.2012.14.2/akersting.

Korenromp, M. J., G. C. M. L. Page-Christiaens, J. van den Bout, E. J. H. Mulder, J. A. M. Hunfeld, C. M. A. A. Potters, J. J. H. M. Erwich, et al. 2007. "A Prospective Study on Parental Coping 4 Months after Termination of Pregnancy for Fetal Anomalies." *Prenatal Diagnosis* 27 (8): 709–16. https://doi.org/10.1002/pd.1763.

Lafarge, Caroline, Kathryn Mitchell, and Pauline Fox. 2017. "Posttraumatic Growth Following Pregnancy Termination for Fetal Abnormality: The Predictive Role of Coping Strategies and Perinatal Grief." *Anxiety, Stress, & Coping* 30 (5): 536–50. https://doi.org/10.1080/10615806.2016.1278433.

Lafarge, Caroline, Lee Usher, Kathryn Mitchell, and Pauline Fox. 2020. "The Role of Rumination in Adjusting to Termination of Pregnancy for Fetal Abnormality: Rumination as a Predictor and Mediator of Posttraumatic Growth." *Psychological Trauma: Theory, Research, Practice, and Policy* 12 (1): 101–9. https://doi.org/10.1037/tra0000440.

Short, Susanne, and Linda Weidlinger. 1989. "Hidden Secrets of Childhood." *Psychological Perspectives* 21 (1): 100–117. https://doi.org/10.1080/00332928908407598.

The medical part of pregnancy loss

American College of Obstetricians and Gynecologists. n.d. "Physician FAQs." https://www.acog.org/clinical-information/physician-faqs.

Bardos, Jonah, Daniel Hercz, Jenna Friedenthal, Stacey A. Missmer, and Zev Williams. 2015. "A National Survey on Public Perceptions of Miscarriage."

Obstetrics & Gynecology 125 (6): 1313–20. https://doi.org/10.1097/aog.00000
00000000859.

Buckley, Sarah J. 2015. "Executive Summary of Hormonal Physiology of Child-bearing: Evidence and Implications for Women, Babies, and Maternity Care." *The Journal of Perinatal Education* 24 (3): 145–53. https://doi.org/10.1891/1058-1243.24.3.145.

Keating, Nancy L., Mary Beth Landrum, Selwyn O. Rogers, Susan K. Baum, Beth A. Virnig, Haiden A. Huskamp, Craig C. Earle, and Katherine L. Kahn. 2010. "Physician Factors Associated with Discussions about End-of-Life Care." *Cancer* 116 (4): 998–1006. https://doi.org/10.1002/cncr.24761.

Kilshaw, Susie. 2017. "How Culture Shapes Perceptions of Miscarriage." SAPIENS. July 27, 2017. https://www.sapiens.org/biology/miscarriage-united-kingdom-qatar/.

Leis-Newman, Elizabeth. 2012. "Miscarriage and Loss." *Https://Www.Apa.org* 43 (6): 56. https://www.apa.org/monitor/2012/06/miscarriage.

Nikcevic, A. V., S. A. Tunkel, and K. H. Nicolaides. 1998. "Psychological Outcomes Following Missed Abortions and Provision of Follow-up Care." *Ultrasound in Obstetrics and Gynecology* 11 (2): 123–28. https://doi.org/10.1046/j.1469-0705.1998.11020123.x.

Nynas, Johnna, Puneet Narang, Murali K. Kolikonda, and Steven Lippmann. 2015. "Depression and Anxiety Following Early Pregnancy Loss." *The Primary Care Companion For CNS Disorders* 17 (1). https://doi.org/10.4088/pcc.14r01721.

Sensky, Tom, Marie Dennehy, Alexa Gilbert, Richard Begent, Edward Newlands, Gordon Rustin, and Christopher Thompson. 1989. "Physicians' Perceptions of Anxiety and Depression Among Their Outpatients: Relationships with Patients and Doctors' Satisfaction with Their Interviews." *Journal of the Royal College of Physicians of London* 23 (1): 33–38. https://www.ncbi.nlm.nih.gov/pmc/articles/PMC5387439/.

Tenore, Josie L. 2000. "Ectopic Pregnancy." *American Family Physician* 61 (4): 1080–1088. https://pubmed.ncbi.nlm.nih.gov/10706160/.

Wong, Michael K, Trevor J. Crawford, Linda Gask, and Anne Grinyer. 2003. "A Qualitative Investigation into Women's Experiences after a Miscarriage: Implications for the Primary Healthcare Team." *The British Journal of General Practice* 53 (494): 697–702. https://www.ncbi.nlm.nih.gov/pmc/articles/PMC1314692/.

Shock, guilt, shame, loneliness, anger, despair, anxiety— the gang's all here

American Psychiatric Association. 2013. *Diagnostic and Statistical Manual of Mental Disorders: DSM-5.* 5th ed. Arlington, VA: American Psychiatric Association.

Bardos, Jonah, Daniel Hercz, Jenna Friedenthal, Stacey A. Missmer, and Zev Williams. 2015. "A National Survey on Public Perceptions of Miscarriage." *Obstetrics & Gynecology* 125 (6): 1313–20. https://doi.org/10.1097/aog.00000 00000000859.

Bracha, H. Stefan. 2004. "Freeze, Flight, Fight, Fright, Faint: Adaptationist Perspectives on the Acute Stress Response Spectrum." *CNS Spectrums* 9 (09): 679–85. https://doi.org/10.1017/s1092852900001954.

Clarke, David M., and David W. Kissane. 2002. "Demoralization: Its Phenomenology and Importance." *Australian & New Zealand Journal of Psychiatry* 36 (6): 733–42. https://doi.org/10.1046/j.1440-1614.2002.01086.x.

deMontigny, Francine, Chantal Verdon, Sophie Meunier, and Diane Dubeau. 2017. "Women's Persistent Depressive and Perinatal Grief Symptoms Following a Miscarriage: The Role of Childlessness and Satisfaction with Healthcare Services." *Archives of Women's Mental Health* 20 (5): 655–62. https://doi.org/10.1007/s00737-017-0742-9.

Farren, Jessica, Maria Jalmbrant, Nora Falconieri, Nicola Mitchell-Jones, Shabnam Bobdiwala, Maya Al-Memar, Sophie Tapp, et al. 2019. "Posttraumatic Stress, Anxiety and Depression Following Miscarriage and Ectopic Pregnancy: A Multicenter, Prospective, Cohort Study." *American Journal of Obstetrics and Gynecology* 222 (4). https://doi.org/10.1016/j.ajog.2019.10.102.

Farren, Jessica, Maria Jalmbrant, Lieveke Ameye, Karen Joash, Nicola Mitchell-Jones, Sophie Tapp, Dirk Timmerman, and Tom Bourne. 2016. "Post-Traumatic Stress, Anxiety and Depression Following Miscarriage or Ectopic Pregnancy: A Prospective Cohort Study." *BMJ Open* 6 (11): e011864. https://doi.org/10.1136/bmjopen-2016-011864.

Gilbard, Jeffrey P. 1986. "Crying: The Mystery of Tears." *Archives of Ophthalmology* 104 (3): 343–44. https://doi.org/10.1001/archopht.1986.01050150037021.

Gold, Katherine J., Irving Leon, Martha E. Boggs, and Ananda Sen. 2016. "Depression and Posttraumatic Stress Symptoms After Perinatal Loss in a Population-Based Sample." *Journal of Women's Health (2002)* 25 (3): 263–269. https://doi.org/10.1089/jwh.2015.5284.

Freidenfelds, Lara. 2019. Introduction to *The Myth of the Perfect Pregnancy: A History of Miscarriage in America*. New York, NY: Oxford University Press.

Hoyert, Donna L., and Elizabeth C. W. Gregory. 2016. "Cause of Fetal Death: Data From the Fetal Death Report, 2014." *National Vital Statistics Reports: From the Centers for Disease Control and Prevention, National Center for Health Statistics, National Vital Statistics System* 65 (7): 1–25. https://pubmed.ncbi.nlm.nih.gov/27805550/.

Imperial College London. 2016. "Miscarriage, Ectopic Pregnancy May Trigger Post-

Traumatic Stress Disorder." ScienceDaily. November 2, 2016. https://www. sciencedaily.com/releases/2016/11/161102080121.htm.

Kilshaw, Susie. 2017. "How Culture Shapes Perceptions of Miscarriage." SAPIENS. July 27, 2017. https://www.sapiens.org/biology/miscarriage-united-kingdom-qatar/.

Krosch, Daniel Jay, and Jane Shakespeare-Finch. 2017. "Grief, Traumatic Stress, and Posttraumatic Growth in Women Who Have Experienced Pregnancy Loss." *Psychological Trauma: Theory, Research, Practice, and Policy* 9 (4): 425–33. https://doi.org/10.1037/tra0000183.

Lok, Ingrid Hung, Alexander Shing-Kai Yip, Dominic Tak-Sing Lee, Daljit Sahota, and Tony Kwok-Hung Chung. 2010. "A 1-Year Longitudinal Study of Psychological Morbidity After Miscarriage." *Fertility and Sterility* 93 (6): 1966–75. https://doi.org/10.1016/j.fertnstert.2008.12.048.

Mutiso, Steve Kyende, Alfred Murage, and Abraham Mwaniki Mukaindo. 2018. "Prevalence of Positive Depression Screen Among Post Miscarriage Women- A Cross Sectional Study." *BMC Psychiatry* 18 (1). https://doi.org/10.1186/s12888-018-1619-9.

Rice, William R. 2018. "The High Abortion Cost of Human Reproduction." *bioRxiv*, July. https://doi.org/10.1101/372193.

Schumaker, John. 2016. "The Demoralized Mind." New Internationalist. April 1, 2016. https://newint.org/columns/essays/2016/04/01/psycho-spiritual-crisis.

Weng, S.C., J.C. Chang, M.K. Yeh, S.M. Wang, C.S. Lee, and Y.H. Chen. 2018. "Do Stillbirth, Miscarriage, and Termination of Pregnancy Increase Risks of Attempted and Completed Suicide within a Year? A Population-Based Nested Case-Control Study." *BJOG: An International Journal of Obstetrics & Gynaecology* 125 (8): 983–90. https://doi.org/10.1111/1471-0528.15105.

Understanding your grief process

Barr, Peter, and Joanne Cacciatore. 2008. "Problematic Emotions and Maternal Grief." *OMEGA - Journal of Death and Dying* 56 (4): 331–48. https://doi.org/10.2190/om.56.4.b.

Betz, Gabrielle, and Jill M. Thorngren. 2006. "Ambiguous Loss and the Family Grieving Process." *The Family Journal* 14 (4): 359–65. https://doi.org/10.1177/1066480706290052.

Bradbeer, Mark, Robert D. Helme, Hua-Hie Yong, Hal L. Kendig, and Stephen J. Gibson. 2003. "Widowhood and Other Demographic Associations of Pain in Independent Older People." *The Clinical Journal of Pain* 19 (4): 247–54. https://doi.org/10.1097/00002508-200307000-00008.

Buck, Harleah G., Paula Cairns, Nnadozie Emechebe, Diego F. Hernandez, Tina M. Mason, Jesse Bell, Kevin E. Kip, Philip Barrison, and Cindy Tofthagen. 2020. "Accelerated Resolution Therapy: Randomized Controlled Trial of a Complicated Grief Intervention." *American Journal of Hospice and Palliative Medicine®* 37 (10): 104990911990064. https://doi.org/10.1177/1049909119900641.

Fagundes, Christopher P., Ryan L. Brown, Michelle A. Chen, Kyle W. Murdock, Levi Saucedo, Angie LeRoy, E. Lydia Wu, et al. 2019. "Grief, Depressive Symptoms, and Inflammation in the Spousally Bereaved." *Psychoneuroendocrinology* 100 (February): 190–197. https://doi.org/10.1016/j.psyneuen.2018.10.006.

Hannibal, Kara E., and Mark D. Bishop. 2014. "Chronic Stress, Cortisol Dysfunction, and Pain: A Psychoneuroendocrine Rationale for Stress Management in Pain Rehabilitation." *Physical Therapy* 94 (12): 1816–25. https://doi.org/10.2522/ptj.20130597.

Harris, Catherine L., Jean Berko Gleason, and Ayşe Ayçiçeɢi. 2006. "10. When Is a First Language More Emotional? Psychophysiological Evidence from Bilingual Speakers." Edited by Aneta Pavlenko. *Bilingual Minds*, December, 257–83. https://doi.org/10.21832/9781853598746-012.

Hutti, Marianne H., and Rana Limbo. 2019. "Using Theory to Inform and Guide Perinatal Bereavement Care." *MCN, The American Journal of Maternal/Child Nursing* 44 (1): 20–26. https://doi.org/10.1097/nmc.0000000000000495.

Maciejewski, Paul K., Baohui Zhang, Susan D. Block, and Holly G. Prigerson. 2007. "An Empirical Examination of the Stage Theory of Grief." *JAMA* 297 (7): 716. https://doi.org/10.1001/jama.297.7.716.

Mughal, Saba, Yusra Azhar, and Waqas J. Siddiqui. 2019a. "Grief Reaction." Nih. Gov. StatPearls Publishing. March 25, 2019. https://www.ncbi.nlm.nih.gov/books/NBK507832/.

"Overview - The Center for Complicated Grief." 2018. Columbia School of Social Work. 2018. https://complicatedgrief.columbia.edu/professionals/complicated-grief-professionals/overview/.

Toedter, Lori J., Judith N. Lasker, and Hettie J. E. M. Janssen. 2001. "International Comparison of Studies Using the Perinatal Grief Scale: A Decade of Research on Pregnancy Loss." *Death Studies* 25 (3): 205–28. https://doi.org/10.1080/074811801750073251.

Grieving in a society that sucks at grief

Burden, Christy, Stephanie Bradley, Claire Storey, Alison Ellis, Alexander E. P. Heazell, Soo Downe, Joanne Cacciatore, and Dimitrios Siassakos. 2016. "From Grief, Guilt Pain and Stigma to Hope and Pride—a Systematic Review and

Meta-Analysis of Mixed-Method Research of the Psychosocial Impact of Still-birth." *BMC Pregnancy and Childbirth* 16 (1). https://doi.org/10.1186/s12884-016-0800-8.

Centre for Clinical Interventions. "What Is Distress Intolerance?" *Centre for Clinical Interventions*. Government of Western Australia, n.d. https://www.cci.health.wa.gov.au/-/media/CCI/Mental-Health-Professionals/Distress-Intolerance/Information-Sheets/Info-What-is-Distress-Intolerance.pdf.

Connecting with your baby

Leon, Irving G. 2008. "Helping Families Cope with Perinatal Loss." *The Global Library of Women's Medicine* 6. https://doi.org/10.3843/glowm.10418.

Sloan, Denise M., Alice T. Sawyer, Sara E. Lowmaster, Jeremy Wernick, and Brian P. Marx. 2015. "Efficacy of Narrative Writing as an Intervention for PTSD: Does the Evidence Support Its Use?" *Journal of Contemporary Psychotherapy* 45 (4): 215–25. https://doi.org/10.1007/s10879-014-9292-x.

Connecting with your partner

2015 U.S. Trans Survey. "2015 U.S. Trans Survey." 2015 U.S. Trans Survey, 2015. http://www.ustranssurvey.org.

Australian Psychological Society. "Information Sheet: LGBT Pregnancy Loss," n.d. https://www.psychology.org.au/getmedia/9ea8dd55-7c2b-4653-8371-b1f732b70b58/LGBT_pregnancy_loss.pdf.

Brandt, Justin S., Amy J. Patel, Ian Marshall, and Gloria A. Bachmann. 2019. "Transgender Men, Pregnancy, and the 'New' Advanced Paternal Age: A Review of the Literature." *Maturitas* 128 (October): 17–21. https://doi.org/10.1016/j.maturitas.2019.07.004.

Burden, Christy, Stephanie Bradley, Claire Storey, Alison Ellis, Alexander E. P. Heazell, Soo Downe, Joanne Cacciatore, and Dimitrios Siassakos. 2016. "From Grief, Guilt Pain and Stigma to Hope and Pride—a Systematic Review and Meta-Analysis of Mixed-Method Research of the Psychosocial Impact of Stillbirth." *BMC Pregnancy and Childbirth* 16 (1). https://doi.org/10.1186/s12884-016-0800-8.

Cacciatore, Joanne, and Zulma Raffo. 2011. "An Exploration of Lesbian Maternal Bereavement." *Social Work* 56 (2): 169–77. https://doi.org/10.1093/sw/56.2.169.

Carmichael, Cheryl L., Harry T. Reis, and Paul R. Duberstein. 2015. "In Your 20s It's Quantity, in Your 30s It's Quality: The Prognostic Value of Social Activity across 30 Years of Adulthood." *Psychology and Aging* 30 (1): 95–105. https://doi.org/10.1037/pag0000014.

Chapman, Gary. n.d. "Discover Your Love Language." The 5 Love Languages®. https://www.5lovelanguages.com.

Charter, Rosie, Jane M. Ussher, Janette Perz, and Kerry Robinson. 2018. "The Transgender Parent: Experiences and Constructions of Pregnancy and Parenthood for Transgender Men in Australia." *International Journal of Transgenderism* 19 (1): 64–77. https://doi.org/10.1080/15532739.2017.1399496.

Craven, Christa, and Elizabeth Peel. 2017. "Queering Reproductive Loss: Exploring Grief and Memorialization." In *Interrogating Pregnancy Loss: Feminist Writings on Abortion, Miscarriage, and Stillbirth*, edited by Angie Deveau, 225–245. Demeter Press.

Ellis, Simon Adriane, Danuta M. Wojnar, and Maria Pettinato. 2014. "Conception, Pregnancy, and Birth Experiences of Male and Gender Variant Gestational Parents: It's How We Could Have a Family." *Journal of Midwifery & Women's Health* 60 (1): 62–69. https://doi.org/10.1111/jmwh.12213.

Gold, Katherine J., Ananda Sen, and Rodney A. Hayward. 2010. "Marriage and Cohabitation Outcomes After Pregnancy Loss." *PEDIATRICS* 125 (5): e1202–7. https://doi.org/10.1542/peds.2009-3081.

Leis-Newman, Elizabeth. 2012. "Miscarriage and Loss." *American Psychological Association* 43 (6): 56. https://www.apa.org/monitor/2012/06/miscarriage.

Love, Heather. 2009. *Feeling Backward: Loss and the Politics of Queer History*. Cambridge, Mass.; London: Harvard University Press.

Obedin-Maliver, Juno, and Harvey J. Makadon. 2015. "Transgender Men and Pregnancy." *Obstetric Medicine* 9 (1): 4–8. https://doi.org/10.1177/1753495x15612658.

Riggs, Damien W., Clemence Due, and Jennifer Power. 2014. "Gay Men's Experiences of Surrogacy Clinics in India." *Journal of Family Planning and Reproductive Health Care* 41 (1): 48–53. https://doi.org/10.1136/jfprhc-2013-100671.

Rodríguez-González, Martiño, Jessica Lampis, Nancy L. Murdock, Maria L. Schweer-Collins, and Emma R. Lyons. 2020. "Couple Adjustment and Differentiation of Self in the United States, Italy, and Spain: A Cross-Cultural Study." *Family Process* 59 (4): 1552–1568. https://doi.org/10.1111/famp.12522.

Sapra, K. J., A. C. McLain, J. M. Maisog, R. Sundaram, and G. M. Buck Louis. 2014. "Successive Time to Pregnancy among Women Experiencing Pregnancy Loss." *Human Reproduction* 29 (11): 2553–59. https://doi.org/10.1093/humrep/deu216.

Schliep, Karen C., Emily M. Mitchell, Sunni L. Mumford, Rose G. Radin, Shvetha M. Zarek, Lindsey Sjaarda, and Enrique F. Schisterman. 2016. "Trying to Conceive After an Early Pregnancy Loss." *Obstetrics & Gynecology* 127 (2): 204–12. https://doi.org/10.1097/aog.0000000000001159.

Swanson, Kristen M., Zahra A. Karmali, Suzanne H. Powell, and Faina Pulvermakher. 2003. "Miscarriage Effects on Couples' Interpersonal and Sexual Relationships During the First Year After Loss: Women's Perceptions." *Psychosomatic Medicine* 65 (5): 902–10. https://doi.org/10.1097/01.psy.0000079381.58810.84.

Turton, Penelope, William Badenhorst, Patricia Hughes, Julia Ward, Samantha Riches, and Sarah White. 2006. "Psychological Impact of Stillbirth on Fathers in the Subsequent Pregnancy and Puerperium." *British Journal of Psychiatry* 188 (2): 165–72. https://doi.org/10.1192/bjp.188.2.165.

Verbanas, Patti. 2019. "Pregnant Transgender Men at Risk for Depression and Lack of Care, Rutgers Study Finds." Www.Rutgers.Edu. August 15, 2019. https://www.rutgers.edu/news/pregnant-transgender-men-risk-depression-and-lack-care-rutgers-study-finds#.XVGaNZJKi4Q.

Walks, Michelle. 2007. "Breaking the Silence: Infertility, Motherhood, and Queer Culture." *Journal of the Motherhood Initiative for Research and Community Involvement* 9 (2). https://jarm.journals.yorku.ca/index.php/jarm/article/view/13808/0.

Wojnar, Danuta. 2007. "Miscarriage Experiences of Lesbian Couples." *Journal of Midwifery & Women's Health* 52 (5): 479–85. https://doi.org/10.1016/j.jmwh.2007.03.015.

Ziv, Ido, and Yael Freund-Eschar. 2014. "The Pregnancy Experience of Gay Couples Expecting a Child Through Overseas Surrogacy." *The Family Journal* 23 (2): 158–66. https://doi.org/10.1177/1066480714565107.

Connecting with others

Cesare, Nina, Olubusola Oladeji, Kadija Ferryman, Derry Wijaya, Karen D. Hendricks-Muñoz, Alyssa Ward, and Elaine O. Nsoesie. 2020. "Discussions of Miscarriage and Preterm Births on Twitter." *Paediatric and Perinatal Epidemiology* 34 (5): 544–52. https://doi.org/10.1111/ppe.12622.

Desalvo, Louise A. 1999. *Writing as a Way of Healing: How Telling Our Stories Transforms Our Lives*. Boston, Mass.: Beacon Press.

Lambert, Michael J., and Dean E. Barley. 2001a. "Research Summary of the Therapeutic Relationship and Psychotherapy Outcome." *Psychotherapy: Theory, Research, Practice, Training* 38 (4): 357–61. https://doi.org/10.1037/0033-3204.38.4.357.

Returning to "normal" life (whatever that means)

Herz, Rachel S., James Eliassen, Sophia Beland, and Timothy Souza. 2004. "Neuro-imaging Evidence for the Emotional Potency of Odor-Evoked Memory."

Neuropsychologia 42 (3): 371–78. https://doi.org/10.1016/j.neuropsychologia.
2003.08.009.

Jung, C.G.. *Four Archetypes*. United Kingdom: Taylor & Francis, 2014. https://www.
google.com/books/edition/Four_Archetypes/2bXgBQAAQBAJ

Rediscovering (and loving) who you are

Allahdadian, Maryam, and Alireza Irajpour. 2015. "The Role of Religious Beliefs in
Pregnancy Loss." *Journal of Education and Health Promotion*, December. https://
doi.org/10.4103/2277-9531.171813.

Ducharme, Jamie. 2018. "About Half of Americans Say They're Trying to Lose
Weight." Time. July 12, 2018. https://time.com/5334532/weight-loss-ameri-
cans/.

Kilshaw, Susie. 2017. "How Culture Shapes Perceptions of Miscarriage." SAPIENS. July
27, 2017. https://www.sapiens.org/biology/miscarriage-united-kingdom-qatar/.

Krosch, Daniel Jay, and Jane Shakespeare-Finch. 2017. "Grief, Traumatic Stress, and
Posttraumatic Growth in Women Who Have Experienced Pregnancy Loss." *Psychological Trauma: Theory, Research, Practice, and Policy* 9 (4): 425–33. https://doi.org/
10.1037/tra0000183.

Nynas, Johnna, Puneet Narang, Murali K. Kolikonda, and Steven Lippmann. 2015.
"Depression and Anxiety Following Early Pregnancy Loss." *The Primary Care
Companion For CNS Disorders* 17 (1). https://doi.org/10.4088/pcc.14r01721.

Trying again … or not

Allen, Jennifer. "The Long Road: An Article on Anticipatory Grief." web.archive.org, 2008.
https://web.archive.org/web/20120222111722/http:/www.jenniferallenbooks.
com/grief/pdf/longroad.pdf.

Nynas, Johnna, Puneet Narang, Murali K. Kolikonda, and Steven Lippmann. 2015.
"Depression and Anxiety Following Early Pregnancy Loss." *The Primary Care
Companion For CNS Disorders* 17 (1). https://doi.org/10.4088/pcc.14r01721.

Getting pregnant after a loss

Bateman, Anthony, and Peter Fonagy. 2013. "Mentalization-Based Treatment."
Psychoanalytic Inquiry 33 (6): 595–613. https://doi.org/10.1080/07351690.20
13.835170.

Blackmore, Emma Robertson, Denise Côté-Arsenault, Wan Tang, Vivette Glover,
Jonathan Evans, Jean Golding, and Thomas G. O'Connor. 2011. "Previous

Prenatal Loss as a Predictor of Perinatal Depression and Anxiety." *British Journal of Psychiatry* 198 (5): 373–78. https://doi.org/10.1192/bjp.bp.110.083105.

Fonagy, Peter, and Elizabeth Allison. 2012. "What Is Mentalization? The Concept and Its Foundations in Developmental Research and Social-Cognitive Neuroscience." In *Minding the Child: Mentalization-Based Interventions with Children, Young People and Their Families*, edited by Nick Midgley and Ioanna Vrouva, 11–34. New York: Routledge. https://discovery.ucl.ac.uk/id/eprint/1430329/7/Fonagy_chapter1_draft_pfrevised_protected.pdf.

Markin, Rayna D. 2018. "'Ghosts' in the Womb: A Mentalizing Approach to Understanding and Treating Prenatal Attachment Disturbances during Pregnancies after Loss." *Psychotherapy* 55 (3): 275–88. https://doi.org/10.1037/pst0000186.

O'Leary, Joann. 2003. "Grief and Its Impact on Prenatal Attachment in the Subsequent Pregnancy." *Archives of Women's Mental Health* 7 (1): 7–18. https://doi.org/10.1007/s00737-003-0037-1.

Ross-White, Amanda. 2018. "How Remembering Your Baby Helps You Bond with the next One." *Pregnancy After Loss Support* (blog). September 18, 2018. https://pregnancyafterlosssupport.org/remembering-helps-bond/.

Having a baby after a loss

Blackmore, Emma Robertson, Denise Côté-Arsenault, Wan Tang, Vivette Glover, Jonathan Evans, Jean Golding, and Thomas G. O'Connor. 2011. "Previous Prenatal Loss as a Predictor of Perinatal Depression and Anxiety." *British Journal of Psychiatry* 198 (5): 373–78. https://doi.org/10.1192/bjp.bp.110.083105.

Buckley, Sarah J. 2015. "Executive Summary of Hormonal Physiology of Childbearing: Evidence and Implications for Women, Babies, and Maternity Care." *The Journal of Perinatal Education* 24 (3): 145–53. https://doi.org/10.1891/1058-1243.24.3.145.

Dekel, Sharon, Caren Stuebe, and Gabriella Dishy. 2017. "Childbirth Induced Posttraumatic Stress Syndrome: A Systematic Review of Prevalence and Risk Factors." *Frontiers in Psychology* 8 (April). https://doi.org/10.3389/fpsyg.2017.00560.

Farren, Jessica, Maria Jalmbrant, Lieveke Ameye, Karen Joash, Nicola Mitchell-Jones, Sophie Tapp, Dirk Timmerman, and Tom Bourne. 2016. "Post-Traumatic Stress, Anxiety and Depression Following Miscarriage or Ectopic Pregnancy: A Prospective Cohort Study." *BMJ Open* 6 (11): e011864. https://doi.org/10.1136/bmjopen-2016-011864.

National Institute of Mental Health. n.d. "NIMH » Perinatal Depression." National Institute of Mental Health. https://www.nimh.nih.gov/health/publications/perinatal-depression/index.shtml#pub3.

Nynas, Johnna, Puneet Narang, Murali K. Kolikonda, and Steven Lippmann. 2015. "Depression and Anxiety Following Early Pregnancy Loss." *The Primary Care Companion For CNS Disorders* 17 (1). https://doi.org/10.4088/pcc.14r01721.

Weil, Andrew. 2019. "Breathing Exercises: Three to Try | 4-7-8 Breath | Andrew Weil, M.D." DrWeil.com. January 7, 2019. https://www.drweil.com/health-wellness/body-mind-spirit/stress-anxiety/breathing-three-exercises/.

When grief gets (more) complicated

Berinato, Scott. 2020. "That Discomfort You're Feeling Is Grief." Harvard Business Review. March 23, 2020. https://hbr.org/2020/03/that-discomfort-youre-feeling-is-grief.

Ford, Holly B., and Danny J. Schust. 2009. "Recurrent Pregnancy Loss: Etiology, Diagnosis, and Therapy." *Reviews in Obstetrics & Gynecology* 2 (2): 76–83. https://pubmed.ncbi.nlm.nih.gov/19609401/.

Geronimus, Arline T., Margaret T. Hicken, Jay A. Pearson, Sarah J. Seashols, Kelly L. Brown, and Tracey Dawson Cruz. 2010. "Do US Black Women Experience Stress-Related Accelerated Biological Aging?" *Human Nature (Hawthorne, N.Y.)* 21 (1): 19–38. https://doi.org/10.1007/s12110-010-9078-0.

Gunter, Jen. 2016. "What You Learn Doing Abortions after 20 Weeks." Dr. Jen Gunter. June 22, 2016. https://drjengunter.com/2016/06/22/what-you-learn-from-doing-abortions-after-20-weeks/.

Jacobsen, R. H. 1986. "Unresolved Grief of 25 Years Duration Exacerbated by Multiple Subsequent Losses." *The Journal of Nervous and Mental Disease* 174 (10): 624–627. https://pubmed.ncbi.nlm.nih.gov/3760854/.

Kersting, Anette, Michaela Dorsch, Carmen Kreulich, Michael Reutemann, Patricia Ohrmann, Edinef Baez, and Volker Arolt. 2005. "Trauma and Grief 2–7 Years after Termination of Pregnancy Because of Fetal Anomalies – a Pilot Study." *Journal of Psychosomatic Obstetrics & Gynecology* 26 (1): 9–14. https://doi.org/10.1080/01443610400022967.

Kiguli, Juliet, Ian G. Munabi, Eric Ssegujja, Joyce Nabaliisa, Consolata Kabonesa, Sarah Kiguli, and Byamugisha Josaphat. 2016. "Stillbirths in Sub-Saharan Africa: Unspoken Grief." *The Lancet* 387 (10018): e16–18. https://doi.org/10.1016/s0140-6736(15)01171-x.

Law, Tara. 2019. "Ohio Bill Suggests Doctors Who Perform Abortions Could Face Jail, Unless They Perform a Non-Existent Treatment." Time. December 2019. https://time.com/5742053/ectopic-pregnancy-ohio-abortion-bill/.

Lind, Emily R.M., and Angie Deveau. 2017. *Interrogating Pregnancy Loss: Feminist Writings on Abortion, Miscarriage, and Stillbirth*. Bradford, Ontario: Demeter Press.

Meyer, Ilan H. 2003. "Prejudice, Social Stress, and Mental Health in Lesbian, Gay, and Bisexual Populations: Conceptual Issues and Research Evidence." *Psychological Bulletin* 129 (5): 674–97. https://doi.org/10.1037/0033-2909.129.5.674.

Piazza, Jared, and Justin F. Landy. 2019. "Folk Beliefs about the Relationships Anger and Disgust Have with Moral Disapproval." *Cognition and Emotion* 34 (2): 229–41. https://doi.org/10.1080/02699931.2019.1605977.

Ridaura, Isabel, Eva Penlo, and Rosa M. Raich. 2017. "Depressive Symptomatology and Grief in Spanish Women Who Have Suffered a Perinatal Loss." *Psicothema* 29 (1): 43–48. https://doi.org/10.7334/psicothema2016.151.

Van, Paulina, and Afaf I. Meleis. 2003. "Coping With Grief After Involuntary Pregnancy Loss: Perspectives of African American Women." *Journal of Obstetric, Gynecologic & Neonatal Nursing* 32 (1): 28–39. https://doi.org/10.1177/0884217 502239798.

Appendix

CHARITIES AND ORGANIZATIONS

Share Pregnancy and Infant Loss Support | Nationalshare.org
The mission of Share is to serve those whose lives are touched by the tragic death of a baby through pregnancy loss or stillbirth, or in the first few months of life.

March of Dimes | MarchofDimes.org
The March of Dimes supports moms throughout pregnancy, even when everything doesn't go according to plan. They advocate for policies that prioritize women's health, and they pioneer research to find solutions to the biggest health threats to moms and babies.

International Stillbirth Alliance | Stillbirthalliance.org
ISA's mission is to raise awareness and promote global collaboration for the prevention of stillbirth and newborn death, and to provide the best care possible for all those affected.

Miscarriage Association | Miscarriageassociation.org.uk
The Miscarriage Association offers support and information to anyone affected by the loss of a baby in pregnancy, with the goal of raising awareness and promoting good practice in medical care.

Sands (Stillbirth and Neonatal Death Charity) | Sands.org.uk
Sands is the leading stillbirth and neonatal death charity in the UK. Their mission is to reduce the number of babies dying and ensure that anyone affected by the death of a baby receives the care and support they need.

Center for Loss in Multiple Birth (CLIMB) | Climb-support.org
The mission of CLIMB is to provide parent-to-parent support for those who have experienced the death of one or more twins (or higher multiple birth children) at any time from conception through birth, infancy, and early childhood.

HAND (Helping After Neonatal Death) | Handonline.org
HAND aims to help parents, their families, and their health-care providers cope with the loss of a baby before, during, or after birth.

The Ectopic Pregnancy Trust | Ectopic.org.uk
The Ectopic Pregnancy Trust strives to provide information, education, and support to those affected by early pregnancy complications and to the health professionals who care for them.

HELPFUL WEBSITES

Still Standing Magazine | Stillstandingmag.com
Designed specifically for parents grieving the loss of a child or coping with infertility

Remembering Our Babies | October15th.com
The official site of Pregnancy and Infant Loss Remembrance Day

BOOKS

These are some of our favorites:

Nonfiction
- *An Exact Replica of a Figment of My Imagination: A Memoir* (Elizabeth McCracken)
- *Poor Your Soul* (Mira Ptacin)
- *Ask Me His Name: Learning to Live and Laugh Again After the Loss of My Baby* (Elle Wright)
- *About What Was Lost: Twenty Writers on Miscarriage, Healing, and Hope* (Jessica Berger Gross, editor)
- *Sunshine After the Storm: A Survival Guide for Grieving Mothers* (Alexa Bigwarfe, editor)
- *What God Is Honored Here?: Writings on Miscarriage and Infant Loss by and for Native Women and Women of Color* (Shannon Gibney and Kao Kalia Yang, editors)
- *Empty Cradle, Broken Heart* (Deborah Davis)
- *The Brink of Being: Talking About Miscarriage* (Julia Bueno)
- *Coming to Term: Uncovering the Truth About Miscarriage* (Jon Cohen)
- *The Art of Waiting: On Fertility, Medicine, and Motherhood* (Belle Boggs)
- *The Myth of the Perfect Pregnancy: A History of Miscarriage in America* (Lara Freidenfelds)

Fiction

- *What Alice Forgot* (Liane Moriarty)
- *The Light Between Oceans* (M. L. Stedman)
- *A Thousand Splendid Suns* (Khaled Hosseini)
- *The End of Miracles* (Monica Starkman)
- *You Were There Too* (Colleen Oakley)
- *The Mother's Promise* (Sally Hepworth)
- *Interpreter of Maladies* (Jhumpa Lahiri)

Three of Kim's novels include pregnancy loss in the storylines:

- *Cherry Blossoms*
- *Tiny*
- *All the Acorns on the Forest Floor*

RESOURCES FOR HEALTH-CARE PROVIDERS

If you are a health-care provider, the following websites may help you learn more about how to support patients going through infertility and pregnancy loss:

Association of Women's Health, Obstetric and Neonatal Nurses
awhonn.org

Canadian Pediatric Society
cps.ca

Global Library of Women's Medicine
glowm.com

Mental Health Professional Group: A Professional Group of the American Society for Reproductive Medicine (MHPG)
connect.asrm.org/mhpg

National Association of Perinatal Social Workers
napsw.org

National Council for Behavioral Health/ Center of Excellence for Integrated Health Solutions/Health Substance Abuse and Mental Health Administration (SAMHSA)
thenationalcouncil.org/integrated-health-coe

National Perinatal Association

nationalperinatal.org

Resolve: The National Infertility Association

Resolve.org

We also recommend this publication:

Markin, Rayna D. "What clinicians miss about miscarriages: Clinical errors in the treatment of early term perinatal loss." *Psychotherapy*, 2016.

Questionnaires
and screeners

PERINATAL GRIEF SCALE

This thirty-three-item questionnaire was developed by Lori J. Toedter, PhD, and Judith N. Lasker, PhD.

Each of the items is a statement of thoughts and feelings some people have concerning a loss such as yours. There are no right or wrong responses to these statements. For each item, circle the number that best indicates the extent to which you agree or disagree with it at the present time. If you are not certain, use the "neither" category. Please try to use this category only when you truly have no opinion.

	Strongly Agree	Agree	Neither Agree nor Disagree	Disagree	Strongly Disagree
1. I feel depressed.	1	2	3	4	5
2. I find it hard to get along with certain people.	1	2	3	4	5
3. I feel empty inside.	1	2	3	4	5
4. I can't keep up with my normal activities.	1	2	3	4	5
5. I feel a need to talk about the baby.	1	2	3	4	5
6. I am grieving for the baby.	1	2	3	4	5
7. I am frightened.	1	2	3	4	5
8. I have considered suicide since the loss.	1	2	3	4	5
9. I take medicine for my nerves.	1	2	3	4	5
10. I very much miss the baby.	1	2	3	4	5

	Strongly Agree	Agree	Neither Agree nor Disagree	Disagree	Strongly Disagree
11. I feel I have adjusted well to the loss.	1	2	3	4	5
12. It is painful to recall memories of the loss.	1	2	3	4	5
13. I get upset when I think about the baby.	1	2	3	4	5
14. I cry when I think about him/her.	1	2	3	4	5
15. I feel guilty when I think about the baby.	1	2	3	4	5
16. I feel physically ill when I think about the baby.	1	2	3	4	5
17. I feel unprotected in a dangerous world since he/she died.	1	2	3	4	5
18. I try to laugh, but nothing seems funny anymore.	1	2	3	4	5
19. Time passes so slowly since the baby died.	1	2	3	4	5
20. The best part of me died with the baby.	1	2	3	4	5
21. I have let people down since the baby died.	1	2	3	4	5
22. I feel worthless since he/she died.	1	2	3	4	5
23. I blame myself for the baby's death.	1	2	3	4	5
24. I get cross at my friends and relatives more than I should.	1	2	3	4	5
25. Sometimes I feel like I need a professional counselor to help me get my life back together again.	1	2	3	4	5
26. I feel as though I'm just existing and not really living since he/she died.	1	2	3	4	5
27. I feel so lonely since he/she died.	1	2	3	4	5

	Strongly Agree	Agree	Neither Agree nor Disagree	Disagree	Strongly Disagree
28. I feel somewhat apart and remote, even among friends.	1	2	3	4	5
29. It's safer not to love.	1	2	3	4	5
30. I find it difficult to make decisions since the baby died.	1	2	3	4	5
31. I worry about what my future will be like.	1	2	3	4	5
32. Being a bereaved parent means being a "second-class citizen."	1	2	3	4	5
33. It feels great to be alive.	1	2	3	4	5

Scoring instructions: Reverse *all* of the items EXCEPT 11 and 33 (eg, a "1" would become a "5," a "4" would become a "2," etc). By reversing the items, higher scores now reflect more intense grief.

There are three subscales to assess "active grief," "difficulty coping," and "despair." The three subscales consist of the sum of the scores of 11 items each, with a possible range of 11–55.

Subscale	Subscale 2	Subscale 3
ACTIVE GRIEF	DIFFICULTY COPING	DESPAIR
1	2	9
3	4	15
5	8	16
6	11*	17
7	21	18
10	24	20
12	25	22
13	26	23
14	28	29
19	30	31
27	33*	32

*Do not reverse.

Please consult a licensed mental health provider to discuss your responses.

GENERALIZED ANXIETY DISORDER 7-ITEM (GAD-7) SCALE

The Generalized Anxiety Disorder Scale is designed to help screen, diagnose, and assess anxiety disorders.

Over the last 2 weeks, how often have you been bothered by the following problems?	Not at all sure	Several days	Over half of the days	Nearly every day
Feeling nervous, anxious, or on edge	0	1	2	3
Not being able to stop or control worrying	0	1	2	3
Worrying too much about different things	0	1	2	3
Trouble relaxing	0	1	2	3
Being so restless that it's hard to sit still	0	1	2	3
Becoming easily annoyed or irritable	0	1	2	3
Feeling as if something awful might happen	0	1	2	3
Add the score for each column				
Total score (add your column scores) =				

If you checked off any problems, how difficult have these made it for you to do your work, take care of things at home, or get along with other people?

_____ Not difficult at all
_____ Somewhat difficult
_____ Very difficult
_____ Extremely difficult

Please consult a licensed mental health provider to discuss your responses.

PATIENT HEALTH QUESTIONNAIRE-9
(PHQ-9)

The Patient Health Questionnaire (PHQ) is a self-administered diagnostic tool for common mental health disorders. The PHQ-9 is the depression module.

Over the last 2 weeks, how often have you been bothered by the following problems?	Not at all	Several days	Over half of the days	Nearly every day
Little interest or pleasure in doing things	0	1	2	3
Feeling down, depressed, or hopeless	0	1	2	3
Trouble falling or staying asleep, or sleeping too much	0	1	2	3
Feeling tired or having little energy	0	1	2	3
Poor appetite or overeating	0	1	2	3
Feeling bad about yourself, or that you are a failure or have let yourself or your family down	0	1	2	3
Trouble concentrating on things, such as reading the newspaper or watching television	0	1	2	3
Moving or speaking so slowly that other people could have noticed; or the opposite—being so fidgety or restless that you have been moving around a lot more than usual	0	1	2	3
Thoughts that you would be better off dead, or of hurting yourself	0	1	2	3
Add the score for each column				
Total score (add your column scores) =				

If you checked off any problems, how difficult have these made it for you to do your work, take care of things at home, or get along with other people?

_____ Not difficult at all
_____ Somewhat difficult
_____ Very difficult
_____ Extremely difficult

Please consult a licensed mental health provider to discuss your responses.

PTSD CHECKLIST FOR DSM-5
(PCL-5)

The Posttraumatic Stress Disorder Checklist (PCL) is designed to measure PTSD symptoms.

Instructions: Below is a list of problems that people sometimes have in response to a very stressful experience. Please read each problem carefully and circle one of the numbers to the right to indicate how much you have been bothered by that problem in the past month.

In the past month, how much were you bothered by:	Not at all	A little bit	Moderately	Quite a bit	Extremely
Repeated, disturbing, and unwanted memories of the stressful experience?	0	1	2	3	4
Repeated, disturbing dreams of the stressful experience?	0	1	2	3	4
Suddenly feeling or acting as if the stressful experience were actually happening again (as if you were actually back there reliving it)?	0	1	2	3	4
Feeling very upset when something reminded you of the stressful experience?	0	1	2	3	4
Having strong physical reactions when something reminded you of the stressful experience (for example, heart pounding, trouble breathing, sweating)?	0	1	2	3	4
Avoiding memories, thoughts, or feelings related to the stressful experience?	0	1	2	3	4
Avoiding external reminders of the stressful experience (for example, people, places, conversations, activities, objects, or situations)?	0	1	2	3	4
Trouble remembering important parts of the stressful experience?	0	1	2	3	4
Having strong negative beliefs about yourself, or other people, or the world (for example, having thoughts such as: I am bad, there is something seriously wrong with me, no one can be trusted, the world is completely dangerous)?	0	1	2	3	4

In the past month, how much were you bothered by:	Not at all	A little bit	Moderately	Quite a bit	Extremely
Blaming yourself or someone else for the stressful experience or what happened after it?	0	1	2	3	4
Having strong negative feelings such as fear, horror, anger, guilt, or shame?	0	1	2	3	4
Loss of interest in activities that you used to enjoy?	0	1	2	3	4
Feeling distant or cut off from other people?	0	1	2	3	4
Trouble experiencing positive feelings (for example, being unable to feel happiness or have loving feelings for people close to you)?	0	1	2	3	4
Irritable behavior, angry outbursts, or acting aggressively?	0	1	2	3	4
Taking too many risks or doing things that could cause you harm?	0	1	2	3	4
Being "superalert" or watchful or on guard?	0	1	2	3	4
Feeling jumpy or easily startled?	0	1	2	3	4
Having difficulty concentrating?	0	1	2	3	4
Trouble falling or staying asleep?	0	1	2	3	4

Please consult a licensed mental health provider to discuss your responses.

LIFE EVENTS CHECKLIST
(LEC)

The LEC is designed to screen for potentially traumatic events in a person's lifetime.

Listed below are a number of difficult or stressful things that sometimes happen to people. For each event check one or more of the boxes to the right to indicate that: (a) it *happened to you* personally, (b) you *witnessed it* happen to someone else, (c) you *learned about it* happening to someone close to you, (d) you're *not sure* if it fits, or (e) it *doesn't apply* to you.

Be sure to consider your *entire life* (growing up as well as adulthood) as you go through the list of events.

Event	Happened to me	Witnessed it	Learned about it	Not sure	Doesn't apply
Natural disaster (for example, flood, hurricane, tornado, earthquake)					
Fire or explosion					
Transportation accident (for example, car accident, boat accident, train wreck, plane crash)					
Serious accident at work, home, or during recreational activity					
Exposure to toxic substance (for example, dangerous chemicals, radiation)					
Physical assault (for example, being attacked, hit, slapped, kicked, beaten up)					
Assault with a weapon (for example, being shot, stabbed, threatened with a knife, gun, bomb)					
Sexual assault (rape, attempted rape, made to perform any type of sexual act through force or threat of harm)					

Event	Happened to me	Witnessed it	Learned about it	Not sure	Doesn't apply
Other unwanted or uncomfortable sexual experience					
Combat or exposure to a war zone (in the military or as a civilian)					
Captivity (for example, being kidnapped, abducted, held hostage, prisoner of war)					
Life-threatening illness or injury					
Severe human suffering					
Sudden, violent death (for example, homicide, suicide)					
Sudden, unexpected death of someone close to you					
Serious injury, harm, or death you caused to someone else					
Any other very stressful event or experience					

Please consult a licensed mental health provider to discuss your responses.

PATIENT STRESS QUESTIONNAIRE

The Patient Stress Questionnaire is used to screen for behavioral health symptoms.

Over the last 2 weeks, how often have you been bothered by the following problems?	Not at all	Several days	Over half of the days	Nearly every day
Little interest or pleasure in doing things	0	1	2	3
Feeling down, depressed, or hopeless	0	1	2	3
Trouble falling or staying asleep, or sleeping too much	0	1	2	3
Feeling tired or having little energy	0	1	2	3
Poor appetite or overeating	0	1	2	3
Feeling bad about yourself, or that you are a failure or have let yourself or your family down	0	1	2	3
Trouble concentrating on things, such as reading the newspaper or watching television	0	1	2	3
Moving or speaking so slowly that other people could have noticed. Or the opposite—being so fidgety or restless that you have been moving around a lot more than usual.	0	1	2	3
Thoughts that you would be better off dead, or of hurting yoursel fin some way	0	1	2	3
Add the score for each column				
Total score (add your column scores) =				

Over the last 2 weeks, how often have you been bothered by the following problems?	Not at all	Several days	Over half of the days	Nearly every day
Feeling nervous, anxious, or on edge	0	1	2	3
Not being able to stop or control worrying	0	1	2	3
Worrying too much about different things	0	1	2	3
Trouble relaxing	0	1	2	3
Being so restless that it's hard to sit still	0	1	2	3
Becoming easily annoyed or irritable	0	1	2	3
Feeling afraid as if something awful might happen	0	1	2	3
Add the score for each column				
Total score (add your column scores) =				

	NO	YES
Are you currently in any physical pain?		
In your life, have you ever had any experience that was so frightening, horrible, or upsetting that, in the past month, you:		
Have had nightmares about it or thought about it when you did not want to?		
Tried hard not to think about it or went out of your way to avoid situations that reminded you of it?		
Were constantly on guard, watchful, or easily startled?		
Felt numb or detached from others, activities, or your surroundings?		

Drinking alchohol can affect your health. This is especially important if you take certain medications. We want to help you stay healthy and lower your risk for the problems that can be caused by drinking.

These questions are about your drinking habits. We've listed the serving size of one drink below. Please circle your answer.

	0	1	2	3	4
How often do you have one drink containing alcohol?	Never	Monthly or less	2-4 times a month	2-3 times a week	4+ times a week
How many drinks containing alcohol do you have on a typical day when you are drinking?	1 or 2	3 or 4	5 or 6	7 to 9	10 or more
How often do you have four or more drinks on one occasion?	Never	Less than monthly	Monthly	Weekly	Daily or almost daily
How often during the last year have you …					
… found that you were not able to stop drinking once you had started?	Never	Less than monthly	Monthly	Weekly	Daily or almost daily
… failed to do what was normally expected from you because of drinking?	Never	Less than monthly	Monthly	Weekly	Daily or almost daily
… needed a first drink in the morning to get yourself going after heavy drinking?	Never	Less than monthly	Monthly	Weekly	Daily or almost daily

	0	1	2	3	4
. . . had a feeling of guilt or remorse after drinking?	Never	Less than monthly	Monthly	Weekly	Daily or almost daily
. . . been unable to remember what happened the night before because you had been drinking?	Never	Less than monthly	Monthly	Weekly	Daily or almost daily

	0	2	4
Have you or someone else been injured as a result of your drinking?	No	Yes, but not in the last year	Yes, in the last year
Has a relative, friend, doctor, or other health worker been concerned about your drinking or suggested you cut down?	No	Yes, but not in the last year	Yes, in the last year

Standard serving of one drink:

12 ounces of beer or wine cooler

1.5 ounces of 80 proof liquor

5 ounces of wine

4 ounces of brandy, liquer, or aperitif

Please consult a licensed mental health provider to discuss your responses.